STRATEGIC POINT

Harpers Ferry saw as much of the Civil War as any other point. Even before secession it was the scene of fighting when John Brown seized the national arsenal with only a handful of men and held it three days. When Virginia left the Union, the Southerners immediately took over the town, and from then on it changed hands so often that the arsenal was left in ruins.

THE CIVIL WAR

THE PICTURE CHRONICLE

Washington City.
Sep. 10. 10⅕Hh. 1862.

Major Genl. McClellan.
        Rockville, Md.
                How does it look now?
                        A. Lincoln

THE
CIVIL WAR

VOLUME II
THE
PICTURE CHRONICLE
of the Events, Leaders and
Battlefields of the War

BY

RALPH NEWMAN
and E. B. LONG

Introduction by
ALLAN NEVINS

GROSSET & DUNLAP, INC.
Publishers, New York

This volume

is humbly dedicated to the late

FOREMAN "Mike" LEBOLD

*who, out of his love for his country North
and South, collected the original manuscripts
relating its dramatic story, and unselfishly
shared his vast collection with so many and
helped us gain a greater appreciation
for our country and its citizens.*

FOREWORD

The Civil War presents itself in many forms of today's literature, comprehensive histories, biographies, studies of single battles and campaigns, picture books or eyewitness accounts such as those found in Volume I of *The Civil War*. But the war should also be seen as a whole as it unrolls, day to day, month to month, year to year. It was a pageant of action and the events of each day merge together to form a complete chronicle. This chronicle as here presented will, we hope, open up vistas of future study and enjoyment for the reader. It is to serve as a concise, brief guide giving the major and some of the minor events and giving them in a connected way so that the reader, while watching the war progress before his eyes will also grasp the overall scene, as it is seldom possible to do in more detailed studies.

But the events alone are not enough, for men make the events. So the facts of the lives of one hundred of the outstanding personalities, along with a summary of the story of the common soldier himself, have been included to round out the picture. What these men did is of course important, but to know what they looked like is equally as rewarding as reading of their deeds. Each biography is accompanied by a representative portrait. So too the chronology of the war is illustrated. There are the battlefields, behind the lines operations and, in order to bring the war even closer to the reader, headlines from newspapers of the day, reproductions of historic letters by important actors in the drama, and the broadsides and posters which played so prominent a part in advertising the Civil War.

To give the reader a doorway to greater enjoyment and knowledge there is also presented a reading list of some of the outstanding books on the subject, regardless of date of publication. Civil War literature is so vast that guidance is needed. The reader will find here our recommendations for a basic Civil War library containing the histories, the campaign studies, the major biographies as well as some special publications. Here is a path to greater appreciation of American history. It also serves as a bibliography for this volume, since these works were used to compile the chronology, the biographies, and the lineup of the armies which comprise the major elements of this guide.

The problem of how many fought in a given battle and how many men were killed, wounded, and missing on each side has seldom if ever been settled. The authors have made the best estimates available, as it seemed to them, and generally speaking casualty figures and troop numbers are taken from Thomas L. Livermore, *Numbers and Losses in the Civil War in America*, 1861-1865.

The majority of the photographic portraits are by Mathew B. Brady and some of his talented contemporaries, from the great private collection of Frederick Hill Meserve, with others supplied by the Chicago Historical Society. Other illustrative material came from two of the rarest collections of Civil War photographs: George N. Barnard's *Photographic Views of Sherman's Campaign, from Negatives taken in the field*; New York, 1866, and Alexander Gardner's *Gardner's Photographic Sketch Book of the War*, Washington, 1865; and from Philip Van Doren Stern, Charleston (S. C.) Public Library, Chicago *Tribune* Library, Emory University Library, Illinois State Historical Library, Historical Society of Pennsylvania, The Library of Congress and Virginia State Library. Among the private collectors who made priceless manuscripts available to us for study and reproduction were David H. Annan, Newton C. Farr, C. Norton Owen, Philip D. Sang, Alfred Whital Stern and the late Foreman M. Lebold. The recently uncovered Ellsworth Eliot, Jr.-Wiley R. Reynolds collection and the manuscript resources of the Abraham Lincoln Book Shop were also placed at our disposal.

While the material was selected and written entirely by the authors and is their responsibility, there are many persons who played an important role in the preparation of this volume. We owe especial thanks to Ezra J. Warner of LaJolla, California, outstanding authority on the lives of Civil War military personalities, for his painstaking reading and correction of the manuscript, pointing out of errors or misconceptions and many, many hours of work. Carl Haverlin, of California and New York, not only lent us his valuable Barnard and Gardner photographic collections, but as a renowned collector and student has aided in ways too numerous to mention. Our

FOREWORD

deep appreciation for advice and inspiration goes to Dr. Allan Nevins, author of the introduction to this volume.

Others who aided include Arnold and Marda Alexander, Margaret H. April, Edward E. Barthell, Jr., Robert Buchbinder, Olive Carruthers, Bruce Catton, Richard E. Clark, Glenn Dolberg, Otto Eisenschiml, Charles Godwin, Patricia K. Lynch, Earl Schenck Miers, the late Fletcher Pratt, Don Russell, Carl Sandburg, Tessie Santos, Georgia Schenk, John Y. Simon, Clyde C. Walton, Frieda Weisbach and Bell Irvin Wiley.

To our wives Estelle Newman and Barbara Long who allowed us to enlist for the "duration" and permitted us to go off to "war" again until the final proof corrections were made, we owe more than we can express and if we ever forget, we are certain that they will remind us of this.

We realize full well that it is impossible to produce a book of this kind, or for that matter, any book, completely free from errors, and we apologize in advance for any that may be found. We hope that we have achieved a volume as accurate as possible that will give the everyday reader a guidepost, and the student a handbook, to the greatest crisis and drama in the nation's history.

RALPH NEWMAN
E. B. LONG

Oak Park,
Illinois,

Hd. Qrs Army Northern Virginia
April 10th 1865

Gen'l Order
No. 9

After four years of arduous service marked by unsurpassed courage and fortitude the Army of Northern Virginia has been compelled to yield to overwhelming numbers and resources.

I need not tell the survivors of so many hard fought battles who have remained steadfast to the last that I have consented to this result from no distrust of them.

But feeling that valour and devotion could accomplish nothing that could compensate for the loss that would have attended the continuance of the contest I determined to avoid the useless sacrifice of those whose past services have endeared them to their country.

By the terms of the agreement officers and men can return to their homes and remain until exchanged.

You will take with you the satisfaction that proceeds from the consciousness of duty faithfully performed, and I earnestly pray that a merciful God will extend to you his blessing and protection.

With an unceasing admiration of your constancy and devotion to your country and a grateful remembrance of your kind and generous consideration for myself, I bid you an affectionate farewell

R E Lee
Genl

General Robert E. Lee bids farewell to his army following his surrender at Appomattox.

(NOTE: Full texts of all the letters reproduced in this volume may be found starting on page 223.)

CONTENTS

FOREWORD v

INTRODUCTION xi

A CHRONICLE 1

    1860 3

    1861 7

    1862 23

    1863 53

    1864 84

    1865 121

THE LINEUP 139

MEN WHO MADE WAR 153

TEXTS OF THE LETTERS 223

THE WAR IN BOOKS 225

INDEX 237

Head Quarters, Mil. Div. of the Miss.

Chattanooga, Ten. Nov. 22nd 1863.

Maj. Gen. G. H. Thomas,

Comdg Army of the Cumb.d

General.

The bridge at Brown's Ferry being down to-day, and the excessively bad roads since the last rain, will render it impossible for Sherman to get up either of his two remaining divisions in time for the attack to-morrow morning. With one of them up and, which would have been there now but for the accident to the bridge I would still make the attack in the morning, regarding a day gained as of especial advantage to a single division of troops.

You can make your arrangements for this delay.

Very respectfully
U. S. Grant
Maj. Gen.

General Grant explains to Thomas in Chattanooga that attack must be delayed due to bad roads and a wrecked bridge.

INTRODUCTION

"The battle pictures etched most deeply on our souls," wrote Theodore Roosevelt, "are those of our own land." He was complaining of a New England essayist who had dwelt on Crecy and Sebastopol to the neglect of American combats. T. R. went on:

"Farragut, lashed in the rigging of the *Hartford*, as, with her great guns leaping and bellowing, she steamed past the forts to try her oaken stem on the ironclad hull of the ram; Stonewall Jackson dying at the head of his men in the last of his many triumphs; Cushing victoriously steering his frail craft through the night against the huge *Albemarle;* the little Confederate torpedo boat lying beside the Union sloop of war on the sea-bottom off Charleston harbor, wrapped in the doom she had brought on her foe; the mighty wrestle at Gettysburg; the stormers scaling Lookout Mountain in the battle above the clouds—these, and a hundred others like them, are the memories which make our hearts throb quickest."

These, albeit the list is somewhat conventional, are indeed stirring pictures; and how many more we could add! The mighty panorama of the years 1861-65 is the richest single picture gallery in our history.

The Civil War was, of course, far more than a succession of tableaux. But if we do not give ample attention to the pictorial record— the gathering of the troops, the sketches of march and camp, the scenes of pomp and devastation, the poignant photographs of shapeless bundles of flesh and clothing in clumps and huddles of the slain, the portraits of generals whose characters are written in deeply lined faces—we miss one of the most revealing parts of the war's history. A photograph by Mathew Brady or Alexander Gardner has two distinct values. It shows us a fragment of the war with a vividness which words cannot achieve, and it awakens the imagination in a way that only the greatest prose narrators, such as Parkman or G. M. Trevelyan, can match. We are fortunate that in 1861 field photography, carried far beyond the point to which Roger Fenton had taken it in the Crimea, was put in the hands of the devoted Brady, who later wrote: "A spirit in me said 'Go,' and I went."

The veracity of such work makes its mere surface values important. These pictures do not lie. Various observers tell us how smart McClellan's cavalry was after he reorganized the Army of the Potomac in 1861. But W. H. Russell writes that "he had the very dirtiest and most unsoldierly dragoons, with filthy accoutrements and un-groomed horses, I ever saw." A few photographs decide between two such conflicting witnesses. Photographs give precise details on how troops were embarked at Aquia Landing, how Napoleon guns were served in action, and how various kinds of winter barracks were built.

But the greater value lies in the food which well-chosen pictorial material offers to the imagination. Some of the battle-scenes in this volume will start many a reader on a train of grim fantasy. The scene of a battle-line breaking, a command in flight, is always particularly haunting. The exploding shells, the soldiers scurrying pell-mell through billowing smoke, the mangled men in their pools of blood, the wrecked field-pieces, the mounted officers vainly trying to stem the tide, usually against a background of sullen sky and seared trees—this was a story told at Bull Run, at Shiloh, at Second Manassas, at Chancellorsville, at Cedar Creek, and on many another field. The contrast with brighter scenes drives home the meaning of war. All too often the grim clashes of the war went without a photographic record. Armies going into action could not wait for the photographer's heavy, complicated equipment. But from the stark scenes of devastation recorded after the battles, our imagination can fill in the action. The portraits in this book are equally a challenge to the imagination. Pondering the image of Longstreet, for example, we divine his mixture of shrewdness, tenacity, and heaviness; scrutinizing that of Farragut, so serene, thoughtful, and determined, we understand why tars called him "Old Heart of Oak."

This collection of pictures, so industriously made, so astutely arranged, and so conscientiously annotated by Mr. Newman and Mr. Long, is not a mere supplement to history; it *is* history. The authors have searched zealously for the letters, broadsides, and posters here included; they have weighed carefully the relative merits of Gardner, Barnard, and Brady photographs, some not before used; they have found material in private collections never before opened. They make a fresh addition of value to our resources on the war. Their admirable work should be studied, not merely scanned, and studied for the two cardinal values we have mentioned, veracity of detail and inspiration to the imagination.

For without careful and sustained attention, these values will not be won. What would we not give to stand a moment (preferably behind a thick tree) at Antietam or Spotsylvania? If every element of a battle photograph is studied minutely, we are on such a field. What would we not give to see one of the great captains in camp habiliments? If we look long and earnestly at the portrait of George H. Thomas, we see his reserve, self-control, painstaking care about details ("The fate of a battle may depend on a buckle"), tenacity ("We will hold the town till we starve"), and modesty ("His face would color with blushes when his troops cheered him") quite as plainly as if he walked through the room. If we brood long enough over the various war scenes, our imaginations may catch something of a deeper vision, until we find them as real as H. H. Brownell's sailor found "The River Fight"—

'Twas lightning and black eclipse,
With a bellowing roll and crash!—

or as Edmund Clarence Stedman's trooper found the cavalry charge, dashing under "a smoky dome" against incessant "level lightnings"; or as W. E. Henley's blockade runner found the drummer thudding on the Charleston wharves to summon the last recruits, "Poor old Dixie's bottom dollar." That is, we may begin to see the war with the perception of the poets who shared or touched it.

The fact that the war grew steadily in intensity and grimness as well as scope is evident to anyone who studies its pictures. The fresh-faced, honest-eyed farm boys who made up so large a part of the armies had become hard-jawed, stern-eyed veterans by 1864. For more than a year most men believed it would be a short conflict. When McClellan set forth for Richmond in the spring of 1862, many Northerners feared it would be over before slavery could be put to death; when McClellan reeled back in defeat from the Seven Days, many Southerners saw the end at hand. A good many of the early scenes had a touch of lightness: wheezy, ponderous Winfield Scott, huge of frame, brow, and epaulets, falling asleep in the midst of an important conference at his 17th Street headquarters; the Third Alabama marching into their Virginia camp with a hundred body-servants to brush their glossy blue uniforms; Price's men rolling bales of hemp forward to the easy capture of Lexington, Mo. By the time of Fredericksburg and the 'mud march' all levity had gone out of the struggle. The armies were fighting like tigers. "All," wrote General T. W. Hyde, "were like athletes trained down to the last limit for some great contest of brawn and muscle." Behind the armies the two populations, save for a few fainthearts, were ready to expend the last ounce of strength for their causes.

No pen, no pencil, no camera, could catch more than a small fraction of the multitudinous aspects of the Civil War. What photographer was at hand at Vicksburg on July 4, 1863, for the glorious scene when, the stars and stripes having been hoisted over city hall, the gunboats moved in line past the town, bands playing, crews cheering, guns saluting? Who could justly have pictured the evening scene at Atlanta on November 15, 1864, the city in flames, and the munitions warehouses exploding, but the band of the Thirty-third Massachusetts playing "John Brown's Body" by the light of the burning buildings? Not a thousandth part of the acts of devotion and heroism ever found a chronicler. At Fredericksburg, as the Fifth New Hampshire fell back, seven or eight men died in succession trying to rescue their fallen banner; and at last one saved it under the shelter of the heap of dead. At Gaines Mill five young Confederates similarly died trying to bring out the colors of the First South Carolina, and finally the sixth bore them away. We can only be thankful that the record of this tragic but heroic era, so rich in lessons of patriotism, is as full as it is.

Mr. Newman and Mr. Long—the one the proprietor of that delightful resort of bibliophiles and historians, the Abraham Lincoln Book Shop in Chicago, the chief organizer of the Chicago Civil War Round Table now copied all over the land, and the initiator of the Civil War Book Club; the other an experienced journalist, a deeply-read student of military history, and research chief for Mr. Bruce Catton's *Centennial History of the Civil War*—have added to the value of their combined narrative and pictorial history by three excellent editorial features. One is a section containing biographical sketches of a hundred leaders North and South; one is a bibliography listing accurately and fully the works needed for a substantial Civil War library; and the third is a careful record of the major units of command on both sides, with their generals, areas of operation, and battles. All three represent long and careful work. We thus have in these two volumes, a comprehensive work of reference as well as a vivid running narrative of events. Readers will find the set one of the best available keys to the history which coming centenary observances will revive in the national memory.

New York   ALLAN NEVINS

THE CIVIL WAR

THE PICTURE CHRONICLE

The Charleston Mercury.

CHARLESTON, S. C., SATURDAY, APRIL 13, 1861.

THE MERCURY.

SATURDAY, APRIL 13, 1861.

April Twelfth, 1861.

We stated yesterday that on Thursday, at three o'clock, p. m., General BEAUREGARD had made a demand upon Major ANDERSON for the evacuation of Fort Sumter through his Aids, Colonel CHESNUT, Captain LEE, and Colonel CHISOLM, and that Major ANDERSON had regretfully declined, under the circumstances of his position. It was, however, understood that unless reinforced he would necessarily yield the post in a few days—say by the fifteenth. An effort was, therefore, made to avoid an engagement, without incurring greater risk of reinforcement. At one and a half, a. m., Colonel CHESNUT and Captain LEE reached Fort Sumter from General BEAUREGARD, and, we gather, were prepared to enter into any arrangement for non action as to Fort Sumter, if no assistance were given to the efforts of reinforcement; but postponement merely to mature hostile plans was impossible. No satisfactory agreement being proposed, and time being important, at three and a half o'clock a. m., Major ANDERSON was notified that, at the expiration of an hour, the batteries would open their fire upon him. The Aids then passed thence in a boat to Fort Johnson, and Col. CHESNUT ordered the fire to begin. Precisely at four and a half o'clock a shell was fired from the signal battery on James' Island, which, making a beautiful curve, burst immediately above Fort Sumter. Within fifteen minutes all the Carolina batteries were in full play. The inhabitants of Charleston forthwith thronged to the East Bay Battery and other points of observation, and excitement prevailed through the day amid various and stirring rumors put afloat from time to time. Major ANDERSON, having no oil to light up his casemates, and the morning being slightly murky and drizaly, did not respond until broad day. At a quarter before six he opened his fire by a shot at the Iron Battery on Cumming's point; then at Fort Moultrie, the Floating Battery, located at the west end of Sullivan's Island, the Dahlgren battery; the Enfilade Battery, Major TRAPIER's Battery, and Fort Johnson, interspersing his attentions by paying respects to the numerous mortar batteries, by which he, enclosed in brick, is surrounded. Hour after hour has the fire on both sides been kept up, deliberate and audgaging. The steady, frequent shock of the cannon's boom, accompanied by the hiss of balls, and the horrid, hurtling sound of the flying shell, are now perfectly familiar to the people of Charleston. While the early sun was veiled in mist, we saw shell-bursting within and illuminating Fort Sumter, or exploding in the air above, leaving a small thick cloud of white smoke to mark the place. We saw solid shot striking the dark walls, and in each instance followed by a fume of dust from the battered surface. One man was visibly stricken prostrate on the wharf, and carried in the fort; and several guns were dismounted. The walls, too, in several spots, were damaged. And while Sumter has certainly and manifestly been injured, no loss is yet sustained on our part. Fort Moultrie is intact, so far as its fighting capacity is concerned. The Iron Battery is ready for continued work, after a full and fair trial of its powers of resistance; also the Floating Battery. The practice of our soldiers, as marksmen, has been excellent and highly satis-

BOMBARDMENT
OF
FORT SUMTER!
Splendid Pyrotechnic Exhibition.
FORT MOULTRIE
IMPREGNABLE.
THE FLOATING BATTERY
AND
Stevens' Battery a Success.
"Nobody Hurt" on Our Side.
ETC., ETC., ETC.

As may have been anticipated from our notice of the military movements in our city yesterday, the bombardment of Fort Sumter, so long and anxiously expected, has at length become a fact before was gradually worn down, the citizens who had thronged the battery through the night, anxious and weary, had sought their homes, the Mounted Guard which had kept watch and ward over the city, with the first grey streak of morning were preparing to retire, when two guns in quick succession from Fort Johnson announced the opening of the drama. Upon that signal, the circle of batteries with which the grim fortress of Fort Sumter is beleaguered opened fire. The outline of this great volcanic crater was illuminated with a line of twinkling lights; the clustering shells illuminated the sky above it; the balls clattered thick as hail upon its sides; our citizens, aroused to a forgetfulness of their fatigue through many weary hours, rushed again to the points of observation; and so, at the break of day, amidst the bursting of bombs, and the roaring of ordnance, and before thousands of spectators, whose homes, and liberties, and lives were at stake, was enacted this first great scene in the opening drama of what, it is presumed, will be a most momentous military act. It may be a drama of but a single act. The madness which inspires it may depart with this single paroxysm. It is certain that the people of the North have ranking at their hearts no sense of wrong to be avenged; and exhibiting to those who expect power to reconstruct the shattered Union, its utter inadequacy to accomplish a single step in that direction, the Administration of the old Government may abandon at once and forever its vain and visionary hope of forcible control over the Confederate States. But it may not be so; they may persist still longer in assertions of their power, and if so, they will arouse an independent spirit in the South, which will effect a merciless and fearful retribution.

But to return to our report. The act which we have undertaken to record was so unique as might be supposed there were few incidents to mark it. Below we have presented the reports as we...

CAMP BOMAR, SULLIVAN'S ISLAND, 1 P. M.

No fleet in sight yet. Sumter badly damaged in parapet guns and buildings. Lieutenants RHETT and MITCHEL are at Moultrie in command of the battery bearing on Sumter. Captain HAM. ILTON has a DAHLGREN gun at the Cove, doing great mischief, and gets, with the Floating Battery, commanded by Lieutenants YATES and HARLESTON, nearly all ANDERSON's attention. No one killed yet on our side or injured.

RIPLEY is in his shirt sleeves, working his guns himself. The work is progressing finely.

LETTER FROM AN OFFICER IN COMMAND OF THE SUMTER GUNS ON FORT MOULTRIE.

FORT MOULTRIE, 4 o'clock.

We are all unhurt, and if the war steamers now off the bar do not give us trouble to night, I have great expectation of success.

RIPLEY is every inch a soldier. Indeed, I cannot speak in too high terms of our officers and men.

Our gun practice has been fine. It has been satisfactory to Col. RIPLEY. Every now and then whilst I write seated between two of my Columbiads a shot from ANDERSON hisses spitefully over my head.

To Lieut. MITCHEL, under my command, belongs the honor of having first dismounted two guns for ANDERSON at one shot.

In haste, yours,

FORT MOULTRIE, 4½ p. m.

We commenced firing this morning at 4¾ a. m., and have continued a steady fire until the present, and are still firing. The balls from Fort Sumter are doing little or no damage to our forts, having been injured. The Morris Island batteries appear to be doing a great deal of injury to that side of Sumter.

Major ANDERSON has one gun bearing on Fort Johnson, one on each of the lower batteries on this Island, and five on Fort Moultrie. At present there are three United States war-vessels off the harbor. All the guns bearing on them are loaded and manned, ready for action.

MORRIS ISLAND, 8 a. m.

The batteries are doing great execution, and have received no injury.

STEVENS' BATTERY, MORRIS ISLAND, 10 a. m.

Everything going on well. The battery has been struck ten times without being injured. Every body in good spirits, and no one hurt.

MORRIS ISLAND, 12 m.

Two of the guns on the iron battery have been partially disabled, but no one injured.

MORRIS ISLAND, 3½ p. m.

We have repaired the injury done to iron battery, and have commenced firing with the same success. No one injured.

FORT JOHNSON, 3 o'clock.

ANDERSON has fired two shots, but without effect.

The official reports made to Headquarters last night from the several forts and batteries, state that no person was injured; and that for instance, every six shells fired, fell inside Fort Sumter.

The schooner Petrel, J. L. JONES, commanding, while lying off the mouth of Hog Island Channel, was fired into from Fort Sumter, about half-past 8 o'clock. One shot took effect in the bow of the schooner, and several passed over her. Captain JONES reports that the fire of Sumter is principally directed against the Floating Battery, the Four Gun Battery, and the DAHLGREN Battery on Sullivan's Island, with little apparent effect. Most of the shell from the Mortar Battery on Morris...

A CHRONICLE

Nearly a century ago the United States of America ceased for a time to be united, and for four years a record of tragedy and glory was traced in lightning on the North American continent. Nothing quite like it had happened before nor can happen again. The United States that people spoke of before 1860 had an emphasis on the "States," it was a confederation of governments, not quite independent, not quite interdependent. After 1865 the people spoke of the United States with emphasis on "United."

What happened may be found in the dusty records of the government and in the stacks of libraries, in the private collections of collectors, but mainly in books of the time and books of now. Yesterday's newspaper is gone; the day by day record is sinking into time, and only the overall picture composed of high points remains. But it was more than just a time of major battles, of great events. Things happened in between and men fought in over 10,000 places between 1861 and 1865. The multitudinous names of those places are forgotten today —Wet Glaze, Missouri; Convalescent Corrall, Mississippi; Gum Swamp, North Carolina; Droop Mountain, Virginia; Bear Wallow, Kentucky, and thousands more. With the forgotten places are forgotten men—hundreds of thousands of men and boys, some who went out and did not return, others who returned to live out their lives in memories. They too are gone now. In today's rapid world we cannot be concerned with those little places nor concerned enough with the little men.

But we can pause and glance behind us into the shadows. We can watch a young country in its infancy, suffering its growing pains and wrestling with itself. We can see the germs of the sores in the body of the nation planted one by one. We can see them mature into cancers that, although cut, return to erupt into one final gigantic ulcer. We can look at those four years month by month as if reading a news magazine of the past. We can feel a bit of the anxiety, the confidence, the satisfaction and the despair. We can watch the nation in November of 1860 tremble in the excitement of it knew not what, we can watch it fall apart with increasing velocity until it bursts in fiery shells. We can watch the armies prepare for battle, march to the conflict; see the fight itself and the march back.

Slavery, state's rights, individual rights, sectional rights, economic pressures, personal antagonisms, all and much more rolled into over seventy-five years of mounting tension were the causes of it all. But no one can lay his finger today on one broken pulse and say this was the flaw. The tangle of what led up to the war remains locked in the minds of those long gone, and even they couldn't answer. But we do know much of what happened during the four years of fighting. We cannot relate it all, no written record can, but we can give the running account and set the chronological pattern for those who wish to visit those widely separate fields of battle, for those who wish to look into one event or one man, and for those who just want to know what happened. Here, then, is the American Civil War, the War Between the States, the War of Northern Aggression, the War of the Rebellion, the War for Southern Independence, the War of the American States, the Confederate War, the Brothers' War.

1860

S	M	T	W	T	F	S
				1	2	3
4	5	6	7	8	9	10
11	12	13	14	15	16	17
18	19	20	21	22	23	24
25	26	27	28	29	30	

Election day, Tuesday, Nov. 6, 1860, for the sixteenth President of the still-United States saw four candidates, sectional parties, threats and counter-threats. If a Republican were elected there was sure to be secession, said the South. And a Republican seemed certain of victory. Abraham Lincoln, Illinois Republican, and Hannibal Hamlin of Maine got 1,866,452 votes to win; Stephen A. Douglas, Illinois Democrat, and Herschel V. Johnson of Georgia got 1,376,957 votes; John C. Breckinridge, Southern Democrat of Kentucky, and Joseph Lane of Oregon, 849,781 votes; John Bell, Tennessee Constitutional Unionist, and Edward Everett of Massachusetts, 588,879 votes. President-elect Lincoln had less than half the popular vote— a minority President. But in the all-important electoral count Lincoln had 180 votes, Breckinridge 72, Bell 39, and Douglas 12. Therefore, the expected result and the expected excitement.

The sections had spoken and the strain on the Union was telling. There were those in North and South who called for calm, but the cry was not heard. Indignation meetings in Southern cities, the Palmetto flag raised at Charleston, S. C., and Maj. Robert Anderson of the United States Army was assigned Nov. 15 to command defenses in Charleston Harbor. South Carolina Senators James Chesnut, Jr., and James H. Hammond resigned their seats on the 9th and a convention was called by the South Carolina legislature. There was talk of troops and arms, conventions and secession. But did secession mean war? Could something yet be done?

S	M	T	W	T	F	S
						1
2	3	4	5	6	7	8
9	10	11	12	13	14	15
16	17	18	19	20	21	22
23	24	25	26	27	28	29
30	31					

Dec. 4 and fading President James Buchanan told Congress that the South had no legal right to secede, but that the government had no power to prevent it. A crisis arose in the cabinet,

[3]

FORT SUMTER, SOUTH CAROLINA

The bombardment of this Federal fort, set in Charleston's harbor, touched off the Civil War. Major Anderson's Union troops had occupied the fort on Dec. 26, 1860. The Confederate bombardment by Beauregard's troops took place on April 12-13, 1861. Following the fall of the fort on April 13, the bastion remained in Confederate hands throughout most of the war.

and two Southerners resigned: Secretary of Treasury Howell Cobb quit Dec. 8 and Secretary of War John B. Floyd left Dec. 29 under a cloud that suggested charges of treason. Secretary of State Lewis Cass also resigned Dec. 12, but he left because the President refused to reinforce the Charleston forts. Sen. John J. Crittenden of Kentucky made an effort on the 18th to compromise, with a resolution that called for five amendments to protect slavery in states where it was legal, and to revive the Missouri Compromise line, but it failed. The South Carolina convention gathered in Charleston and on Dec. 20 the state left the Union by a vote of 169 to 0. The threats of many years were now fact. Commissioners were named by the Sovereign State of South Carolina Dec. 22 to talk to President Buchanan. It was Christmas, and the day after the holiday U.S. Army Major Robert Anderson abandoned undefendable Fort Moultrie and occupied Fort Sumter, an island in Charleston Harbor. The next day South Carolina troops took over the other now abandoned fortifications. The breaking of a nation had begun.

1861

S	M	T	W	T	F	S
		1	2	3	4	5
6	7	8	9	10	11	12
13	14	15	16	17	18	19
20	21	22	23	24	25	26
27	28	29	30	31		

A new year and the states were no longer united. South Carolina had led the way and others made their moves toward secession. Questions, turmoil, doubt and hysteria gripped the nation both North and South. There was high self-confidence and optimism in much of the South, at least in the surface utterings and events; much more doubt in the North. The legislature of the slave state of Delaware voted Jan. 3 to remain in the Union. In New York pro-Southern Mayor Fernando Wood proposed on Jan. 6 that the nation's largest center declare itself a free city and remain neutral. The proposal came to nothing. Off Charleston, focal point of secession, an unarmed U. S. merchant ship, *Star of the West*, arrived Jan. 9 to strengthen and re-supply Fort Sumter. It was fired on by South Carolina guns and returned North. Many said it was the first actual shot of the war. Jan. 9 and Mississippi withdrew from the Union by a vote of 84 to 15; Florida departed on the 10th, 62 to 7; Alabama acted on the 11th, 61 to 39. Georgia Jan. 19 passed an ordinance of secession 208 to 89, while on the 26th Louisiana joined the deep South 113 to 7. On Jan. 3 Georgia state troops seized Fort Pulaski in Savannah harbor. Arsenal after arsenal, fort after fort fell to the seceded states. In the House of Representatives a committee Jan. 14 recommended enforcement of the Fugitive Slave Act, repeal of the hated state personal liberty laws of the North, and an amendment to the Constitution to protect slave states from interference with slavery. The amendment was adopted but not ratified. Six children had left the parental home for the world of strife and battle. South Carolina, Florida, Mississippi, Alabama, Georgia and Louisiana were all from the deep South and expressed the "fire-eating" of some of the "Gulf Squadron" leaders. But it went deeper than that, much deeper. Politicians alone could never have accomplished it. Who would follow their example? Could these six states fight a war? Martial music, martial speech, and martial action resounded from the Mississippi River to the Atlantic. Talk, talk, talk, for so long; but finally there was action. Where would it all lead?

[7]

INSIDE FORT SUMTER

This shows the inside defenses of the fort. In the summer of 1863, it was threatened by the Union forces under Gillmore moving on Charleston. During Aug.-Oct., 1863, it was under constant Union bombardment, but both it and Charleston withstood the Union siege. The city and the fort finally fell to Federal troops late in the war—Feb. 18, 1865. The last troops to march out of Charleston came from Fort Sumter.

FEBRUARY, 1861

S	M	T	W	T	F	S
					1	2
3	4	5	6	7	8	9
10	11	12	13	14	15	16
17	18	19	20	21	22	23
24	25	26	27	28		

Texas, in convention assembled, voted 166 to 7 for secession on the first day of February—seven states were now gone. The Texans confirmed the decision at the polls on the 23rd. But there were those who still had hopes of peace. On Feb. 4 a conference of 21 states assembled at Washington. On the 27th it presented a plan for seven amendments to the Constitution with slavery to be protected south of the old Missouri Compromise line, but nothing came of the plan in Congress. But even while there was talk of peace there was another convention at Montgomery, Ala., to form a provisional government for the seceded states. A constitution was adopted, patterned on that of the United States except that slavery was recognized and protected. On the 9th the Provisional Congress of the Confederate States of America named Jefferson Davis of Mississippi as Provisional President and Alexander H. Stephens of Georgia, Provisional Vice President. On the 18th Davis and Stephens were inaugurated, a cabinet was named and a new government was in operation. In Tennessee and Virginia there was opposition to secession —for the moment. Arsenals, forts, federal buildings were taken over by the fledgling Confederacy. On Feb. 11 a

worried man left Springfield, Ill., "not knowing when or whether I ever may return." After speeches en route the President of the now dis-United States secretly arrived in Washington.

MARCH, 1861

S	M	T	W	T	F	S
					1	2
3	4	5	6	7	8	9
10	11	12	13	14	15	16
17	18	19	20	21	22	23
24	25	26	27	28	29	30
31						

Abraham Lincoln became President of a divided nation facing an uncertain future on March 4, 1861. Secession would not be tolerated; the nation could not be separated, he said. But there would be no violence unless it was forced on the Union. A few uncertain days and Lincoln showed his cabinet and the nation that he was President in fact as well as name. The Union cabinet included such men as William H. Seward of New York, the Secretary of State, who for a short time expected to be "Prime Minister;" Salmon P. Chase of Ohio, whose treasury made the wheels of war spin; Simon Cameron of Pennsylvania, who was forced upon Lincoln as War Secretary; Gideon Welles of Connecticut, who was to run the Navy. But there were many problems. Could the "border states" such as Virginia, Kentucky, Maryland and Missouri be saved? On the same March 4 the Confederate flag of Stars and Bars was adopted by a committee and used officially for two years. On the 11th the Constitution of the Confederacy was unanimously adopted at Montgomery. The cast of characters was drawing to completion; the dress rehearsal was over and the first act was ready for the curtain and drama would unroll.

APRIL, 1861

S	M	T	W	T	F	S
	1	2	3	4	5	6
7	8	9	10	11	12	13
14	15	16	17	18	19	20
21	22	23	24	25	26	27
28	29	30				

The nation was asunder, but despite all the hot words, all the long years of events, crises, compromises, irritations and prophecies, would blood be let? Could there be a settlement or at least another postponement? Lincoln had decided to support Maj. Robert Anderson at Fort Sumter in Charleston Harbor and the United States now held only three other major points in the South: Fort Pickens and Key West in Florida; and Fort Monroe in Virginia. The United States April 6 told South Carolina that an expedition was on its way to provision, not to reinforce, the lightly held fort. Off Charleston by April 12—it was too late. South Carolina on the 11th requested Anderson to surrender, and he offered to do so as soon as supplies ran out, or if he received new orders. The Confederate government and the state said no; surrender now. At 4:30 on the morning of April 12, 1861, guns under the command of Gen. Pierre Gustave Toutant Beauregard opened fire. The last old-fashioned—or perhaps the first modern—war had begun. All the years, all the talk, all the hopes, all the work of lives spent in seeking a solution was over. The sputtering and smoke of pol

itics and statecraft were cleared away by the storm of war. Claims were made that Lincoln maneuvered the South into fighting; other claims held that the South alone had done the deed. No matter where the blame, the guns of North and the guns of South were answering each other in Charleston Harbor. For 34 hours the bombardment continued until 2:30 p.m. April 13, and Major Anderson surrendered his partially ruined fort. Not a man died in the opening battle, a bloodless beginning to what no man really knew. April 15 Lincoln said "insurrection" existed; 75,000 volunteers needed for three months to put it down. A hysterical pause before the plunge ahead. On the 17th the Virginia state convention adopted an ordinance of secession 103 to 46, but not without opposition from her western counties. Harpers Ferry, Va., arsenal was abandoned by the U. S. April 18, and on the 19th a blockade of ports of the Gulf States was proclaimed. Merely a proclamation for a while, for the U. S. Navy was far from ready yet to imprison the South. Ships came and went almost at will—for a time. What about the remaining border states: Maryland, Missouri and Kentucky? The 6th Massachusetts on its way to Washington was attacked by a mob in Baltimore April 19. Four volunteers were killed and at least nine civilians left dead. The capital of the United States was cut off from the nation. The Southerners would march into Washington at any moment, some feared and others hoped, but no Confederates came. April 25 the 7th New York came in from Annapolis, Md., with many other troops behind it. April 20 and the forces of Virginia seized the important Navy Yard at Norfolk with its guns, supplies, and

NORFOLK NAVY YARD DESTROYED

The great Navy Yard at Norfolk, Va., was twice razed during the war as it changed hands. First in April, 1861, evacuating Union forces spiked the guns, threw shot and small arms into the river, and set fire to the whole 200 acres of shops and warehouses. Later when the yard was recaptured by the Union, the Confederates added what damage they could before they evacuated. Even so the yard, with shops rebuilt in the midst of ruins, came to be an important depot for Union blockading fleets, for the James River flotilla, and for army gunboats.

some ships. What of the regular soldier of the United States? What would he do? The man in the ranks fought his war mostly in blue but many an officer had to fight a war with his conscience before he took up his uniform. Great deliberation, deep decisions of the soul: and many went South. Col. Robert E. Lee, career soldier, was offered command of the Federal forces. He refused, and April 20 resigned after 36 years of service to give his sword to Virginia and the South.

MAY, 1861

S	M	T	W	T	F	S
			1	2	3	4
5	6	7	8	9	10	11
12	13	14	15	16	17	18
19	20	21	22	23	24	25
26	27	28	29	30	31	

As spring marched into summer the war that had begun in April gradually became a reality to both sides. It was here and it had to be fought. Lincoln became aware that three months was not going to do the job; so on May 3 he called for 42,000 volunteers for three years or the duration. It turned out to be duration for many of those who survived. On the 6th the Confederate Congress formally declared that a state of war existed with the United States. But the North never formally admitted that the Southern government existed. Also on May 6, Arkansas in its convention decided to secede 69 to 1. The ninth star was gone from the flag, and the tenth was to leave May 7 when the Tennessee legislature submitted an Ordinance of Secession to a vote of the people, and approved military alliance with the Confederacy. But the somewhat doubt-

ful slave state of Maryland stayed with the North, although it furnished men to both sides. The armies were not ready yet, so military action was slight. In bitterly torn Missouri pro-Southern militia occupied a training camp in generally pro-Union St. Louis. On May 10 Capt. Nathaniel Lyon and Francis P. Blair, Jr., seized the camp and took the militia prisoners. Street fighting caused at least 28 deaths—a riot observed by U. S. Grant and William T. Sherman, not yet in military roles. Queen Victoria proclaimed May 13 that Britain was neutral, although it recognized the Confederacy as a belligerent. U. S. Minister Charles Francis Adams and Secretary of State Seward protested and laid a course of strength in diplomacy. British Foreign Minister Lord John Russell had received Confederates William L.Yancey and Pierre A. Rost as Commissioners. On the 20th the eleventh and last full state left its sisters when the North Carolina convention adopted secession. By May 29, Richmond, Va., became the second capital of the Confederacy. The Virginia voters had ratified their secession May 23. Kentucky, native state of both presidents, desired to avoid war while between two fires. The Kentucky legislature May 20 resolved that the state should be neutral. How soon that policy would appear to be ridiculous! A politician turned general, Benjamin F. Butler at Fort Monroe declared refugee Negroes "contraband" of war. Union troops moved out from Washington May 24 to clean out Confederates in Alexandria and Arlington, Va. Col. Elmer E. Ellsworth of the 11th New York Volunteers, and a friend of Lincoln, died. There was great mourning, for the nation was not yet used to killing.

JUNE, 1861

S	M	T	W	T	F	S
						1
2	3	4	5	6	7	8
9	10	11	12	13	14	15
16	17	18	19	20	21	22
23	24	25	26	27	28	29
30						

Summer and more preparation. There was no sudden spring to do battle—neither side had much to spring with. Manpower was not a problem, not yet. Of course, not all the troops had guns, but they would get them one way or another. Supplies were built up, contracts let; the business side of the war was in full swing. The U. S. Navy, small and unready, was at least in existence. The Confederacy had to create one—and did. On both sides the populace called for action. There was a little—slight compared with what was to come, but magnified for the moment into real war. Union troops had moved into western Virginia in May, commanded by the 35-year-old, flamboyant Maj. Gen. George B. McClellan. The Confederates met the invaders and lost at the Philippi Races June 3 and the Federals under field command of Brig. Gen. William S. Rosecrans moved forward into the pro-Union territory. At Harpers Ferry the Confederates pulled out of the vital river and railroad point, which had been seized by an obscure Col. T. J. Jackson. Down on the Virginia peninsula there was a scrap June 10 at Big Bethel near Yorktown with the Confederates victorious. Out in Missouri, Lyon, now a brigadier general, moved out from St. Louis and into the capital of Jefferson City June 15 and on to fighting at Boonville June 17. On June 3 Sen. Stephen A. Douglas died, and the nation was the loser. On the 11th the loyal element of western Virginia seceded from Virginia in a Wheeling convention and a new Union state was born. June 8 Tennessee confirmed secession in a popular vote two to one.

JULY, 1861

S	M	T	W	T	F	S
	1	2	3	4	5	6
7	8	9	10	11	12	13
14	15	16	17	18	19	20
21	22	23	24	25	26	27
28	29	30	31			

The small engagements still looked like big battles, both sides were positive that after two or three really major fights it would all be over. The Union push in West Virginia continued successfully in fights at Rich Mountain July 11 and at Carrick's Ford July 13. The major part of West Virginia fell to Union hands. But the cry was for more successes. Serious, inexperienced Union Brig. Gen. Irvin McDowell advanced from Washington with about 30,000 toward Manassas Junction, and against Beauregard, hero of Sumter. Another column under Robert Patterson headed south in the Shenandoah toward Joseph E. Johnston to keep him from joining Beauregard. Patterson failed and Johnston, warned of McDowell's advance, set out to join Beauregard. South of little Bull Run creek were the Confederates. McDowell planned to swing around their left and hit them in the flank. Beauregard planned primarily a move to his right

BULL RUN

This stone bridge over the little creek known as Bull Run was a key point in the Union disaster on July 21, 1861, known as the First Battle of Bull Run or Manassas. The Confederates held the bridge as well as a ford nearby. Union General McDowell intended to force the Confederates from the road so he could get to the railroad and cut Confederate lines. His plan was to demonstrate against the bridge with one division and against Blackburn's Ford, two miles away, with another force. Meanwhile, he sent other units on a broad flanking movement up the creek a mile or two to strike the Confederate left. But his flanking movement was delayed and Confederate General Beauregard was ready. Even so, the Union forces managed to gain control of the road beyond the bridge—but not for long. Reinforcements under Johnston struck the Union right and McDowell's army was routed. Men, horses, and wagons jammed the bridge trying to escape. The bridge was destroyed to hinder pursuit by the Confederates.

against the Union left flank. Identical wheeling movements, but the Union troops started their end run first and early on July 21 crossed the creek and moved down against the Confederate flank. The blue troops surged forward confidently; the Confederates fell back. But on Henry house hill the gray lines held and fighting surged. Brig. Gen. Barnard Bee, later mortally wounded, saw Colonel Jackson's Confederate brigade holding firm and shouted, "There stands Jackson like a stone wall." Words that gave the former mathematics professor a symbolic name forever. Late afternoon saw a sag in the Confederate lines, but slowly Johnston's forces moved into line and now the South advanced. The Federals broke. It was rout with roads to the capital clogged with running soldiers, officers attempting a rally or themselves running, and carriages of ladies and politicians who had come to view the victory. Washington cringed. The Confederates were coming. The war might be over. But they did not come and the war was not over. Demoralized by victory, the Confederates thought winning the day enough. First of a long series of failures of both sides to follow through. Union effectives: 28,452 with 481 killed, 1,011 wounded and 1,216 missing. Confederates engaged: 32,232 with 387 killed, 1,582 wounded, 12 missing. July 27 and winning general McClellan replaced beaten McDowell in field command. Things would be all right now that "Little Mac" was at his post. July 5 another Union defeat out in Missouri at Carthage. July 2 Lincoln empowered General Scott, still nominally in command, to suspend the writ of habeas corpus in certain areas. The Thirty-Seventh Congress met in spe-

cial session July 4 to approve Lincoln's moves already made and to provide the muscles of war. The blockade slowly moved into action, but there were many, many holes in the screen of ships off Southern ports.

AUGUST, 1861

S	M	T	W	T	F	S
				1	2	3
4	5	6	7	8	9	10
11	12	13	14	15	16	17
18	19	20	21	22	23	24
25	26	27	28	29	30	31

The big battle had been fought, but there was still war, as the public was reminded by the casualty lists of First Bull Run or Manassas just issued. McClellan in Washington began his preparations for no one knew what. Gen. Robert E. Lee took command of Confederates in West Virginia. Down on the North Carolina coast Gen. Ben Butler took Forts Clark and Hatteras on Pamlico Sound. Little action in the central West and minor engagements across the Mississippi, except for one —the biggest battle of the war in Missouri. On Aug. 10 at Wilson's Creek, also called Oak Hills or Springfield, Union forces under Lyon were badly beaten just south of Springfield by Confederates Benjamin McCulloch and Sterling Price. Union force: 5,400 with 223 killed, 721 wounded, 291 missing. Confederates: 11,600 with 257 killed, 900 wounded and 27 missing. Biggest loss was the death of Lyon, the most promising officer of the West. The Federal Congress prepared for war and promoted officers, including Col. Ulysses S. Grant, on outpost duty in

Missouri at the time. Aug. 30 in St. Louis, flamboyant Gen. John Charles Frémont ordered martial law and declared that slaves of all Missourians taking up arms against the North were free. A terrific furore, and on Sept. 2 Lincoln modified the Frémont ruling considerably. In Richmond the Confederate Congress voted money and arms for the struggle.

SEPTEMBER, 1861

S	M	T	W	T	F	S
1	2	3	4	5	6	7
8	9	10	11	12	13	14
15	16	17	18	19	20	21
22	23	24	25	26	27	28
29	30					

In West Virginia, Robert E. Lee failed in miserable weather. Way down on the Gulf of Mexico, Ship Island, Miss., fell to the Union Sept. 17—another base nibbled away from the South. The Kentucky fiction of neutrality came to end Sept. 3 when Confederates occupied fortress-like Columbus, Ky., on its bluffs overlooking the Mississippi just south of the Federal base at Cairo, Ill. New Brigadier Grant, now commanding at Cairo, occupied Paducah, Ky., at the mouth of the Tennessee River Sept. 6 in answer. A Confederate defense line now stretched thinly across Kentucky from Columbus through Bowling Green to Cumberland Gap. More fighting in always struggling Missouri—little affairs, neighbor against neighbor for four years. Lexington, on the Missouri River, was besieged by Sterling Price. About 2,800 Federals under Col. James

Mulligan stood hard, but had to surrender Sept. 20.

OCTOBER, 1861

S	M	T	W	T	F	S
		1	2	3	4	5
6	7	8	9	10	11	12
13	14	15	16	17	18	19
20	21	22	23	24	25	26
27	28	29	30	31		

Oct. 21 a Union force crossed the Potomac west of Washington near Leesburg, Va., on reconnaissance in force. Attacked by the Rebels, the Yankees fled beyond the river. Heavy losses included Col. Edward D. Baker, U. S. Senator from Oregon and close friend of Lincoln. Ball's Bluff or Edwards' Ferry, as this battle became known, was an unnecessary fiasco with repercussions against Union commanders. Small fights continued over West Virginia. Confederates failed Oct. 9 in an attack at Pensacola, Fla. Minor action in East Tennessee and in Missouri at places lost even on the maps. Union troops began an expedition into East Tennessee. Across the Mississippi affairs at Wet Glaze or Monday's Hollow, Underwood's Farm and Big Hurricane Creek became names in the official records. Oct. 31 and a "Rebel Legislature" at Neosho voted Missouri out of the Union. Although represented in the Confederate Congress and on the Southern flag, Confederate Missouri was often a government in exile. On Oct. 12 James Mason of Virginia and John Slidell of Louisiana ran the Charleston blockade en route to Britain and France as Commissioners from the Confederacy.

[19]

"ZOUAVE" REGIMENT

This company of "Zouaves," patterned after the corps in the French army, is seen in winter quarters around Culpeper, Va., where it acted as headquarters guard to General Meade. Organized in Philadelphia as the 114th Regiment Pennsylvania Volunteers, they affected the red Zouave pantaloons, which later were changed to red trousers when they moved into the Virginia woods. Their colorful outfits—white turbans and blue-and-scarlet uniforms—made them easy marks in battle, but despite high casualties, the 114th refused to part with their dress. In fact, they participated in several of the war's bloodiest battles, including Gettysburg.

NOVEMBER, 1861

S	M	T	W	T	F	S
					1	2
3	4	5	6	7	8	9
10	11	12	13	14	15	16
17	18	19	20	21	22	23
24	25	26	27	28	29	30

There was skirmishing in Virginia, while in West Virginia the fighting was nearly over and Federals ruled the mountains. Port Royal, S. C., was taken Nov. 7 to become another base for the blockading fleet. On the Mississippi opposite Columbus, Ky., Grant attacked Belmont, Mo., Nov. 7, temporarily succeeding, only to be driven out and back to Cairo. Nov. 1 McClellan was appointed General-in-Chief of Union armies to succeed ailing, infirm, figurehead Winfield Scott. Maj. Gen. Henry Halleck replaced the incompetent Frémont at St. Louis Nov. 19. Jefferson Davis was elected Nov. 6 as actual President of the Confederacy. A group of Kentucky soldiers and Southern leaders adopted secession Nov. 18 and Kentucky had its Confederate government, like Missouri's often on the move. But on the high seas there was real news. On Nov. 8, Confederate Commissioners Mason and Slidell were wrested from a British mail packet in the Bahama channel. The North, at first jubilant, soon began to fear that the impulsive action of Capt. Charles Wilkes might backfire into a shooting war with Britain.

DECEMBER, 1861

S	M	T	W	T	F	S
1	2	3	4	5	6	7
8	9	10	11	12	13	14
15	16	17	18	19	20	21
22	23	24	25	26	27	28
29	30	31				

Desultory action, little of importance, but men still died and it was war. The United States Congress met, and on Dec. 10 the Committee on the Conduct of the War was established to investigate inactivity of Union armies, the Ball's Bluff defeat, and much more in time. Dec. 26 Secretary of State Seward admitted the seizure of Mason and Slidell was an illegal act, and they went on their way. A holiday season, first of the war, and, of course, it would not be the last.

1862

S	M	T	W	T	F	S
				1	2	3	4
5	6	7	8	9	10	11
12	13	14	15	16	17	18
19	20	21	22	23	24	25
26	27	28	29	30	31	

A new year with new hopes and many new fears. The specter of war crept closer home each day and before long the armies would go into action, or at least they should. But now the armies were in winter quarters, or what passed for them. There was, however, the usual "little war." Out in central Kentucky on Jan. 19 was fought the battle of Mill Springs, Fishing Creek, Logan's Crossroads, or Somerset, call it what you will. Union Brig. Gen. George H. Thomas pushed against Confederate amateur Brig. Gen. Felix K. Zollicoffer. The well-handled Union force was victorious and Zollicoffer died. The Confederates withdrew into Tennessee, opening an important break in their Kentucky line. U. S. War Secretary Simon Cameron stepped down Jan. 13 to make room for Edwin M. Stanton. Cameron, the politician, went to Russia as minister. Dictatorial, efficient, hated, and successful Stanton now ruled the war of-

fice. But something had to be done in Virginia; McClellan had to move. On Jan. 27 came an unprecedented order from the President: McClellan was to advance Feb. 22. "Little Mac" ignored it.

S	M	T	W	T	F	S
						1
2	3	4	5	6	7	8
9	10	11	12	13	14	15
16	17	18	19	20	21	22
23	24	25	26	27	28	

Still "all quiet along the Potomac"— much too quiet. On Feb. 8 Burnside captured Roanoke Island off North Carolina. But the West was the winter battleground again. The Kentucky Confederate line was weakly held with but a few strong points. Albert Sidney Johnston had tried too much. Union forces, gunboats and men, shoved south, up the Tennessee from Paducah and attacked Fort Henry just below the Tennessee-Kentucky line. The gunboats took the honors Feb. 6 and Fort Henry fell as U. S. Grant moved his troops up for his first big opportunity. There was a march across the narrow strip of land to Fort Donelson on the Cumberland at Dover. Four days of siege and heavy fighting

ARMY REPAIR SHOP
Here is a field workshop of the Federal Army in Virginia.

through bitter cold nights and warmer days, brought victory for the North over an inert and inept Confederate command Feb. 16. A few Rebels got away but more than 14,000 surrendered. Brig. Gen. Simon Bolivar Buckner, third in command, asked for terms. His superiors, Gideon Pillow and John B. Floyd, had fled. Grant said "Unconditional Surrender"—and coined a watchword for the North, never to be forgotten. The words became a nickname fastened to this colorless little general and his initials. The Kentucky line that should never have been was gone. The drive to split the South had begun. The cost—Federals with 27,000 men, 500 killed, 2,108 wounded, 224 missing. Of 21,000 Confederates, 2,000 killed and wounded, 14,623 missing and captured. Other points crumpled. Bowling Green, Ky., on Feb. 14-15 and finally Nashville on Feb. 25 were occupied by Gen. Don Carlos Buell. In politics, a convention at Wheeling, W. Va., Feb. 18 adopted a pro-Union constitution for the new state. Jefferson Davis was inaugurated Feb. 22. And a poem appeared in *The Atlantic Monthly:* Julia Ward Howe and her "Battle Hymn of the Republic." Was the "jubilant swift sword" of the North already on its way? If so, it was to be dented again and again.

S	M	T	W	T	F	S
						1
2	3	4	5	6	7	8
9	10	11	12	13	14	15
16	17	18	19	20	21	22
23	24	25	26	27	28	29
30	31					

MARCH, 1862

On the James River off Norfolk, Va., a box-like, heavily armored Confederate vessel lumbered laboriously out March 8 in a surprise attack on the Union fleet. *U.S.S. Cumberland* sank and *Congress* burned. The resurrected *Merrimac*, officially the *C.S.S. Virginia*, had begun her new career. Excitement,

cheers and hopes in the South; woe and hand wringing in Washington. Fearful minds in the Capitol imagined the Confederate ironclad in the Potomac itself. But there was an answer —the "cheesebox on a raft." The unproven *U.S.S. Monitor* came down Hampton Roads March 9 and met the Confederate *Merrimac* in a five-hour fight. Shells bouncing on iron did only slight damage amid great noise, and it was a drawn engagement. The *Monitor* pulled back to shallow water, while the *Merrimac* headed back into Norfolk to appear no more. It was destroyed in the May evacuation of the port. The first battle of the ironclads was a tactical draw but a Northern strategic victory. Now the South was alarmed for a new Navy had come into existence. In North Carolina the capture of New Bern March 14 gave Burnside still another base. But the Army of the Potomac—where was it? There was an embarrassing Union foray to Manassas Junction March 7, but Johnston was gone leaving only fake guns. Reorganization, urgings, and frustration for a President with his never-ready McClellan. On March 11 McClellan was relieved of his overall command of the Union armies, retaining his proud possession, the Army of the Potomac. Lincoln urged a direct overland blow at Richmond but bowed

F. Ship Hartford
N Orleans, April 29th
1862

My dearest Wife,

We are now masters of
the Mississippi River, the Forts Jackson &
St. Phillips have surrendered—McIntosh & Mc
Intosh & a host of others are my Prisoners
of course the New Orleans papers abuse me
but I am case hardened to all that, I
dont read the papers except to gain in
formation as to the War—
I find the Forts all along the coast are
surrendering & we will have nothing to
do but occupy them—I will be off
for Mobile in a few days & put it
to them there—I have done all I promised & all I was expected to do—
So thanks to God, I hope I have acquitted
myself to my friends as well as my country
I was recommended by others for the appointment, it was not sought—& I hope
through Gods assistance not to disappoint
either my friends or the country—
Your affectionate husband & father
D. G. Farragut

To
Mrs. D. G. Farragut

Admiral Farragut writes his wife, "We are now masters of the
Mississippi River."

to McClellan's strategy for an attack from the Peninsula east of Richmond. Lincoln agreed only if McClellan promised to protect Washington which of course the general did. On March 17 the troops began embarking. The Confederates decided on diversion and sent to the Shenandoah Valley onetime "Tom Fool" Jackson, now known as "Stonewall." Jackson kept Union forces moving and fighting late in March and prevented them from joining McClellan. Defeated at Kernstown March 23, Jackson retreated with Nathaniel Banks in pursuit. In the West victorious Grant was under a cloud after taking Fort Donelson. He had allegedly failed to keep Halleck in St. Louis properly informed and so Grant's army moved up the Tennessee River without him to Savannah where Grant rejoined his men upon the illness of Gen. C. F. Smith. Twenty miles away in Mississippi the Confederates massed at Corinth under Albert Sidney Johnston. Still farther west in northern Arkansas, Union Gen. Samuel Curtis won his only claim to fame by defeating Confederates at Pea Ridge or Elkhorn Tavern March 6 to 8. Federals: 11,250 with 203 killed, 980 wounded, and 201 missing. Confederates: 14,000 with about 600 killed and wounded and 200 missing. In the forgotten far southwest, Confederates under Henry Hopkins Sibley captured Santa Fe, N. M., March 4, only to be beaten in Apache Canyon at Pigeon's Ranch or Glorieta March 28. The Southerners retreated from the state and the war in New Mexico was over. On the Mississippi, New Madrid, Mo., was taken March 14 by Federals under a rising name, Brig. Gen. John Pope. An important stretch of the river was in Northern hands. On March 13 all persons in Federal service were forbidden to return escaped slaves to Confederate owners under a new Article of War. Also in March Confederate President Jefferson Davis made some cabinet changes. Judah P. Benjamin replaced Robert M. T. Hunter as Secretary of State; George W. Randolph succeeded Benjamin as Secretary of War; and Thomas N. Watts became Attorney General in place of Thomas Bragg.

APRIL, 1862

S	M	T	W	T	F	S
		1	2	3	4	5
6	7	8	9	10	11	12
13	14	15	16	17	18	19
20	21	22	23	24	25	26
27	28	29	30			

It was really spring now and armies were on the move. McClellan was on the Peninsula and Grant was pushing near Mississippi. A mass of a hundred thousand moved toward Yorktown, Va., a scene of Revolutionary glory. At first only 16,000 Confederates under John Magruder, aided by spring rains, held off the Union horde. On April 5 McClellan was notified that McDowell's corps would be held near Washington to fend the threatening Jackson. This was the beginning of the oft-repeated excuse that the loss of McDowell wrecked the entire drive on Richmond. McClellan prepared for siege at Yorktown—big guns, fortifications and waiting. Jackson in the Valley watched and waited to pounce and the Federals wondered in what direction, where and when. In Georgia, Fort Pulaski, on the ap-

Confederate cavalry leader Nathan Bedford Forrest tells in characteristically salty language and faulty spelling how he caught the enemy by surprise near Corinth, Miss. "I look for a fite soon and a big one when it comes off," he concludes.

BATTERY BEFORE YORKTOWN

Union General McClellan took no chances when he moved against Yorktown, Va., on his drive toward Richmond in 1862. He set out to besiege the city with an overwhelming force. This battery of big guns was set up in the orchard of the Farinholt House, near Yorktown. Known as Battery No. 1, this was the best constructed of all the works. It was concealed behind the little crest rising from the shore of the York River. There were five 100-pound guns and one 200 pounder. Outnumbered by McClellan's force, the Confederates abandoned Yorktown and moved up the peninsula toward Richmond.

proaches to the port of Savannah, surrendered to Federals April 11. And on the 26th Fort Macon, N. C., fell to the North. But there was much more going on in the West. On the banks of the Tennessee near old Shiloh Meeting House, Grant and his army were quietly encamped, their back to the river and their position unfortified. Albert Sidney Johnston prepared to move. Organization problems delayed the limping advance until April 3. But Union scouts gave little and unheeded warning and few pickets saw the Confederate outposts coming. Sunday morning April 6 it happened. The sleeping and breakfasting Federals hurriedly organized but were struck from the woods and struck hard. Grant was up the river at Savannah. But he came a-steamboating at the sound of the guns. The Union lines sagged and crumpled — what lines there were. Breaking Federals fled to slight safety under the bluff along the river. A few held—and bravely—in the "Hornet's Nest" and elsewhere. Maj. Gen. Lew Wallace, later to write *Ben Hur*, lost his way. Grant, however, managed to hold on—the entire army was not in the river. Confusion reigned too in Southern ranks, and General Johnston died from a wound in the leg, needlessly bleeding to death. By early evening help came when Buell pushed rapidly in from Nashville and Beauregard, now in Confederate command, could not press home the winning thrust. On the 7th the reinforced Federals held the field and the Battle of Shiloh, or Pittsburgh Landing, was over. Grant's worst battle—and he must have known it—but there were plenty of excuses. Beauregard retreated to Corinth. Union, 42,682 with Grant and 20,000 with Buell: 1,754 killed, 8,408 wounded,

2,885 missing. Confederate: 40,335 with 1,723 killed, 8,012 wounded and 959 missing. A heavy price for carelessness on both sides. Grant was again in a shadow and Halleck took over in person. Assembling 100,000 he inched forward toward Corinth April 29. On the Mississippi, Pope added to his laurels April 7 when Island Number 10, a fortified Confederate post, surrendered. On April 11 Huntsville, Ala., was seized. From this raid Capt. James J. Andrews and 21 soldiers went out to steal the locomotive "General" between Atlanta and Chattanooga. They got the engine all right and attempted to destroy the railroad to give Gen. O. M. Mitchel at Huntsville opportunity to move between Atlanta and Chattanooga. It was a foolhardy stunt and a lost race, but one of the wildest runs in the history of railroading. Finally Andrews and his men were forced to flee into the woods and some died as spies. On the Gulf, the gateway of the Confederacy in the West was New Orleans. April 24 Flag Officer David Glasgow Farragut daringly passed Forts St. Philip and Jackson and smashed a weak opposing fleet. The city itself was penetrated April 25 and occupied on the 29th. Gen. Benjamin F. Butler took over for the Federal army and began his harsh rule that was to bring him hatred in the North as well as the South.

MAY, 1862

With overwhelming Union forces crowding in upon Yorktown, Joseph E. Johnston ordered the Confederates to evacuate May 3 and retreat toward Richmond. The withdrawal ended in the suburbs and countryside near the Southern capital itself. The Norfolk naval base was evacuated May 11 and

BUTLER'S PROCLAMATION.

His outrageous insult to the Women of New Orleans!

Southern Men, avenge their wrongs!!!

Head-Quarters, Department of the Gulf, New Orleans, May 15, 1862.

General Orders, No. 28.

As the Officers and Soldiers of the United States have been subject to repeated insults from the women calling themselves ladies of New Orleans, in return for the most scrupulous non-interference and courtesy on our part, it is ordered that hereafter when any Female shall, by word, gesture, or movement, insult or show contempt for any officer or soldier of the United States, she shall be regarded and held liable to be treated as a woman of the town plying her avocation.

By command of Maj.-Gen. **BUTLER,**
GEORGE C. STRONG,
A. A. G. Chief of Stables.

This is a Confederate broadside that uses Union General Butler's inflammatory proclamation concerning the women of New Orleans to fan the zeal of Southerners. Butler's General Order 28 was the most widely known of many acts during his rule of New Orleans which earned him the epithet, "Beast."

McCLELLAN'S ARMY

Shown is a small part of the vast force that General McClellan led against Richmond in the Peninsula Campaign in 1862. This is a camp at Cumberland Landing, Va., on the Pamunkey River. A writer of the time describes the view of the camp as a whole as "one of the most magnificent spectacles ever seen in the army." The wagon in the foreground is a blacksmith's forge.

the ironclad *Merrimac* destroyed. The North held the peninsula and the James River approaches to Richmond. McDowell began an overland movement southward to join McClellan May 17. McClellan spread his massive

S	M	T	W	T	F	S
				1	2	3
4	5	6	7	8	9	10
11	12	13	14	15	16	17
18	19	20	21	22	23	24
25	26	27	28	29	30	31

army along the swampy Chickahominy with three corps on the north to join with McDowell and two south facing the Confederates. Always fearful of the size of the enemy, McClellan got a good look by sending up captive balloons with officers in small baskets to peer at the lines about the city. Johnston needed no such view to see the separated Federals and May 31 fell upon the two corps at Seven Pines or Fair Oaks. Despite the flooded stream and weakened bridges a third corps managed to cross in time to hold off the Confederate drive. Johnston was wounded and Robert E. Lee took over the army, soon to be given its immortal name, the Army of Northern Virginia. June 1 the Confederate attack continued only to end in withdrawal into the earthworks of Richmond. Union forces available or used: 44,944 with 790 dead, 3,594 wounded and 647 missing. Confederates: 41,816 effectives with 980 killed, 4,749 wounded and 405 missing. Richmond was virtually under siege from the east. Some fear rose in the South, but the army was still between them and the Yankees, although the distance was very short. More complaints from McClellan: he wanted

McDowell's troops and even more; he claimed he was outnumbered. He did not attack. The day of Jackson had come in the Shenandoah. Two Union forces under Banks and John C. Frémont, explorer and defeated Republican presidential candidate, moved on Stonewall at Staunton. A quick thrust west and Jackson defeated Federals at McDowell, Va., May 8 before turning on Banks. He swept north up the Luray valley to win at Front Royal May 23. Banks had been outflanked and he too fell back. Jackson hit him at Middletown and Newton May 24 and again at Winchester May 25. The Yankees fled across the Potomac at Williamsport. But as Jackson demonstrated against Harpers Ferry, Frémont was moving in from the west to cut him off; and McDowell, halted again in his move toward Richmond, started west from Fredericksburg. It was to be a squeeze play. Jackson started from Winchester May 31 up the valley, southward for Strasburg. By month's end Jackson was in full retreat and the Federals crouched outside Richmond. Was there a crisis ahead with victory possible for the North? In New Orleans Butler was earning his title of "Beast" when he ordered any female insulting a Union soldier to be regarded as a "woman of the town plying her avocation." John Hunt Morgan, the Kentucky Confederate raider, suffered a rare defeat at Lebanon, Tenn., May 5. Halleck from Shiloh crept roller-like toward Corinth, fortifying every night—there would not be another Sunday morning surprise. But Beauregard had no intention of repeating Shiloh. Keeping a bold front with noises of trains and troops he pulled out May 29-30 and headed south toward Tupelo. Halleck had won the campaign, such as it was. But among the soldiers at least his first attempt at field operations was considered a bit of a joke. On May 15 the Department of Agriculture was established by the United States Congress although it was not given Cabinet status until 1889. Congress passed a homestead measure which granted farms of 160 acres to any person who would occupy and improve it for five years.

JUNE, 1862

S	M	T	W	T	F	S
1	2	3	4	5	6	7
8	9	10	11	12	13	14
15	16	17	18	19	20	21
22	23	24	25	26	27	28
29	30					

June 1 the Battle of Seven Pines or Fair Oaks ended. In the valley, Jackson rolled south, fighting rearguard actions. At Cross Keys June 8 he struck at the incoming Frémont and won. A quick turn and he hit Shields of Mc-Dowell's corps at Port Republic June 9. The trap had failed and the first Valley Campaign was over. Jackson had marched about 300 miles in 35 days, fought four battles and many smaller encounters with a pitifully small force. He had kept nearly 60,000 Federals more than occupied. A reputation had been made. Rain at Richmond, McClellan got some of his reinforcements but it was never enough, at least in his eyes. June 12 to 15 another name joined the Southern heroes when James Ewell Brown Stuart rode around McClellan's army in a daring raid. "Jeb" gained much knowledge for Lee, lifted the spirits of the South, and won himself a plume. Lee decided to wait no longer. June 25 Fitz-John Porter was on the Union right, north of the Chickahominy. Secretly Jackson transported his Confederates to the aid of Lee, giving the South about 85,000 to 100,000 for McClellan. June 26 Lee crossed the Chickahominy to turn McClellan's right and cut him off from his York River base. The Rebels struck Porter at Mechanicsville or Beaver Dam Creek and Porter sank back a bit only to be hit again June 27 by Lee, joined by Jackson, at Gaines' Mill or First Cold Harbor. Union losses were great, but at high cost to a South that already could ill afford it. McClellan decided to retreat south to the James River under protection of the fleet. Across White Oak Swamp they moved, but the Confederates pressed hard against them. At Savage Station June 29 the Southerners came near to victory, but Jackson was tardy—Jackson of the fast moving valley campaign. On the 30th another fight: White Oak Swamp, Glendale or Frayser's Farm. McClellan held the Confederates off and made a brilliant retreat to Malvern Hill, just north of the James. July 1 and Lee assaulted the low but strongly held rise of ground only to falter with more heavy casualties. McClellan July 2 moved down the James a bit to Harrison's Landing. Richmond was saved. The Seven Days were over and McClellan had failed. Figures for the campaign vary greatly but the Union managed about 91,169 effectives engaged with 1,734 killed, 8,062 wounded and 6,053 missing. Confederates effective and engaged: 85,000, 3,478 killed, 16,261 wounded and 875 missing. A high Southern price. There were many inquiries—why had Jackson been slow? Why had McClellan de-

MECHANICSVILLE

This collection of about a dozen ordinary houses was the scene of some of the heaviest fighting of the war, during the Peninsula Campaign culminating in the Battle of Malvern Hill, July 1, 1862. Mechanicsville, Va., fell into Union hands on June 2. After a struggle at nearby Beaver Dam Creek, the Confederates retreated in disorder down the pike towards Richmond, three and a half miles away. The Confederates counterattacked and recaptured Mechanicsville on June 26 at the start of the Seven Days Campaign. The two-story house at the left was on the turnpike to Richmond. A barricade was thrown across the road in front of the house, with two howitzers placed for defense.

layed and lost? Questions never entirely answered but it didn't matter; the events were history. In Charleston Harbor, Union probes were repulsed June 10 and 16. June 4 Fort Pillow on the Mississippi was evacuated by the South, and on the 6th the important river city of Memphis, Tenn., fell, after a Confederate river squadron of vastly inferior numbers and fire power put up a losing fight. The river campaign in the west was paying off. Could the Confederacy be split? True, much of the river north and south was in Union hands but there was always Vicksburg on its towering, gun-laden bluffs. Farragut June 26-29 brought his fleet from New Orleans north and passed the batteries. The drive against Vicksburg had begun, to end a year later. An attempt to dig a canal June 27 across from Vicksburg to change the course of the river and isolate the city ended in mud and swamps. In staff changes, Gen. Braxton Bragg replaced the ailing Beauregard June 17 in Confederate western command. Lincoln, still fearful of the defenses of Washington, ordered western victor John Pope to command a new Army of Virginia June 26.

JULY, 1862

S	M	T	W	T	F	S
		1	2	3	4	5
6	7	8	9	10	11	12
13	14	15	16	17	18	19
20	21	22	23	24	25	26
27	28	29	30	31		

The Army of the Potomac was safe at Harrison's Landing on the James while Pope was organizing the widespread fragments of his separate force near Washington and making boastful claims. But there was plenty of battling with words. McClellan violently protested the proposal to bring his army back to northern Virginia, and Lincoln went to see him July 9 with many pointed questions. The public was disappointed, their victorious hero had failed them. But the army was happy, they always were with "Little Mac." He took care of them and loyalty became affection. McClellan seemed to glory in his campaign and his men. Small actions marked the month in the West. There was fighting in Arkansas, and on July 13 Nathan Bedford Forrest, now beginning his independent career, took Murfreesboro, Tenn., southeast of Nashville. July 15 and down the Yazoo above Vicksburg came the homemade ironclad *Arkansas*, built at great cost to the Confederates out of railroad iron, faulty engines and pure ingenuity. Under Commander Isaac N. Brown the ram swept through the Yankee fleet, challenging them all to control of the Mississippi. July 4 to 28 John Hunt Morgan raided Kentucky and Tennessee. July 2 Lincoln called for 300,000 volunteers for three years' service and Congress authorized money, and gave its approval to the muscles of war. July 11 Henry Wager Halleck from the West was made General-in-Chief of all land forces of the United States, and on July 17 Grant took over in the west from Halleck. July 30 in a Cincinnati paper the term Copperhead appeared, referring to the pro-Southerners in Indiana and Ohio. On July 16 Confederate Commissioner John Slidell was received by Napoleon III and on the 29th the Confederate cruiser *Alabama* left Liverpool where it been built, more or less secretly. The Confederates managed several ship buildings in England until masterful diplomacy by U. S. Minister Charles Francis Adams aided by the fortunes of war caused a change in British policy. July 22 the Federal cabinet met. President Lincoln had a proposal. He suggested that shortly, when the public climate was right, he proclaim emancipation of all slaves in states "remaining in insurrection" as of the first of January, 1863. The cabinet urged a slight delay. There was more to war than dying.

AUGUST, 1862

S	M	T	W	T	F	S
					1	2
3	4	5	6	7	8	9
10	11	12	13	14	15	16
17	18	19	20	21	22	23
24	25	26	27	28	29	30
31						

McClellan was still within striking distance of Richmond but he did not strike. He was too busy arguing with Washington. Lee now saw that the best defense would be an offensive toward the north. What about Pope who had marched slowly south of the Rappahannock? And if Lee left Richmond what about McClellan? Jackson was sent back to the northwest where he defeated Banks in the battle of Cedar or Slaughter Mountain, south of Culpeper Aug. 9. Pope pulled back. By the 16th the Army of the Potomac was evacuating from the Peninsula. Lee began to move fast now. Jackson led the way up the valley followed by Lee with Longstreet's Corps. Jackson poured out of Thoroughfare Gap in the Bull Run Mountains Aug. 26, having rounded Pope's right, and was now in his rear, back at the old battlegrounds of the year before at First Bull

Run. Aug. 26-27 and the Confederates had a high time destroying Pope's stores at Manassas Junction and Bristoe Station, stuffing themselves on hard-to-get delicacies and lighting huge bonfires. Pope fell back rapidly now toward Washington but arriving at Manassas, he found Jackson had just gone. Pope probed for Jackson and Jackson fought him at Groveton Aug. 28. Pope figured it was over; Jackson must have left now, greatly outnumbered and far from communications as he was. But Lee was coming in rapidly behind Jackson and by the night of the 28th was just east of Thoroughfare Gap. Confusion grew in Pope's command. He know how to fight but this was too hard to figure. By late on the 29th Pope found Jackson and was ready to attack. Pope hit him north of Groveton along an unfinished railroad embankment. Fitz-John Porter of McClellan's army had come up to help and Pope gave him an indefinite order to hit Jackson's exposed right wing. Porter quickly found there was more in front of him than a ragged flank. It was Longstreet with reinforcements for Jackson. The Confederate army was now united under Lee. Porter refrained from full attack but held off Longstreet. He was to stand trial for this action. It was not until the administration of Grover Cleveland that Porter was reinstated and cleared of the charges of failing to attack. Again Pope thought the Confederates had withdrawn and attacked again on the 30th in a badly planned assault that was valiantly and persistently pushed forward. But Longstreet with artillery and infantry rolled up and Pope was badly beaten. Retreat was ordered and the Federals headed back for Washington again. Beaten they were, but full

GAINES' MILL

This is the scene of the battle of June 27, 1862. Following the fierce fighting of that day, it was converted into a hospital for the wounded. The wooden part of the structure was destroyed in a raid on Richmond, leaving only the brick superstructure, scorched by fire.

retreat was hardly necessary. More of McClellan's army was coming in; it was Pope himself who was beaten. Second Bull Run or Manassas was fought with 75,696 Federals, engaged Aug. 27 to Sept. 2: 1,724 killed, 8,372 wounded, 5,958 missing. Confederates: 48,527 engaged, 1,481 killed, 7,627 wounded and 89 missing. In Tennessee "Morgan and his terrible men" were active again, and Aug. 27-28 a main force of Confederates under Braxton Bragg invaded Kentucky in a drive for the Ohio River. Small engagements west of the Mississippi, and Rebel guerrilla William Clarke Quantrill captured Independence, Mo., Aug. 11. In the northwest it wasn't Confederates but Indians that caused the Union troubles, with an uprising starting Aug. 18 in Minnesota. First permission to use Negroes as soldiers was given by Stanton Aug. 25 to South Carolina coastal bases. Aug. 24 and the *C.S.S. Alabama* was commissioned at sea near the Azores. The blockade began to tighten along the Atlantic coast as Federal bases and ships multiplied. But for the South it was a month of victory.

SEPTEMBER, 1862

S	M	T	W	T	F	S
	1	2	3	4	5	6
7	8	9	10	11	12	13
14	15	16	17	18	19	20
21	22	23	24	25	26	27
28	29	30				

Lee with his victorious Army of Northern Virginia tried to cut off the retreat of Pope's inglorious Army of Virginia but Federal Maj. Gens. Phil. Kearny and I. I. Stevens blocked Lee at Chantilly or Ox Hill Sept. 1 and lost their lives. Lincoln stepped in to revive the possibly disintegrating Union army. McClellan, the pride of the army and the bane of those who wanted to win the war, was restored to full command and ordered once more to defend Washington from the invader. Pope went west to fight Indians. The army rejoiced and the people wondered. Maybe McClellan would fight this time. For there was something to fear —the Army of Northern Virginia and its Lee and Jackson—by now a legend. Lee saw attack at Washington was impossible so once more he moved. This time he crossed the Potomac Sept. 5 into Maryland—the North itself heard the sound of Confederate troops. There was hope that Marylanders would join the South but few did. Sept. 7 and Lee entered Frederick, Md., where a little aged lady named Barbara Frietchie lived and that is all. She waved no flag and delivered no taunts to Jackson— that was for the poets. Lee was bold but he knew that McClellan, if he followed at all, would be very cautious. The possibilities spread out: Harrisburg, Pa.; Philadelphia or even Baltimore. Sept. 9 came orders from Lee; the force of 55,000 was to be divided. The whole army would withdraw to the other side of South Mountain. Jackson was to recross the Potomac and take Harpers Ferry with its 12,000 Federals. Other troops spread around Maryland. On Sept. 13 a sergeant and private of the Union army that was probing northward found a piece of paper wrapped around a few cigars. Was it important? Indeed it was—Lee's special orders were in Union hands. McClellan knew it all now, or was it a trick? Maj. Gen. D. H. Hill was sent by Lee to defend South Mountain and McClellan cautiously attacked Sept. 14.

Hill held all the day in the Battle of South Mountain while to the south at another gap Confederate Maj. Gen. Lafayette McLaws held off W. B. Franklin. At Harpers Ferry, Jackson was at work. Lee withdrew from South Mountain across Antietam Creek to the village of Sharpsburg, the Potomac at his back. Lee waited. On the 15th Harpers Ferry, 12,000 strong, surrendered to Jackson. But McClellan waited too. He brought up more troops but did not use them. Jackson hurried north to join Lee, leaving A. P. Hill with a division to complete things at Harpers Ferry. By the 16th Jackson had rejoined Lee. Ponderously and by units McClellan attacked Sept. 17. First he surged against Jackson on the Confederate left and then further along the line McClellan moved in at the East Wood, the West Wood, the Dunkard Church and along Bloody Lane in separate, jerky attacks. On the far right of the Union army Burnside was late at the Stone Bridge but he pushed the thin Confederate line into the outskirts of Sharpsburg. Then through the cornfields came A. P. Hill and his "Light Division," tired from hard marching but ready to save an army. The Confederates held and it was Hill's greatest hour among many. The Battle of Antietam or Sharpsburg, one of the bloodiest of the war, was over. The figures were huge, the controversy heated, and the results vital. Lee had been halted in his invasion although he held the battleground. Union force present: 87,164; effectives, 75,316; killed, 2,108; wounded, 9,549; and 753 missing. Confederates engaged: 51,844; killed, 2,700; wounded, 9,024; and 2,000 missing. Reinforcements joined McClellan but there were none for Lee. The Confederate army waited on the 18th and that

night pulled out without opposition. McClellan rested his army, many of whom had fought well, and some of whom had not fought at all. In Kentucky the Confederate advance continued. Kirby Smith of Bragg's army was at Covington, Ky., just across from Cincinnati, Sept. 15, but quickly retired. Fears swept the Ohio; would Bragg cross? By Sept. 25 Buell had gotten back with his army to Louisville for defense. Still more Confederate attack. In Mississippi Sterling Price and Earl Van Dorn hit William S. Rosecrans at Iuka Sept. 19 and lost. A new Union name, Rosecrans, was rising. Sept. 23 and the issuance of Lincoln's preliminary Emancipation Proclamation put the North on record as to slavery.

OCTOBER, 1862

S	M	T	W	T	F	S
			1	2	3	4
5	6	7	8	9	10	11
12	13	14	15	16	17	18
19	20	21	22	23	24	25
26	27	28	29	30	31	

A second summer of battle and death was over, but war only paused. It never changes seasons. East and west the big battles of the summer were nearly over, but not quite. Van Dorn and Price, defeated at Iuka, weren't through either. On Oct. 3-4 they attacked Rosecrans at Corinth and failed again. Retreating Van Dorn was hit again by Gen. E. O. C. Ord at the Big Hatchie River Oct. 5. In central Kentucky Bragg paused to inaugurate Richard Hawes as Confederate governor of Kentucky at Frankfort, Oct. 4. But the new governor did not occupy

ANTIETAM BRIDGE

This bridge across Antietam Creek on the turnpike leading from Boonesboro to Sharpsburg is one of the memorable spots of the war. Aided by artillery from the surrounding ridges, Federal cavalry attacked the bridge early in the Battle of Antietam and held it against savage counterattacks until infantry was moved up. The Confederates were driven back almost to Sharpsburg, but the arrival of A. P. Hill's "Light Division" enabled them to hold.

his capital for long. Buell had turned and was marching on Bragg to catch him at Perryville or Chaplin Hills Oct. 8 and soundly pummel him. An unknown Brigadier rose with the battle: Gen. Phil Sheridan. Union: 36,940 with 845 killed, 2,851 wounded, 515 missing. Confederates: 16,000 with 510 killed, 2,635 wounded and 251 missing along the quiet valley of Doctor's Creek. Bragg retreated and the Kentucky invasion was over. On the 26th the Confederates pulled out through Cumberland Gap into Tennessee. The proud summer of Southern victories seemed far away now. Richmond had held; Jackson had been in the Valley; Pope was routed at Manassas; Maryland was invaded and then Antietam, and in the west after Shiloh came successful raids and invasion nearly to the Ohio. These Confederate gains were all gone now. Back to Tennessee, back to Virginia, the Rebels came. But they left a farewell card. On Oct. 9, J. E. B. Stuart made his first Pennsylvania raid with 1,800 men. They probed as far as Chambersburg, Pa., and returned Oct. 12 with fresh horses. Lee rested in the northern valley at Winchester before moving south behind the Rappahannock slowly followed by McClellan. Lincoln had gone up to Sharpsburg to urge speed, but it was useless. In the west Grant took over the Department of the Tennessee Oct. 25 and made plans to take the bastion on the river at Vicksburg where the fleets had failed. While Grant was busy with his plans Gen. John A. McClernand of Illinois received confidential orders from Lincoln to raise a separate force to attack the city on the bluff. Politics and war were mixing. More changes and Rosecrans, victor at Iuka and Corinth, succeeded Buell, victor at Perryville, but a

failure for letting Bragg into Kentucky. Oct. 7 in England William E. Gladstone declared that the Confederates "have made a nation," and "we may anticipate with certainty" their success. But emancipation and the early fall news made them look again; recognition did not come. Summer, 1862, was over.

NOVEMBER, 1862

S	M	T	W	T	F	S
						1
2	3	4	5	6	7	8
9	10	11	12	13	14	15
16	17	18	19	20	21	22
23	24	25	26	27	28	29
30						

Still more changes came in the Northern command. On Nov. 7 near Warrenton, Va., slowly moving southward at last, McClellan was superseded by Ambrose Everett Burnside in orders from Lincoln. A great and controversial career was over. The organizer who didn't often fight was through; and his successor didn't want the job: he didn't think he was good enough and he wasn't. In mid-November the Army of the Potomac with its new leader moved to the heights at Falmouth across from Fredericksburg on the direct road to Richmond. No pontoon bridges to cross the Rappahannock and Burnside waited. The next day Lee pulled in also to the hills back of the city and began to dig in although much digging wasn't needed. Fredericksburg was a natural entrenchment with its hills, valleys, stone walls and now its armies. In Arkansas and Mississippi there were several small affairs. On the big river Grant began overland from Corinth toward Vicksburg and took Grand Junction on the Mississippi Central and then occupied Holly Springs, Nov. 13. Northern-born Confederate John C. Pemberton fell back toward Vicksburg. By now Grant had heard of McClernand and his projected operations from Memphis. The first Union regiment of South Carolina volunteers came into existence, recruited on the coast from former slaves.

DECEMBER, 1862

S	M	T	W	T	F	S
	1	2	3	4	5	6
7	8	9	10	11	12	13
14	15	16	17	18	19	20
21	22	23	24	25	26	27
28	29	30	31			

The quiet of winter quarters had not set in, at least not for a while. Burnside was expected to head for Richmond and he did—straight ahead across the Rappahannock and up the hills with Lee in the way. Dec. 11 and 12 he crossed the river under fire and paused. He assaulted on the 13th. It was not a battle but a slaughter. Charge after charge was sent straight ahead against Marye's Heights and further along the line. There was small chance and no sense to it. Burnside failed. Union strength: 106,007 with 1,284 killed, 9,600 wounded, and 1,769 missing. Confederates: 72,497 engaged, only 595 killed, 4,061 wounded and 653 missing. Lee was victorious but nothing happened. Lee held his line and Burnside held his across the Rappahannock and now it was time for winter quarters, past time for the Federals. In North Carolina Dec. 12-18 a Union expedition to Goldsboro was repulsed. There was sparring for keeps in the Mississippi valley and Van Dorn struck boldly against Holly Springs, Miss., destroyed over $1,500,000 of vital supplies and Grant was checked in his designs on Vicksburg, but not for long. Dec. 20, having reached a firm understanding with McClernand, Grant moved Sherman down from Memphis to ascend the Yazoo and attack Vicksburg from Chickasaw Bayou and Haines (or Haynes) Bluff. Assaults on Dec. 27-29 failed with Union forces of 30,720 losing 208 killed, 1,005 wounded and 563 missing against 13,792 defenders with 63 killed, 134 wounded and 10 missing —a miniature Fredericksburg. But the Confederates were worried over Vicksburg. Grant already was showing that he didn't mean to stop. Nathan Bedford Forrest in West Tennessee gave Grant things to worry about, too, tearing up railroads, destroying more supplies and fighting several engagements. Morgan was busy with a Christmas raid into Kentucky as far as Elizabethtown on the 27th, just south of Louisville. In Arkansas at Prairie Grove Dec. 7, Generals J. G. Blunt and F. J. Herron defeated Confederate T. C. Hindman south of Fayetteville and the Southerners gave up advancing into Missouri for a time. After his retreat from Perryville, Bragg retreated to Murfreesboro along Stone's River near Nashville. Rosecrans followed him the day after Christmas. By the night of the 30th both armies faced each other outside Murfreesboro. Bragg made the first move early on the 31st rolling up the Union right against the turnpike and the river. Rosecrans, with Sheridan and George H. Thomas, desperately held the Nashville road. New

FREDERICKSBURG

Some of the most thrilling events of the war took place around this picturesque Virginia city, midway between Washington and Richmond and just below the falls of the Rappahannock River. Union troops captured it in April, 1862, only to surrender it a few months later when Pope's troops had to retreat from Cedar Mountain. In November, the Army of the Potomac marched down from the Antietam campaign and went into winter quarters in the hills along the river. On Dec. 12th Union troops entered Fredericksburg against only token resistance. But the next day, when Burnside threw his troops against Lee's position above the town his army was cut to pieces and the Federals withdrew from Fredericksburg to their previous positions.

Year's day was quiet with little action, but on the 2nd the Confederates hit the other side of the Union line, the left. At first again there was success, but the drive was blunted and driven back. The next day both sides wondered who had won. But on the night of Jan. 3 Bragg withdrew through Murfreesboro to winter quarters 35 miles away at Tullahoma. Effective Federals: 41,400 with 1,667 killed, 7,543 wounded and 3,686 missing. Confederate effectives: 34,732 with 1,294 killed, 7,945 wounded and 2,500 missing. Dec. 1 Congress convened and heard Lincoln's message recommending emancipation in the loyal states and compensation to loyal owners for slaves made free by war. Thirty-eight Indians were hanged at Mankato, Minn., Dec. 26 for participating in the Sioux uprisings. Congress Dec. 31 admitted West Virginia as the 35th state. The unseaworthy ironclad *Monitor* sank off Cape Hatteras Dec. 30 in a storm and 16 died. President Davis Dec. 23 proclaimed Benjamin F. Butler, Federal ruler of conquered New Orleans, a felon, outlaw and enemy of mankind who should be hanged without trial. It was Christmas, 1862.

1863

S	M	T	W	T	F	S
				1	2	3
4	5	6	7	8	9	10
11	12	13	14	15	16	17
18	19	20	21	22	23	24
25	26	27	28	29	30	31

Just where did things stand? So much had happened and yet there was going to be more; anyone could see that. Nothing had been finally decided as far as could be seen. Emancipation was the talk in the North, as the factories hummed. There was talk in the South, too, of victories, but there were too few factories to hum. There was a bit of fear that perhaps the Confederates were only hanging on—at Fredericksburg and on the Mississippi. Time was moving and going the wrong way for the South. Everywhere war was reaching into the heart of the nation: homes with vacant chairs, and wounded soldiers hobbling the streets North and South. But war was not quite all. Cornelius Vanderbilt was beginning to take over eastern railroads. The infamous Tweed Ring was beginning in New York, free mail delivery began in some larger cities, and *The Man Without A Country* by Edward Ev-

erett Hale appeared in a literary magazine. The Emancipation Proclamation Jan. 1 freed slaves in areas still in rebellion and made valuable propaganda. The battle was ending at Murfreesboro, Tenn., Jan. 2 with the retreat of the Confederates. Burnside at Fredericksburg wasn't going to be a McClellan, no sir, he would do something. On Jan. 20 his army, twisted with internal wrangling, marched up the Rappahannock looking for a crossing. Rains, mud, cold and the army came back with the "mud march" over by the 24th and only discontent accomplished. Lincoln wanted to see Burnside and Burnside wanted to see Lincoln. Some generals had to go, said Burnside and Lincoln agreed. On Jan. 25th Maj. Gen. Joseph Hooker replaced Burnside. Hooker was a swaggering, boasting, drinking, fighting man whom Lincoln did not entirely trust but someone had to be tried. Fighting in Virginia was mostly by snowballs. Confederate Magruder of Yorktown reputation was on the Gulf coast and took Galveston Jan. 1, opening it to blockade runners, but there was always the blockade. McClernand, with Sherman, went up the Arkansas river and Jan. 11 captured Fort Hindman. But by the end of January the understanding was clear, Grant was in command on the Mississippi and McClernand had only a corps. In the Gulf waters Jan. 11 the

TRAVELING NEWSROOM

The New York *Herald* was the first newspaper to set up a formal organization of war correspondents to cover the campaigns. Before the *Herald* came onto the scene, newspapermen attached to each army were dependent upon the hospitality of the officers. The *Herald* changed that for its correspondents, for it provided transportation, tents, camp equipment and all other essentials for its men. With the Army of the Potomac it had one correspondent attached to headquarters of each infantry corps and the cavalry, all under a chief at the Commanding General's headquarters. It is this main headquarters at Bealton, Va., that is pictured here.

C.S.S. *Alabama* sunk the U.S.S. *Hatteras* off Galveston. Jan. 15 the *C.S.S. Florida* left Mobile for six months of raiding. Confederates penetrated into central Missouri during the month. The Confederate Congress met in January and on the 29th authorized a loan of $15,000,000 to be placed in Europe through Emil Erlanger of France.

FEBRUARY, 1863

S	M	T	W	T	F	S
1	2	3	4	5	6	7
8	9	10	11	12	13	14
15	16	17	18	19	20	21
22	23	24	25	26	27	28

The winter had seen enough activity. Naval action dominated. The Confederate cruiser *Nashville* was destroyed Feb. 28 by the *U.S.S. Montauk* near Fort McAllister, Ga. At Vicksburg the drive down the Yazoo Pass began and on the river the *Queen of the West* ran past Vicksburg and took several Confederate prizes, only to run aground Feb. 14 and be captured. Now a Confederate, the *Queen* captured the Federal *Indianola* and roused the ire of Union Admiral David D. Porter. The Admiral put out reports of a sensational new Union secret weapon that would destroy the Confederate river fleet and might even take Vicksburg. He then dressed up an unarmed, unmanned coal barge so that it looked like an invincible ironclad. Down the Mississippi one night came the fantastic "ghost ship." Shots failed to halt her. Smoke from smudge fires poured from fake funnels. The Confederates hurriedly blew up the disabled *Indianola*, and the *Queen of the West* fled to escape the harmless former coal barge.

MARCH, 1863

S	M	T	W	T	F	S
1	2	3	4	5	6	7
8	9	10	11	12	13	14
15	16	17	18	19	20	21
22	23	24	25	26	27	28
29	30	31				

Virginia was quiet but for Ranger John S. Mosby and his Confederate partisans. Early on March 9 they captured Federal Brig. Gen. Edwin H. Stoughton at Fairfax Court House. More raiding in Kentucky with Rebel Morgan operating March 22 to April 1. Forrest was busy also late in the month at Brentwood and Franklin, Tenn. The pressure was still on at Vicksburg. The attempt of Union gunboats and soldiers to pass through the Yazoo and get in back of Vicksburg failed March 13 to April 5 at Fort Pemberton. March 16 to 22 another attempt through Steele's Bayou failed. Federal Congress March 3 gave the President power to suspend the Writ of Habeas Corpus as a wartime act, and the same day Congress passed a draft measure allowing exemption from conscription for anyone paying $300 or furnishing a substitute. Congress also approved formation of the Territory of Idaho, additional loans to finance the war, and increasing the number of major and brigadier generals for both the regular army and the volunteer service. The Supreme Court was increased from nine to ten judges. Jay Cooke was appointed a government agent to direct the campaign to sell U. S. bonds. Finishing a busy session March 4, Congress resolved to vigorously prosecute the war until "rebellion" was suppressed.

APRIL, 1863

S	M	T	W	T	F	S
			1	2	3	4
5	6	7	8	9	10	11
12	13	14	15	16	17	18
19	20	21	22	23	24	25
26	27	28	29	30		

Spring again and action was expected. It was certain to come along the Mississippi and out of Fredericksburg. Hooker had planned a move to get around Lee's left flank and cross the Rappahannock, avoiding Burnside's fatal frontal assault of December. April 28-29 Hooker crossed his Federals into the Wilderness of scrub timber and useless land. Federal Cavalry under George Stoneman raided southern Virginia April 27 to May 8. Longstreet's Confederate corps had been detached from the Army of Northern Virginia to put Suffolk, near Norfolk Va., under siege. Union monitors under Admiral Samuel F. Du Pont failed in their April 7 attack on Fort Sumter. In the west the raids continued, this time by Federals. April 17 to May 2 Col. Benjamin H. Grierson and his Union cavalry raided from La Grange, Tenn., to Baton Rouge, La., cutting railroads and penetrating the heart of the Confederacy. Col. A. J. Streight from Rosecrans' command headed from Tuscumbia, Ala., April 27 toward Rome, Ga., only to be captured May 3, by Confederate Forrest on the Coosa River. But Vicksburg was the main goal. Grant, too, had made his plans and on April 16 Admiral Porter's fleet passed below the city while Union troops slogged overland west of the river. April 29 a Union gunboat attack on Grand Gulf was repulsed. But on the 30th, Grant began to cross the Mississippi, landing at Bruinsburg, below Vicksburg. The final drive against the fortress was begun. The cruiser *C.S.S. Georgia*, built in England, hurriedly left Liverpool April 1. Food, never in surplus in the South, was slowly mounting into a real problem, with bread riots in Richmond April 2. The Confederate Congress April 24 levied a new tax including a "tax in kind," a tenth of the land's produce for 1863.

MAY, 1863

S	M	T	W	T	F	S
					1	2
3	4	5	6	7	8	9
10	11	12	13	14	15	16
17	18	19	20	21	22	23
24	25	26	27	28	29	30
31						

The commander of the Army of the Potomac congratulated his 73,000-man army from his headquarters at the farm home called Chancellors the last day of April. Joseph Hooker was on his way around Lee—no fighting and no loss. Maj. Gen. John Sedgwick was left behind at Fredericksburg to demonstrate against the heights held by the Confederates. Everything was going as to plan. But Lee knew and was moving to act despite the absence of Longstreet's corps. Maj. Gen. R. H. Anderson with his division, followed by Jackson's corps and Lafayette McLaws' division, headed out toward Chancellorsville leaving Maj. Gen. Jubal Early with only 10,000 against Sedgwick's 40,000. But Hooker believed the road to Richmond open. His advance probed forward May 1 only to run into some light fighting and was withdrawn to Chancellorsville. The Union Army had suddenly stalled. Had Hooker lost his nerve? Night of May 1 and Lee and Jackson were but a mile and a half away from Chancellorsville. Lee, minus Longstreet and Early, decided to divide again. Jackson with his 26,000 was to pass westward, circling to the south of Hooker and come in from the west along the Rappahannock. Lee with Anderson and McLaws and 17,000 would try to hold the Federals at Chancellorsville. Foolhardy— for dividing one's forces is often fatal. Early May 2 Jackson plunged deeper into the Wilderness. Hooker heard warnings and they were ignored. By late afternoon Jackson's Confederates burst from the woods striking the corps of Maj. Gen. O. O. Howard. Complete surprise! Nothing could stop Jackson now. Panic in the Union corps, confusion in the Southern ranks, too, and in the darkness Jackson fell, shot in the arm by his own men. For fear it was more than just a wound, Jackson was taken from the field. A. P. Hill was also down, so cavalier Jeb Stuart commanded Jackson's victorious corps on Sunday May 3 and drove it again against Hooker's right as Lee, with his few, assaulted the Union center and left. At Fredericksburg, Sedgwick was commanded to attack the weakened defenses and then rush to Hooker's aid. But it wasn't that easy; it took four blows to drive back Early from the heights and even then the Confederates remained between Sedgwick and Hooker. Early made a stand late on the 3rd at Salem Church. Hooker was no longer "Fighting Joe." Uncertain and despondent as he watched the battle he was struck by one of the falling pillars torn off Chancellor's house by a shell.

Injury adding to his panic, Hooker ordered a retreat. Was it too late to achieve success? Would attack with his overwhelming force still possibly succeed? He didn't try. Monday, May 4 Stuart demonstrated against Hooker, and Lee and Early pushed Sedgwick back at Salem Church. The Federals withdrew to the Rappahannock. May 6 and the Army of the Potomac was back near Fredericksburg, its parade to Richmond over. Union effectives engaged: 97,382; killed, 1,575; wounded, 9,594; and missing, 5,676. Confederates engaged: 57,352; killed, 1,665; wounded, 9,081; and missing, 2,018. Another Union general beaten and a great victory for the South. Superb in Southern strategy, superb in tactics—and superbly fought. Great rejoicing, but on May 10 Stonewall Jackson died at Guinea Station and much died with him. Out on the river Vicksburg had withstood a lot; could it take Grant's thrust to the south? Pemberton did his best with little, but it wasn't a very good best. May 1 Grant moved inland, capturing Port Gibson, forcing abandonment May 3 of Grand Gulf and its forts. May 9 Joseph E. Johnston took over Confederate command in Mississippi, but most of the defense was up to Pemberton. Grant rolled inland. He forgot supplies, forgot communications; the land was his feedbox. Eastward he moved to victory at Raymond, Miss., May 12 and Jackson, capital of the state, fell May 14. Johnston with a feeble force had been brushed aside and Grant turned sharply west toward Vicksburg upon Pemberton. May 16 and at Champion's Hill the Confederates were pounded back to the Big Black River crossing in confusion on the 17th. May 18 Pemberton was inside the lines of his city and

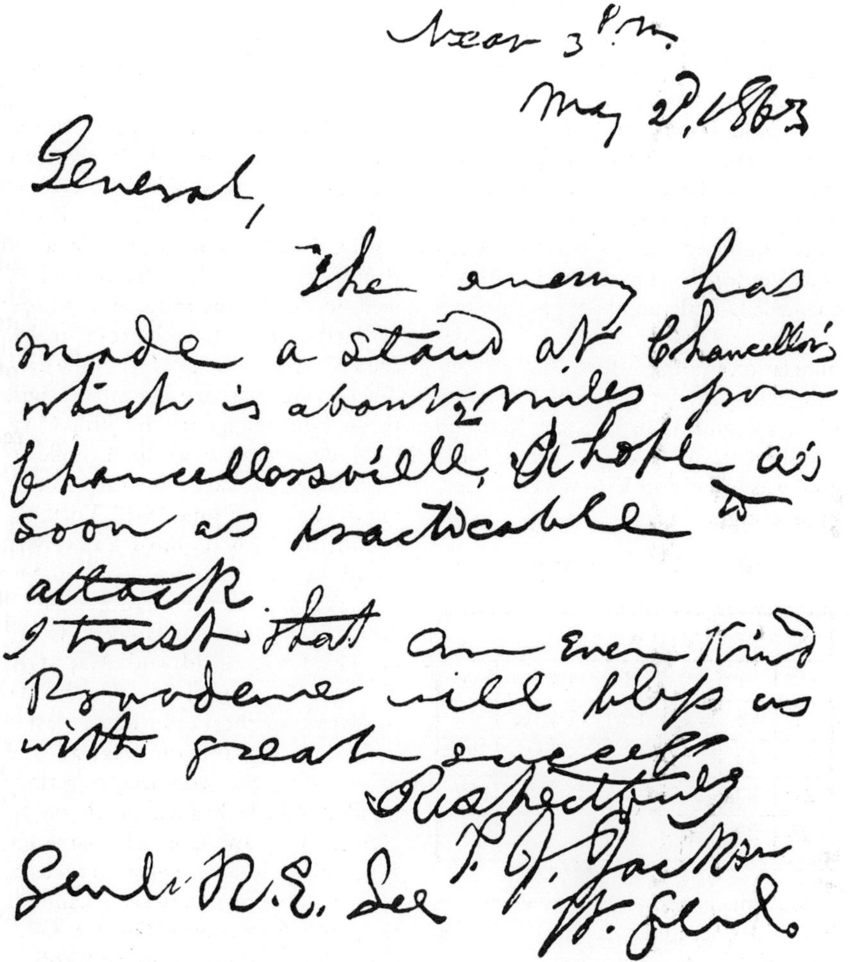

Near 3 P.M.
May 2, 1863

General,

The enemy has made a stand at Chancellor's which is about ½ miles from Chancellorsville, I hope as soon as practicable to attack. I trust that an ever Kind Providence will bless us with great success.

Respectfully

Genl. R. E. Lee   T. J. Jackson
                            Lt. Genl.

The leading division is up & the next two appear to be well closed.

T. J. J.

This was "Stonewall" Jackson's last dispatch before he met his death in the Battle of Chancellorsville. He tells Lee, "I trust an ever kind Providence will bless us with great success."

Grant had ringed Vicksburg. Before declaring it a siege the Federals assaulted May 19 and 22 only to fail. A little farther south on the Mississippi at Port Hudson, Nathaniel Banks had stormed at the only other important point remaining and he, too, had failed. In the midwest the Copperheads were agitating for the end of war. On May 5 Clement L. Vallandigham of Ohio was arrested in Dayton, Ohio, for his denunciation of the conflict. May 19 Lincoln changed the order of imprisonment to send Vallandigham south in banishment. At Alder Gulch, Mont., gold was found and Virginia City grew up overnight.

JUNE, 1863

S	M	T	W	T	F	S
	1	2	3	4	5	6
7	8	9	10	11	12	13
14	15	16	17	18	19	20
21	22	23	24	25	26	27
28	29	30				

Movement and siege and worry on both sides. Lee had staved off Federal attacks at Fredericksburg and Chancellorsville, but he would have to move ahead on his own now. Again it was to be invasion of Pennsylvania with an eye on Philadelphia, Baltimore, or even the capital itself. Richard Ewell and A. P. Hill led off from Fredericksburg June 3, followed by Longstreet, back from Suffolk; the Army of Northern Virginia was in full motion up the Shenandoah. Hooker fell forward with his cavalry under Maj. Gen. Alfred Pleasanton, but ran into Stuart June 9 at Brandy Station or Beverly Ford. One of the few real cavalry charges of

the war—horses and men in shock. Pleasanton fell back. The Federals were pushed out of Winchester June 14 and the Confederates began crossing the Potomac on the 15th. Hooker was forced to follow and left Fredericksburg with Lee well ahead of him. Again, Lincoln had to worry about Pennsylvania, and he called for volunteers to defend the state. Stuart broke off again. Once more he rode around the Federals but he left Lee in the dark. There were sharp cavalry fights throughout the month. By June 27 the Confederates were within 13 miles of Harrisburg. Hooker trailed after, crossing the Potomac June 25-27. York, Pa., fell on the 28th to Jubal Early, with badly needed supplies for Southern men. Again a change was urgent in the North. On June 28th Hooker was relieved of command and Maj. Gen. George Gordon Meade commanded the Army of the Potomac, the last of its leaders. Beginning his task at Frederick, Md., the competent, serious-minded Meade headed north on the 29th probing for Lee. The same day Lee, well spread out, began to focus his army at Cashtown between Chambersburg and Gettysburg. On the 30th a Confederate division moved toward Gettysburg looking for shoes. Armies were poised in the east. At Vicksburg lines tightened, as did Confederate belts. But it would be only time, and Johnston on the edges of the siege could do little but nibble. There was life on the Vicksburg bluffs, but it was in caves and trenches, mines and tunnels, and outside there were always the Federals. Port Hudson, too, felt the stranglehold. In Tennessee it was time to move forward and Rosecrans from June 23 to July 7 brilliantly maneuvered Confederate Bragg out of middle

Washington, D. C., June 10.   1863

Major General Hooker

Your long despatch of to-day is just received. If left to me, I would not go South of the Rappahannah upon Lee's moving North of it. If you head Richmond invested to-day, you would not be able to take it in twenty days; meanwhile your communications, and with them, your Army, would be ruined. I think Lee's Army, and not Richmond, is your true objective point. If he comes towards the Upper Potomac, follow on his flank, and on the inside track, shortening your lines whiles he lengthens his. Fight him too, when opportunity offers. If he stays when he is, fret him, and fret him.

A. Lincoln

This letter from Lincoln to General Hooker shows how seriously the President took his role as commander-in-chief and what a large part he played in determining strategy.

THE "SHEBANG"

Establishments for the U. S. Sanitary Commission, such as this one at Brandy Station, Va., were called "shebangs." The Commission's job was to alleviate the hardships of military life by providing aid and comfort to the sick and the wounded and supplying necessary personal items. Funds for the Commission were raised through "Sanitary Fairs" in the principal Union cities and through individual contributions. In addition to a Relief Bureau, the Commission also had a Claim Bureau, which handled pensions and problems of pay and gave general information and advice to the soldiers.

Tennessee and back toward Chattanooga. Small midsummer fights sputtered throughout the area of war, and peace talk was strong in the North.

JULY, 1863

S	M	T	W	T	F	S
			1	2	3	4
5	6	7	8	9	10	11
12	13	14	15	16	17	18
19	20	21	22	23	24	25
26	27	28	29	30	31	

Pennsylvania and the Mississippi—was this to be the climax: July 1863? Midsummer heat on the first day of the month in Pennsylvania and Confederates under A. P. Hill probed into Gettysburg. But the probes hit Federal troops to the west of the little college community. Neither army had picked its spot and neither army had chosen its time. There was hard fighting that July morning and capable Maj. Gen. John F. Reynolds of the Union died. But Howard, victim of Chancellorsville, moved rapidly into Gettysburg with more behind him. Confederates under Ewell came in from the north and Howard fell back, through the village to the rise of land south and east. It wasn't quite a big battle—not yet. But the actors were arriving on the stage and the Union forces settled in a position picked by Maj. Gen. Winfield Scott Hancock. Low heights, east and southeast of Gettysburg with the highest point to the south, Round Top. Then there was Little Round Top and on the north Cemetery Ridge with its village burying ground, running to the east into Culp's Hill, making a gigantic question mark or a fish hook. But whatever it was it was a strong position. To the west the Confederates were on a parallel but slightly lower rise, site of a Lutheran seminary. There must be a fight now; retreat was impossible. And Lee, so often victorious of late, knew the move was up to him. It was July 2 and Ewell's corps was on the left, A. P. Hill in the center and Longstreet on the right. Longstreet was to make the main drive against the Round Tops and the Union left. There was argument, indecision, and a controversy not yet settled. It was four o'clock in the afternoon before Longstreet pushed ahead against the unoccupied Round Tops. Still more hesitation, and an attack up the Emmitsburg Road between Seminary and Cemetery Ridges. Federal Dan Sickles out front at the Peach Orchard was crushed and the Federals hurled back at the Devil's Den and the lower slopes of Little Round Top. Brig. Gen. G. K. Warren saw it and rushed troops to the unprotected rocky mound. The Confederates had lost their chance and on the far left Ewell accomplished little against Culp's hill. The second day of Gettysburg was over with the armies battered but in line. On July 3rd there was an hour of quiet before noon. The roar of cannon from Seminary Ridge and an answering Union fire foretold advance. Gray lines moved out to the open plain. George E. Pickett, J. J. Pettigrew, and I. R. Trimble led divisions in line of march. Across the Emmitsburg Road under fire and up the slant of Cemetery Hill. Brig. Gen. Lewis Armistead leading the van climbed a wall to fall before a Federal volley. Union lines were penetrated but not broken. The tide was high at Gettysburg. And then it washed back toward Seminary Ridge and the broken gray line was no longer on parade. Pickett's charge was over. Gettysburg was over. Over northeast of Gettysburg cavalry fought that same July 3rd. Stuart was trying to rejoin the Confederates,but the battle meant little. The over-all record—Union: 88,289 engaged, 3,155 dead, 14,529 wounded, and 5,365 missing. Confederate effectives: 75,000; dead, 3,903; wounded, 18,735; and missing, 5,425. Lincoln announced the victory and on Independence Day, 1863, Lee once more turned south toward the Potomac. Again there was slowness in follow-up. Meade was very cautious. Southern cavalry covered the retreat with fights at Manassas Gap and Chester Gap in the Blue Ridge July 21 and 23. By month's end Lee was near Warrenton and then crossed the Rappahannock to a triangle of ground between that river and the Rapidan at Culpeper. There was Northern victory in the east and now victory in the west. A telegram to Washington on July 4 in midmorning announced that Vicksburg had fallen. No relief, no food, no hope; Pemberton and 27,000 had surrendered to U. S. Grant. Port Hudson, La., after six weeks, could not withstand the loss of Vicksburg and it, too, gave up July 8. The Mississippi was open to the Union, and Lincoln said it "ran unvexed to the sea." The trans-Mississippi states of Missouri, Arkansas, Louisiana and Texas were split from their sisters in Confederacy. There was mopping up along the Mississippi and again John Hunt Morgan was riding. This time through Kentucky, southern Indiana and Ohio, north along the West Virginia line to near New Lisbon where he surrendered July 26. But victories were not all in the North. On July 13-14 three to five hundred died in New York City in anti-draft riots; police

were overpowered, Negroes beaten to death, buildings set afire. Troops that had been rushed to Gettysburg rushed back and by July 16 New York was quiet but restless.

AUGUST, 1863

S	M	T	W	T	F	S
						1
2	3	4	5	6	7	8
9	10	11	12	13	14	15
16	17	18	19	20	21	22
23	24	25	26	27	28	29
30	31					

There was still time for summer campaigning but for the moment North and South had had enough. There was a catching of breath after the big battles, but as always, somewhere the guns roared. In Charleston Harbor the Federals continued to bombard Forts Wagner and Sumter. Cavalry fought in Virginia. At Lawrence, Kan., strongly pro-Union since the days of its struggle in the Kansas civil war, Quantrill's bandits raiders struck August 21, burned and pillaged, and 140 citizens died. Successful at Vicksburg, Grant suggested that his mighty army, concentrated as it was, should push on south to take Mobile. But his great force was broken up, dispersed to Texas, Arkansas, Natchez and other garrisons. Grant himself was injured in a fall from a horse in New Orleans. Rosecrans, after his Tullahoma victory of movement, looked for a means of flanking Bragg out of Chattanooga. Crossing the Tennessee River Aug. 20 to Sept. 3, he headed south into the mountains just west and south of Chattanooga. He would have to cross those mountains to get back of the city.

GETTYSBURG, PENNSYLVANIA

The battle that is often called the beginning of the end was fought here July 1-3, 1863. This photograph was taken from Cemetery Ridge, where the Confederate Army aimed its strongest assaults on the final day of the struggle. In back of this place, the first skirmish of the battle was fought on the 1st, when Federal cavalry engaged Confederate infantry. At the left of the picture is Seminary Ridge, where Union General Reynolds was killed.

GETTYSBURG HEADQUARTERS

General Meade moved into this house as headquarters on July 1, 1863, after having transferred his base from Taneytown, ten miles away. In the afternoon of the second day of the Battle of Gettysburg, a heavy artillery barrage was concentrated around this house. Shot and shell plunged through the building, killing a number of men inside and forcing the general and his staff to make a hasty exit. The following day, even more severe fire raged around the house. This scene shows it after the battle, when the owner returned and repaired the damages.

"THE SLAUGHTER PEN"

This portion of the Gettysburg battlefield, known as "Devil's Den," located in front of Little Round Top, was also called the "Slaughter Pen" because of the incredible carnage wrought here while control of the area was changing back and forth between Northern and Southern forces. Some of the dead can be seen strewn on the field; the wounded had been removed to hospitals.

AFTER THE BATTLE

This scene shows the battlefield at Gettysburg in July, 1863, shortly after Lee's broken army headed south in retreat. Many of these bodies have already had their feet stripped of shoes by needy survivors and their pockets rifled of everything valuable.

SEPTEMBER, 1863

S	M	T	W	T	F	S
		1	2	3	4	5
6	7	8	9	10	11	12
13	14	15	16	17	18	19
20	21	22	23	24	25	26
27	28	29	30			

Early fall and a quiet one in Virginia, except for those usual cavalry fights. Fort Wagner outside Charleston was evacuated by the Rebels Sept. 6, but on the 8th Fort Sumter repulsed another night attack. The conquest of Tennessee continued, with Burnside occupying Knoxville Sept. 4, while on the 9th Cumberland Gap and its garrison were captured. Rosecrans moved though the mountain passes south of Chattanooga toward the all-important Confederate supply line to Atlanta. Bragg was forced once more to pull back without a fight for the moment and he left the city Sept. 8, and the Federals moved in. But help was coming to Bragg as he waited at Lafayette, Ga. Lee had detached Longstreet from Virginia again and sent him west. Both armies gathering forces. And on the 18th Bragg began his move against the Federals and Chattanooga. Both armies moved north and west down the valley of the Chickamauga, Bragg trying to get between the left flank of Rosecrans and the city on the 19th. But George H. Thomas was able to extend his lines by a night march toward Chattanooga to protect the Union left. The Chickamauga was crossed and the Confederates launched their drive Sept. 19 in bunches, fits and starts, hitting Thomas, and Thomas stood. That night Longstreet arrived with his Virginia veterans. Bragg had Polk on the right wing and Longstreet on the left with orders for Polk to start things on the 20th. Once again there was badly needed lost time and no dawn attack. The Confederate right wing pushed in against the Federal wall and Rosecrans ordered help to Thomas on the Union left. Brig. Gen. T. J. Wood's division went to the aid but left a gap near the center of the Union lines and Longstreet poured through. The Union right fell apart and was swept away, fleeing to Chattanooga, Rosecrans with the men. But Thomas remained, fighting on Snodgrass hill against attack after attack. The Union army was beaten, but saved, and Thomas, the Union Virginian, had earned his title, "Rock of Chickamauga." Confederate victory, but again no follow-up and Rosecrans, a whipped general with a whipped army, was locked in Chattanooga. Never popular, Bragg, although successful, was the center of dissatisfaction among his officers and men of the Army of Tennessee. The record of the Battle of Chickamauga—Union engaged and effective: 58,222; killed, 1,657; wounded, 9,756; missing, 4,757. Confederates engaged: 66,326; killed, 2,312; wounded, 14,674; missing, 1,468. Rosecrans needed help. On Sept. 24 Hooker, late of the Army of the Potomac, went west with the 11th and 12th Corps in a brilliantly managed railroad shipment pulled off by Secretary of War Stanton and his crew. Federals captured Fort Smith, Ark., Sept. 1 and Little Rock was evacuated by the Confederates on the 10th. But Confederate Jo Shelby raided into Missouri Sept. 27 to Oct. 28. Charles Francis Adams Sept. 5 threatened war against Britain if shipbuilding for the Confederacy was not halted. The British clamped down. The Laird rams never got to the South and were eventually taken over by the British fleet. Russian warships appeared in New York and San Francisco on visits of friendship. President Lincoln suspended the writ of habeas corpus Sept. 15, throughout the country when necessary.

OCTOBER, 1863

S	M	T	W	T	F	S
				1	2	3
4	5	6	7	8	9	10
11	12	13	14	15	16	17
18	19	20	21	22	23	24
25	26	27	28	29	30	31

The fighting continued slim in Virginia, but there was more movement. With Longstreet gone west, Meade advanced and Lee withdrew behind the Rapidan. Then, when Hooker took his two Union corps west also, Lee planned to move around Meade's flank and on Oct. 9 swung west and north of the Rapidan. Meade left Oct. 11 from Culpeper and on the 14th arrived at Centreville, while Lee stopped near the old Manassas fighting ground. Lee returned to the Rapidan followed once more by Meade, after an engagement Oct. 14 at Bristoe Station and other rearguard actions. As the Confederates bickered near Chattanooga, the Union army, pocketed in the city by mountains and Confederates, was near starvation. There was only a horrible mountain road of sixty miles for a supply line. But help was coming. Hooker's two corps moved into Bridgeport, Ala., and Sherman from Grant's army headed for the beleaguered city

late in September. Then, on October 17, in a meeting at Louisville with Secretary of War Stanton, Grant was named to command the armies of the Tennessee, Cumberland and Ohio in the Division of the Mississippi, while Rosecrans was replaced as commander of the Army of the Cumberland by Thomas. "The Rock" simply stated he would hold Chattanooga until starvation. On the 23rd Grant reached the city. Plans were made for bringing troops and supplies around the foot of Lookout Mountain, crossing the Tennessee at Brown's Ferry. By the 27th, with fighting at Wauhatchie, Oct. 28, an all-important pontoon bridge was set up across the river and the city was partially relieved of siege. Unsuccessful attacks continued at Fort Sumter Oct. 26 to Nov. 4, and there were minor fights in Tennessee and Mississippi. Shelby's raid succeeded until he was beaten Oct. 13 near Arrow Rock, Mo. In Arkansas the Rebels were beaten at Pine Bluff Oct. 25 and fell back toward the Red River.

NOVEMBER, 1863

S	M	T	W	T	F	S
1	2	3	4	5	6	7
8	9	10	11	12	13	14
15	16	17	18	19	20	21
22	23	24	25	26	27	28
29	30					

Nov. 19 and a new cemetery for the war dead at Gettysburg was dedicated. Orator Edward Everett was the principal speaker on the scene of battle of four months before. And then President Lincoln added less than 300 words, the Gettysburg Address, that

CHATTANOOGA, TENNESSEE, FROM THE NORTH

This city, seen from across the Tennessee River, was the center of a crucial struggle in the late summer and fall of 1863. Rosecrans' attempt to outflank Bragg met with defeat at nearby Chickamauga, Ga., on Sept. 19-20. However, the Confederates were unable to hold Grant in Chattanooga. The Federals went on the attack, Hooker assaulting Lookout Mountain on Nov. 24 and Thomas taking Missionary Ridge on Nov. 25. By the latter date Chattanooga was secure for the Union forces.

joined the history of a place, a war and a people. Movement continued in Virginia with Meade on the offensive in the Mine Run Campaign. The Army of the Potomac was to cross the Rapidan on Lee's right and attack the Confederates from the east before they could be regathered after their movement south from Centreville. But Stuart's cavalry gave warning of the crossing at Germanna Ford Nov. 26 and Meade found Lee in strong entrenchments in the Wilderness on the west bank of Mine Run. Surprise a failure, Meade withdrew to the north bank of the Rapidan and Culpeper Dec. 1 and 2. Still the main attention was at Chattanooga. Could Grant get out of the city or could he be held? Bragg detached Longstreet north against Knoxville and Burnside. The Federals would have to do something if Knoxville and east Tennessee were to be saved. Sherman pushed into Chattanooga by mid-November, swinging around to form a north and left wing of the Union forces with Thomas in the center and Hooker on the right at Lookout Valley. Thin supply lines and heavy rains caused more delay but on the 23rd Thomas was able to occupy the rise of Orchard Knob in front of Missionary Ridge, and about noon on the 24th Hooker assaulted Lookout Mountain. There was more climbing than fighting in the mists which gave it the name "the Battle Above the Clouds." By morning of the 25th the U. S. flag was on Point Lookout. Sherman Nov. 24 occupied the slimly held northern edge of Missionary Ridge. On the 25th Sherman hit again against Confederate Pat Cleburne at Tunnel Hill but was unable to crush the Confederates. Hooker on the right had been delayed in advancing from Lookout Mountain by

road blocks and broken bridges. Grant gave Thomas orders to move ahead a bit to the first line of rifle pits on Missionary Ridge. Mid-afternoon of the 25th the rifle pits were taken but that was not all. No halt and the Federals moved right on up the hill, official orders or not. There was confusion in Confederate ranks and the ridge was taken. Bragg's center was licked and so were his right and left. Slowly he withdrew into Georgia with rearguard actions against Hooker on the 27th. Grant and Thomas were victorious at Missionary Ridge where on Nov. 23-25 Federals engaged numbered 56,-359; killed, 753; wounded, 4,722; and missing, 349. Confederates: 46,165 engaged with 361 killed, 2,160 wounded, and 4,146 missing. Low Confederate losses, but a nearly broken army. Longstreet arrived before Knoxville Nov. 17 and Burnside pulled inside the city. Attacks on Fort Sanders were beaten off Nov. 29 and as Sherman moved north from Chattanooga in relief, Longstreet retreated towards Virginia. Siege had been lifted at Knoxville, Chattanooga was lost, and was the war being lost by the South in the West? Many Southerners felt that Davis had neglected that area or had supported his friend Braxton Bragg too long. Down on the Gulf Coast Federal forces occupied Brownsville, Tex., Nov. 6 and Corpus Christi on the 16th as well as other important points. There was considerable fighting by lesser forces in Tennessee, aside from the Chattanooga area. On Nov. 12 there was a meeting at Little Rock, Ark., to consider measures for the restoration of Arkansas to the Union. Confederate John Hunt Morgan escaped from the penitentiary at Columbus, Ohio, Nov. 27, for more raiding.

DECEMBER, 1863

S	M	T	W	T	F	S
		1	2	3	4	5
6	7	8	9	10	11	12
13	14	15	16	17	18	19
20	21	22	23	24	25	26
27	28	29	30	31		

The third Christmas of the war and a stalemate on the Virginia front with defeat in the west for the Confederates. The usual raiding parties and skirmishes from the Trans-Mississippi to St. Augustine, Fla. Dec. 8 Lincoln promised pardon to all Confederates who would take a prescribed oath, excepting, of course, certain high officials and generals. There were also plans for restoration of loyal governments in seceded states when one tenth of those qualified to vote in 1860 took another oath. On Dec. 1 Bragg stepped down from command of the Army of Tennessee, only to be named military advisor to President Davis. Bragg had failed in battle and failed in relations with his army; but not with Davis. On Dec. 16 Joseph E. Johnston took over command, and tried to reassemble the demoralized forces.

RINGGOLD, GEORGIA

This small town lay near Chickamauga Creek. It was toward here
that Crittenden followed up Bragg's supposed retreat on Sept.
10, 1863. However, Crittenden retreated when he found a strong
concentration of the enemy. The battle at nearby Chickamauga
followed shortly after (Sept. 19-20).

MISSIONARY RIDGE, TENNESSEE

General Thomas sent the Federal troops up Missionary Ridge on Nov. 25. The unrelenting advance threw Bragg's center into confusion, and soon the Confederate Army gave up the hill and fled in retreat.

1864

S	M	T	W	T	F	S
					1	2
3	4	5	6	7	8	9
10	11	12	13	14	15	16
17	18	19	20	21	22	23
24	25	26	27	28	29	30
31						

It was a different New Year's. While in the North there was a bit of cautious optimism, there was a realization that much remained to be done. The Confederate armies were intact and had demonstrated what they could do. In the South there was the haunting realization that a lot of territory was gone despite their victories on individual fields of honor. But there was always hope. Everyone everywhere was sure of one thing—the war was with them still and would not soon depart. Fighting as a big thing was almost non-existent in January. Jonesville, Va., Jan. 3; Jan. 29-Feb. 1 at Medley, W. Va.; Dandridge, Tenn., Jan. 16-17 were all names, small names but big at the moment to those who fought there. Reconstruction plans were being readied on the fringes of the Confederacy. Arkansas in a convention Jan. 19 adopted an anti-slavery constitution for its pro-

Northern elements, and named a provisional governor. Similar moves began in Louisiana and Tennessee.

FEBRUARY, 1864

S	M	T	W	T	F	S
	1	2	3	4	5	6
7	8	9	10	11	12	13
14	15	16	17	18	19	20
21	22	23	24	25	26	27
28	29					

The pace stepped up in February but involved mostly raiding. Brig. Gen. Judson Kilpatrick and young Col. Ulric Dahlgren made a cavalry sortie on Richmond Feb. 28 to March 4, penetrating to within five miles of the Confederate capital before turning back. Dahlgren was killed. Youthful, glamorous Brig. Gen. George A. Custer rode around Albemarle County, Va., Feb. 28 to March 1. In Florida, Federals were beaten at Olustee or Ocean Pond on the 20th. Off Charleston Feb. 17 a Confederate submarine, the *Hunley*, sank the *Housatonic*. In the west Feb. 3 William T. Sherman led an expedition from Vicksburg and Jackson to occupy Meridian, Miss., Feb. 14, after destroying railroads and supplies in the heart of the Confederacy. Brig. Gen. William Sooy Smith took his Union cavalry Feb. 10 to 25 from

[84]

Memphis to Meridian but was driven back by Forrest from Okolona, Miss., on the 22nd. There was fighting at Tunnel Hill, Buzzard Roost and Rocky Face Ridge, Ga., Feb. 22-25 against Joseph E. Johnston. On Feb. 29 Congress revived the military grade of Lieutenant General and had Grant in mind for three stars, highest in the Federal army. More than a hundred Federal prisoners escaped from Libby Prison in Richmond through tunnels Feb. 9 and on the 15th Union prisoners began arriving at Andersonville, deep in Georgia.

MARCH, 1864

S	M	T	W	T	F	S
		1	2	3	4	5
6	7	8	9	10	11	12
13	14	15	16	17	18	19
20	21	22	23	24	25	26
27	28	29	30	31		

March 9 Major General Grant became Lieutenant General and on March 10, he became commander of all Union armies. The country had long looked for a general and now had found him—from the West. Victor in many battles, possibly a loser in others; at any rate there was now a fighting leader. Halleck was named Chief of Staff, a desk job well fitted for him; Meade continued to command the Army of the Potomac, but Grant chose to be with him in the field. W. T. Sherman was to command in the West with the Military Division of the Mississippi; Maj. Gen. J. B. McPherson had the Army of the Tennessee; George H. Thomas remained with the Army of the Cumberland and John M. Schofield had the Army of the Ohio. Nathaniel Banks led his army and gunboats up the Red River in Louisiana March 12 and on the 14th captured Fort De Russy. Once more in Tennessee and Kentucky Forrest was on the move, raiding Paducah, Ky., on the Ohio March 25.

APRIL, 1864

S	M	T	W	T	F	S
					1	2
3	4	5	6	7	8	9
10	11	12	13	14	15	16
17	18	19	20	21	22	23
24	25	26	27	28	29	30

Another spring and another time for preparation. Phil Sheridan took over the cavalry of the Army of the Potomac April 4, cavalry that had been far outclassed by the horsemen in gray. April 17 Grant refused to exchange any more prisoners. A very unpopular decision on both sides, but war was reality and the South was already suffering from lack of manpower; the North could stand the loss as far as numbers went. In Louisiana, Banks ran into shallow water on the Red River and Confederate soldiers as well, being defeated on the 8th and 9th at Sabine Cross Roads and Pleasant Hill near Mansfield, La. Banks retreated to New Orleans with a few tangles on the way and the expedition was a failure. A cooperating force under Frederick Steele was supposed to join Banks through Arkansas. Steele fought several engagements and was back in Little Rock by the 30th. On the Mississippi above Memphis was Fort Pil-

[85]

WAGON PARK

This wagon park at Brandy Station, Va., represents the grand total of vehicles used for transportation by the Quartermaster's Department and attached to the Army of the Potomac. Here equipment was made and mended, mules were shod, wagons repaired, etc.

low, Tenn., now a Federal stronghold with some Negro troops in its garrison. Forrest on his raid attacked the Fort, capturing it April 12. There was unnecessary bloodshed and Congressmen investigating called the alleged massacre of colored soldiers an "atrocity." Casualties were high, but records tended to show that it was just war and not slaughter. But the propaganda effect was great. Pro-Federal residents of Virginia April 11 voted for a constitution which abolished slavery.

MAY, 1864

S	M	T	W	T	F	S
1	2	3	4	5	6	7
8	9	10	11	12	13	14
15	16	17	18	19	20	21
22	23	24	25	26	27	28
29	30	31				

It was to be overland against Richmond and the Army of the Potomac wondered if it would be just another attempt without the deed as so often before. But Grant had his plans; Franz Sigel was to attack in the Shenandoah; Sherman would attack Johnston in Georgia; Banks would attack Mobile; Butler was to attack Richmond from south of the James and the Army of the Potomac under Grant and Meade was to attack straight ahead. But it didn't go according to plan; there was too much attack set up for three of the generals. Banks never got started; Sigel retreated quickly; and Butler bogged down completely. But there was actually attack enough—in Virginia and Georgia. Grant at Culpeper Court House with about 119,000; Lee at Orange Court House with about

64,000. Grant started in the now almost traditional way on May 3, across the Rapidan and into the Wilderness to the west of the Chancellorsville battleground of the year before. But as he crossed the river into the nearly flat, scrub-timbered land of undergrowth he was on Lee's right flank. The Army of Northern Virginia dashed eastward to head him off. Morning of May 5 Dick Ewell's corps of the Confederates was up and at the attack. The Union advance was upset by the drive coming at right angles along the Orange Turnpike. There was heavy fighting in the brush. But Ewell and now A. P. Hill were ordered to avoid a general major battle as Longstreet was not yet up to help. So late on the 5th the Confederates fended off strong Union blows and held their lines. May 6 at daybreak the Rebels began to give way along the Plank Road after furious Federal assault. But by mid-morning Longstreet was in position and the Union army eased back. Longstreet suffered a severe wound, but on the Confederate left John B. Gordon of Ewell's corps found a hole in the Federal line and only darkness prevented serious trouble to the North. Quiet on the 7th and Lee thought Grant, like those before him, would retreat. The Battle of the Wilderness, May 5-7, had a toll of 101,895 Union men engaged with 2,246 dead, 12,037 wounded and 3,383 missing. The Confederates with 61,025 effectives had around 7,750 killed and wounded but even fairly accurate reports of Southern losses from now on are impossible. But it was not over: a big battle with more to come. Grant slipped to his left, moving southeasterly off Lee's right toward Spotsylvania Court House. Maj. Gen. R. H.

Anderson with Longstreet's corps got there first and faced the Army of the Potomac. The armies rushed in and it became almost like trench warfare of World War I days. Thirteen days of assaults, fighting and dying. May 8 to 21 at the Bloody Angle and in the woods, small meadows, and secondary growth they fought. A stubborn Grant telegraphed Halleck in Washington on May 10, "I propose to fight it out along this line if it takes all summer." Tremendous Federal losses and Confederate losses too—only about a third of those of the North, but much harder to replace. Union 6,020 killed and wounded with 800 missing in the assaults of May 12 and for the campaign from 5th to 12th, 26,815 killed and wounded, and 4,183 or about 263 out of every thousand a casualty—over one out of four. The cavalry would also be different now under Phil Sheridan. The new commander headed toward Richmond May 8 with about 10,000. Jeb Stuart harassed him again and again and on May 11 delayed Sheridan in the fight at Yellow Tavern just north of Richmond. But James Ewell Brown Stuart, pride of the South, fell mortally wounded and another dashing fighting man was gone. Richmond pushed Sheridan away and he rejoined Grant May 24. On the James, Beauregard faced his toughest job of the war trying to stop Butler south of the river at Bermuda Hundred. But Beauregard did it and stuck a cork on the bottle of land and trapped Butler by the 16th of May. Sigel also failed in the valley. At New Market May 15, John C. Breckinridge gathered a few scattered troops along with lads from the Virginia Military Institute. Sigel was beaten, and VMI had a tradition to clothe its noble halls forever. But the core was in the Wilderness. Again Grant slid leftward May 20 and Lee shifted in another block. May 23 Grant tried to cross the North Anna. But Lee was there and again the slide to the southeast all the way to the Chickahominy at Cold Harbor, near scenes of the Seven Days of '62, but Lee was still ahead of him. Out of Chattanooga early in May came Sherman to drive Joseph E. Johnston to and through Atlanta if he could. Sherman protected his railroad line in the rear and marched ahead. Two of his three armies under Schofield and Thomas demonstrated at Tunnel Hill and Rocky Face Ridge near Dalton while McPherson crept in behind at Snake Creek Gap. But the Army of the Tennessee under McPherson halted and Johnston moved back to be attacked at Resaca May 13-15. May 17 the Union pursuit was checked at Adairsville, Ga. At Cassville Johnston halted May 19-20 and then retreated to Allatoona and strong fortifications. Sherman moved around Johnston's left, once more headed for Dallas. May 25 to 29 brought four days of fighting around New Hope Church, northeast of Dallas. Sherman was maneuvering Johnston back, or was Johnston steadily pulling him deep into Georgia readying for a crushing blow? May 28 and Maximilian of Hapsburg landed at Vera Cruz, backed by France and Napoleon III, to attempt to seize the throne of Mexico. Nathaniel Hawthorne died at Plymouth, N. H., May 19. A convention of discontented radical Republicans met at Cleveland, O., May 31 to protest the administration's war policy. John C. Frémont was nominated for president but withdrew from the race in September when support of the group faltered.

THE "HELL HOLE"

A furious battle was fought here near New Hope Church, Ga., May 25-28, 1864. This battle was one of a series of brilliant moves and countermoves which the advancing Union army under Sherman and the retreating Confederate army under Johnston engaged in. Johnston refused to be caught in the traps which Sherman laid. In this battle the Union forces were repulsed by the embattled Southern troops in an action so fierce that Union troops dubbed this the "Hell Hole."

JUNE, 1864

S	M	T	W	T	F	S
			1	2	3	4
5	6	7	8	9	10	11
12	13	14	15	16	17	18
19	20	21	22	23	24	25
26	27	28	29	30		

A bloody summer was begun and June soon showed it would continue. It was assault: cold, ruthless, straight attack once more as at Fredericksburg. This time it was a crossroads tumble of houses known as Cold Harbor. June 1 to 3 and horror swept the North. Grant the victor was becoming Grant "the butcher." It was a mistake and he knew it but those who fell did not live to condemn it. June 3 was the worst with its charging Union troops against Confederates in their strong earthen breastworks. Confusion about who fell, confusion about how many, confusion about how long the carnage took, but no confusion about the result. From June 1 to 3 the Federals had 107,907 engaged with about 12,-000 killed and wounded. Richmond was closer now, but was victory? Grant had lost almost as many men in the entire campaign as Lee's whole army. Grant momentarily now entrenched; assault was over for the moment. But on June 14 he showed that the campaign was not over. Few outside of the Federal army knew it at first. The Grant of Vicksburg was back. Keeping the whereabouts of 100,000 men secret is a difficult task, but Grant did it. Stealthily he shifted south across the James River to rush boiling in at Petersburg. Beauregard desperately called for help. Lee believed Grant was going to attack north of the James and delayed. Beauregard with his record of ups and downs back of him was at his best now. The Union 18th Corps under William F. Smith hit at Petersburg early on June 15 against Beauregard's puny 3,000. But Smith delayed until late in the afternoon and as Hancock with the 2nd Corps came up some advance was made, only to be halted on a bright moonlight night. Beauregard got a little help—possibly 14,000. Richmond could have fallen and should have, but Union command delay and Beauregard saved it for a time. Grant was busy at the James getting the army across, but he should have been pushing the attack. June 16 and Hancock failed to break the Confederates. Slow withdrawal by the South on the 17th but Lee was coming now. Federal blows fell off and the campaign was over with Richmond still in Confederate hands and blood spread over Virginia. Now came siege again. June 22-23 attempts to break and take the Weldon Railroad south of Petersburg failed. Maj. Gen. David Hunter, replacing Sigel, tried again in the Shenandoah. The Confederates, mainly old men and boys, fell back slowly. Hunter moved to Staunton and Sheridan went to help him only to be battered at Trevilian Station June 11. But someone had to stop Hunter. It was to be Jubal Early. Hunter fled into West Virginia with Early after him June 18 and Early headed north toward the Potomac down the avenue so often traversed. John Hunt Morgan made his last raid into Kentucky, entering Lexington June 11, but was driven out after a fight at Cynthiana

June 11. Morgan was killed Sept. 4 at Greeneville,Tenn., when his headquarters was surrounded. There was sparring in front of Atlanta, and on June 1 Allatoona was captured. June 4 and Johnston retreated from New Hope church toward Marietta and Kennesaw. June 14 fighting Bishop-General Leonidas Polk of the Confederacy died on Pine Mountain. June 27 Sherman tried assault and also failed at Kennesaw Mountain with losses of about 3,000 contrasted with 500 Confederate casualties. But Sherman continued to move, shifting right the last of June. Brig. Gen. S. D. Sturgis tried to keep Forrest busy in Mississippi only to be badly beaten June 10 at Guntown or Brice's Cross Roads. It was off the coast of France June 19 that the Confederate Navy's proud cruiser *Alabama* with Semmes in command fought ship to ship, gun to gun with the *U. S. S. Kearsarge*. In the glory of single combat the *Alabama* went down and with her went a record of 68 merchant vessels and one gunboat sunk. But even with war there is always politics. The Republican Party, known as the Union Party, met June 7 at Baltimore and nominated Lincoln and War Democrat Andrew Johnson of Tennessee. But this election wasn't going to be easy. There was discontent over the land. Anti-war Democrats continued their hysterical shouting and now more and more in the North listened as the casualty lists lengthened from Virginia. There was noise for a negotiated peace. Radicals, too, stormed at the President; he was too lenient; he was going to reconstruct, not destroy, the South. From two sides Lincoln felt the pressure and from the front came the unending, never relenting report of war;

burden of state, burden of life, burden of death for the man in the White House. Salmon P. Chase resigned as Secretary of the Treasury June 30 to be replaced by William P. Fessenden. The Fugitive Slave Law of 1850, source of much pre-war grief and now almost forgotten, was repealed June 28.

JULY, 1864

S	M	T	W	T	F	S
					1	2
3	4	5	6	7	8	9
10	11	12	13	14	15	16
17	18	19	20	21	22	23
24	25	26	27	28	29	30
31						

It was to be the story of Vicksburg again with a few differences. Siege at Petersburg and all the diggings, defenses and probing efforts to break through and to break in. It was early morning July 30 and along the eastern fortifications a man crawled down a long tunnel and set a fuse; 4:55 a.m. and the earth roared apart. Men and dirt blazed into the air. A mine set after much labor under the Confederate lines made a huge smoking crater 170 feet long, 60 to 80 feet wide and 30 feet deep. Over 275 Confederates were killed or injured in the blast. The Federals swarmed forward to the hole in the Confederate lines but it didn't work. The crater became a grave for charging Union soldiers. Once in the hole the scrambling infantry could not get out and more and more plowed in. Confederates rallied back of the pit. Artillery began to drop its shells. The

BURIAL PARTY

Union soldiers here are collecting the bodies of their comrades, killed at the battles of Gaines' Mill and Cold Harbor in Virginia.

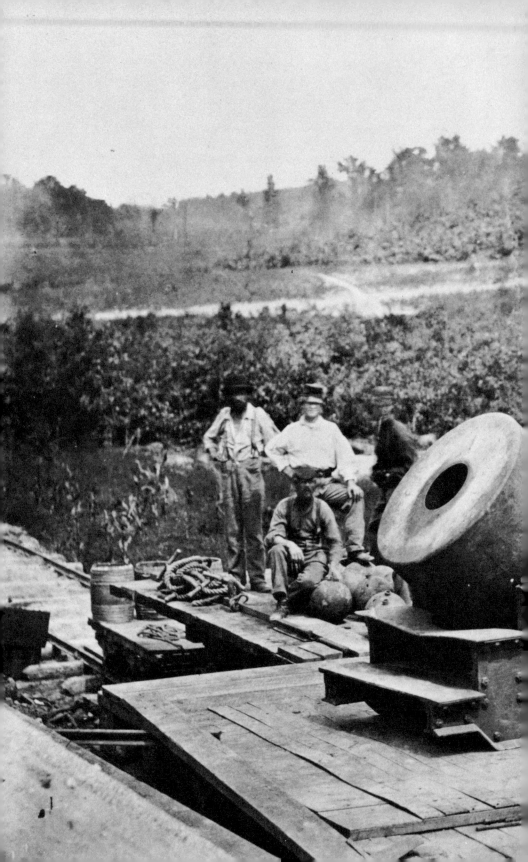

MORTAR DICTATOR

This giant mortar was used in the siege of Petersburg in the summer of 1864. It was transported by a railroad truck, and a side track from the railroad had to be specially constructed to move it into position. Weighing 17,120 pounds, the Dictator was a 13-inch mortar which could fire its 200-pound shell over two and a half miles.

KENNESAW MOUNTAIN, GEORGIA

Sherman attempted to assault this Southern stronghold, here seen from the front, on June 27, 1864. However, he was driven back with heavy casualties.

North retreated and by 1 p.m. 4,000 Federals were killed, wounded or captured. Negro troops suffered most heavily. Sheridan raided north of the James July 27-29. In the Shenandoah the last Confederate advance rolled up the Valley. July 6 and "Old Jube" Early crossed the Potomac at Harpers Ferry and marched into Frederick City, only 14,000 strong. Lew Wallace gathered leftovers and volunteers from garrisons of northern cities and tried to stem Early from his drive on Washington itself July 9. Wallace lost the Battle of Monocacy River but sorely delayed Early. However, by the 11th Early was in the suburbs of Washington. The North and the capital were frightened; was it to fall even temporarily after so much? Lincoln came out to watch from the parapet of Fort Stevens. But reinforcements marched in and through the city to the outposts and Early's valiant demonstration was over. July 14 he crossed the Potomac and moved back into the Valley. There was a Federal attack and failure July 24 at Kernstown and Winchester. Southern cavalry under Brig. Gen. John McCausland raided and partially burned Chambersburg, Pa., July 30 when the town failed to raise $100,000 ransom. In Georgia, Marietta was evacuated July 1 and Johnston was flanked out of Smyrna Station July 2-5. July 7 Schofield crossed the Chattahoochee to force Johnston into the last defenses of Atlanta behind Peachtree Creek. Was "Retreating Joe" Johnston going too far? President Davis thought so and July 17 Johnston turned his command over to rash John Bell Hood. The Federals knew Hood, knew there would be fighting but had worried more over the eva-

sions of Johnston. Sherman, raiding around the city, moved by his left July 17 toward Atlanta's link with Decatur. July 19 and McPherson, near Decatur, turned west toward Atlanta while Thomas crossed Peachtree Creek north of the city and Schofield was in the center, but there were gaps between them. July 20 Hood attacked Thomas at the Battle of Peachtree Creek, only to fall back. The city was ringed north and east. July 22 in the Battle of Atlanta itself Hood attacked McPherson, only to fail again. But brilliant James Birdseye McPherson died, and the North had lost a commander from whom much might have been heard. Maj. Gen. O. O. Howard replaced McPherson in the Army of the Tennessee. Peachtree Creek: 20,139 Union effectives with 1,600 killed and wounded. Confederates: 18,832 with about 2,500 killed and wounded. Atlanta: 34,863 Union forces with 430 killed, 1,559 wounded, and 1,733 missing. Confederates 36,934 effectives with about 7,000 killed and wounded and 1,000 missing. The siege of Atlanta was on, and Sherman pulled his lines close to the city and extended south to cut the railroads to Montgomery and Macon. July 28 and Hood was repulsed near Ezra Church. George Stoneman and Union cavalry raided the railroads but were stopped short at Macon July 30. In Mississippi, Union forces were ordered to keep Forrest busy, off of Sherman's thin, all-important supply line. At Harrisburg, just west of Tupelo July 14, Forrest and Stephen D. Lee attacked Federals in breastworks and A. J. Smith retreated unnecessarily. There was a fruitless secret meeting at Niagara Falls between Editor Horace Greeley and Confederates from Canada, which held rumors of peace. President Lincoln pocket vetoed the Congressional Reconstruction bill which maintained that Reconstruction was a Congressional matter rather than under the President's control.

AUGUST, 1864

S	M	T	W	T	F	S
	1	2	3	4	5	6
7	8	9	10	11	12	13
14	15	16	17	18	19	20
21	22	23	24	25	26	27
28	29	30	31			

At Petersburg the armies glowered and waited. On the fringes, Grant seized the Weldon Railroad Aug. 21 and there was a skirmish at Reams' Station Aug. 25. Sheridan was given command of the Shenandoah Aug. 7 while Early held on with several small actions. Maj. Gen. Joseph Wheeler and his Confederate cavalry raided into Tennessee and Alabama. Union cavalry under Kilpatrick picked at Hood Aug. 18-22. Sherman, late in the month, started his huge wheeling movement to get his armies southwest of Atlanta and strike at Jonesboro. Hood came out to meet him with William Hardee's corps, but the Aug. 31 attack failed. Atlanta was wavering in the late summer heat. Forrest still confounded inept Federals in Mississippi. Aug. 20 he startled the country by entering Memphis and staying a few hours before fleeing. Sterling Price Aug. 29 raided into Missouri. Mobile, aim of many plans and neglected in action, remained open except for the blockade. Aug. 5 Admiral Farragut with four ironclads and 13 wooden vessels steamed into the harbor, with its mines and forts and a pitiful Confederate squadron of three wooden gunboats and the powerful ironclad *Tennessee*. Union monitor *Tecumseh* hit a torpedo or mine and went down. Farragut said or didn't say, "Damn the torpedoes," and the fleet went in to overwhelm the Confederate squadron. Fort Gaines surrendered Aug. 7 and Fort Morgan Aug. 23 but the city itself remained in Southern hands. The Democratic convention at Chicago Aug. 29 nominated George B. McClellan, the fallen general, for president, and the convention said the war was a failure. Noise from the Copperheads and more noise from the radicals bore down upon the harassed President. But did he underestimate the hard core of the people and the importance of the soldier vote?

SEPTEMBER, 1864

S	M	T	W	T	F	S
				1	2	3
4	5	6	7	8	9	10
11	12	13	14	15	16	17
18	19	20	21	22	23	24
25	26	27	28	29	30	

Things looked forlorn in the South and dreary too in the North. Of course Atlanta was tottering, siege was around Richmond and Early was still holding off in the Valley. Grant pushed his lines west of Petersburg a bit and fought at Peebles Farm Sept. 29-30, while north of the James, Federals captured Fort Harrison in the Richmond defense lines Sept. 29. Early was attacked by Sheridan at Winchester in

BATTLEFIELD AT PEACHTREE CREEK, GEORGIA

On July 20, 1864, Hood deployed his troops at this point for the defense of Atlanta. He found that Sherman had divided his forces so that his left wing was too far removed to be of much help to his right wing. Hood attacked but the whole Confederate charge proved abortive.

DEFENSES OF ATLANTA

In July, 1864, Johnston was forced into the last defenses before
Atlanta. Hood became the Confederate commander on July 17,
and for the next month tried desperately to stem Sherman's advance. On Aug. 31, Hood made his last attack before Atlanta,
and then on Sept. 1 he abandoned the city to Sherman.

the Battle of Winchester or Opequon Creek Sept. 19. Early had to retreat and fell back again at Fisher's Hill Sept. 22. Sheridan had the northern valley and he held it tight with his army having almost free rein in pillaging and gorging itself on what was left of crops and supplies. Hood in Georgia turned his back on Atlanta and left Sept. 1 retreating like his predecessor to Lovejoy's Station, but his army was intact. Sherman moved in at once and Atlanta became a vast base. State officials of Georgia began quarreling with the Confederate government and some state troops were withdrawn. Sherman was determined to protect his lines and Sept. 4 ordered all noncombatants to leave and at once. For ten days the civilian victims of war trudged out of the city carrying what little they could. President Davis talked with Hood Sept. 25 and talked to the troops too, hinting that they would soon head back to Tennessee. Thomas was sent back from Georgia late in September to Nashville and Schofield to Knoxville to protect against Forrest who was on another raid, and possibly against any moves by Hood. Price fought often and successfully in Missouri penetrating to the outer defenses of St. Louis itself. Of course victory at Atlanta had helped Lincoln but he still worried over the election, believing that McClellan might be successful. Frémont, nominated by the radical Republicans, had withdrawn from the race. Out in Japan a U. S. steamer was fired on in the straits of Shimonoseka and the U. S. retaliated in July with the *U. S. S. Wyoming* attacking the Japanese. An international squadron finished the job in September and foreign shipping was protected.

OCTOBER, 1864

S	M	T	W	T	F	S
						1
2	3	4	5	6	7	8
9	10	11	12	13	14	15
16	17	18	19	20	21	22
23	24	25	26	27	28	29
30	31					

It was a month of lesser engagements and probing for advantage. At Petersburg there were fights on Darbytown Road Oct. 7 and 13 and at Burgess' Mill or Hatcher's Run Oct. 27. In the Shenandoah cavalry fought Oct. 9 at Fisher's Hill and on the 14th at Strasburg. Sheridan, encamped near Cedar Creek, went to Washington for talks. Early of the Confederates saw his opportunity and attacked boldly Oct. 19 in the Battle of Cedar Creek or Middletown. Rising Confederate Maj. Gen. Stephen Ramseur was killed. At first the Confederates rushed ahead and the Union army with Sheridan away on business fell back in complete surprise. Then a Confederate delay and Sheridan on his way back made his famous ride from Winchester "twenty miles away." The Union troops rallied and turned on Early. The outnumbered Confederates were driven from the field. It was the last big battle of the Shenandoah. Union: 30,829 engaged, 644 killed, 3,430 wounded, and 1,591 missing. Confederates: 18,410 engaged, 320 killed, 1,540 wounded and 1,050 missing. Price, out in Missouri, pushed up the Missouri River to Lexington by Oct. 20 and continued on, but Pleasanton hit Price's army in the rear and

In the Field. Oct 27. 1864

Genl Wilson.

You two dispatches are recvd. I am anxious to learn what Cavalry if any are left back towards Villa-Rica & the Chattahoochee.

I would like you to hit some one body of the Cavalry a good lick if they will stand, for you can prove by that if they are anything like a depot of Horses at Blue Mountain. I would dispond to sens a Brigade of Infantry out som 5 miles tomorrow mong.

Yr
W. T. Sherman
Major Genl.

Sherman advises General Wilson, "I would like you to hit some one body of the cavalry a good lick if they will stand."

CONFEDERATE BLOCKADE RUNNER

The fast Confederate blockade runner *Old Dominion* was fitted out in Bristol, England. The U.S. counsel at Bristol had this photograph made and sent to the Navy Department in Washington so that the blockading squadron could easily identify the vessel and be on the lookout for her. The captain had made a public boast that "the damned Yankees were not smart enough to catch" him.

Courtesy Chicago Historical Society

on Oct. 23 at Westport the Confederates were driven southward along the Missouri-Kansas line with a few minor stands. Major operations in the Trans-Mississippi had ended. Hood, by the 2nd of the month, was on the railroad between Atlanta and the Etowah River aiming at Sherman's communications. Confederates took Big Shanty Oct. 3 and Ackworth Oct. 4. Then Hood's army Oct. 5 attacked the fortified Federals at Allatoona Pass. Sherman pulled some troops out of Atlanta after Hood. Maj. Gen. John M. Corse at Allatoona held on in response to Sherman's message: "hold the fort for we are coming," words later to make a famous hymn. Hood swung to the west across the Coosa River Oct. 11 and took Dalton, Ga. on Oct. 13. He entered Alabama and began the Tennessee campaign from Gadsden Oct. 22. By the 31st he was waiting for Forrest at Tuscumbia. The northernmost "battle" of the war was Oct. 19 when a small group of Confederate raiders came out of Canada into the little town of St. Albans, Vt., robbed the bank, shot up the place and retired. The *U.S.S. Wachusett* sank the Confederate raider *Florida* Oct. 7 at Bahia, Brazil. The cruiser *Shenandoah* left England Oct. 8. In the Roanoke River Oct. 27 the Confederate ram *Albemarle* was destroyed at Plymouth, N. C., by torpedoes launched in a daring raid by Union Lieut. W. B. Cushing and his men. As the election neared in the North a report on Copperhead groups early in October indicated an alleged membership of half a million or more. Chief Justice Roger B. Taney died Oct. 12 in Washington. Maryland ratified an anti-slavery constitution in a popular vote on the 13th. On Oct. 31 Nevada entered the Union of the United States as the official 36th state.

NOVEMBER, 1864

S	M	T	W	T	F	S
		1	2	3	4	5
6	7	8	9	10	11	12
13	14	15	16	17	18	19
20	21	22	23	24	25	26
27	28	29	30			

Abraham Lincoln was elected President of the United States for a second term on Nov. 8, 1864. Andrew Johnson of Tennessee was chosen Vice President. McClellan was defeated in a far stronger victory for Lincoln than many expected. The electoral vote was 212 for the Republican President and 21 for Democrat McClellan, who carried only Delaware, Kentucky and New Jersey. Popular vote was Lincoln 2,330,552 to 1,835,985 for McClellan. The operation of the war had been upheld and Lincoln was given a mandate for victory. At Petersburg there was siege and in the Valley a few minor fights, with Early's few and battered troops unable to stop Sheridan. But in the deep South two armies moved—in opposite directions. Sherman left Atlanta Nov. 16 with about 60,000 for the Atlantic. The "March to the Sea" had begun. But before he left, Atlanta was partially burned. It was to be a campaign of scorched earth in Georgia. Only a few state troops were in front of him. As the Federals spread over the land, the land and all on it gave way before them. Plantations were pillaged and burned; food, horses and even unnecessary luxuries were "procured" from the civilians, sometimes officially, more often not. It was war brought home to the South and many have not forgotten. As Sherman headed east Hood moved north across the Tennessee from Florence, Ala.—the last invasion. Hood hoped that Sherman would be forced to give up his drive to the sea, but Sherman had foreseen it all and Thomas was readying at Nashville. There were dreams for the Army of Tennessee—dreams of seeing the Ohio and perhaps even more. As Hood made his early move, Forrest was out on his last raid into West Tennessee. Schofield was at Pulaski, Tenn. and was ordered back toward Nashville by Thomas. Hood had the opportunity of his career. First, to head off Schofield at the crossing of the Duck River at Columbia, and again at Spring Hill Nov. 29th. As Schofield moved up the pike towards Franklin, Federal advance parties fought briefly with Forrest and pushed on. Hood, within sound of the Union army, did nothing. There was no attack and no victory. And the "Spring Hill Affair" was one of the great lost opportunities of the entire war. The next day, Nov. 30, Schofield with nearly 30,000 effectives, made a stand at the little Tennessee town of Franklin. An aroused and angered Hood plunged out from the low hills crossing the fields towards the town. It was another direct frontal assault, one of the bloodiest of the war, with six Confederate generals dying, including Pat Cleburne. Union army: 27,939 engaged, only 189 killed, 1,033 wounded and 1,104 missing. Confederates: 26,897 effectives, with 1,750 killed, 3,800 wounded and 702 missing. But there was more lost than the men—the campaign really ended at the little town on the Harpeth River in Tennessee. Schofield retired to Nashville and Thomas and a punished Hood followed him. Far out

in Colorado at Sand Creek, Northern Col. J. M. Chivington massacred the Cheyennes Nov. 29, a wanton display of ruthlessness. For over three years there had been rumors and counter-rumors of conspiracy and uprising in the North and nothing much had happened. But Nov. 25 fires were set in eleven New York hotels and Barnum's museum, with most of them sputtering out before much damage was done. There were fantastic plans to capture Chicago, free Southern prisoners at several camps and even take the northwestern states out of the Union. It was a dismal mess. The Copperheads talked big and did little, and most of the Confederate leaders were jailed.

DECEMBER, 1864

S	M	T	W	T	F	S
				1	2	3
4	5	6	7	8	9	10
11	12	13	14	15	16	17
18	19	20	21	22	23	24
25	26	27	28	29	30	31

It was winter again and there was little doing in front of Petersburg. In the Shenandoah, Sheridan moved at will, destroying at will. From the 1st to the 10th Sherman plunged deeper into Georgia, ravaging his way to Savannah. Fort McAllister near Savannah fell Dec. 13. Sherman could forget supply lines for he now had a Union fleet to feed him. Confederate William Hardee did his best with 15,000 inferior troops in Savannah, only to evacuate Dec. 20 and stagger toward South Carolina. President Lincoln received a telegram from Sherman, "I beg to present you as

THE POTTER HOUSE, ATLANTA

In Aug., 1864, Sherman's army bore in on Atlanta. This house shows the devastation which was wrought during the siege.

DOWNTOWN ATLANTA

This scene shows battered downtown Atlanta after Sherman's troops had occupied the city in early September 1864.

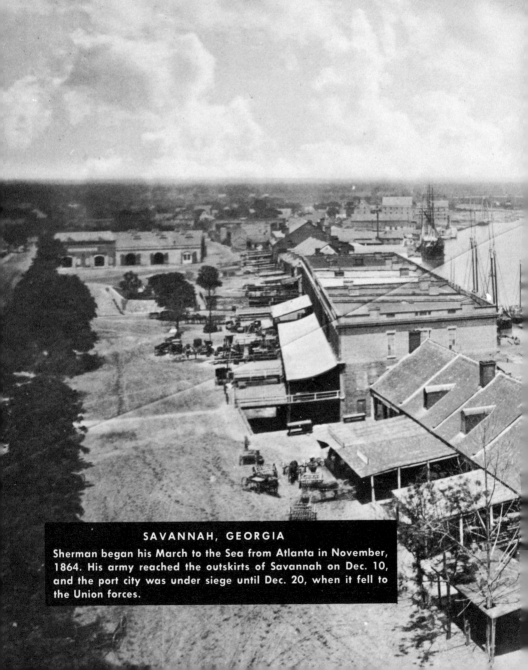

SAVANNAH, GEORGIA

Sherman began his March to the Sea from Atlanta in November, 1864. His army reached the outskirts of Savannah on Dec. 10, and the port city was under siege until Dec. 20, when it fell to the Union forces.

THE CAPITOL, NASHVILLE, TENNESSEE

In November, 1864, General Hood moved north into Tennessee with his Confederate army in an attempt to divert Sherman from his March to the Sea. However, the Confederates were defeated at Spring Hill, Tenn., on Nov. 29, and at Franklin, Tenn., on Nov. 30. The final dashing of Confederate hopes in this campaign occurred in the battle for Nashville, where General Thomas led the Union forces to a smashing victory Dec. 15-16.

a Christmas gift the city of Savannah." Fort Fisher on the North Carolina coast near Wilmington was besieged late in the month. Dec. 6 Salmon P. Chase was named Chief Justice of the United States succeeding the late Justice Taney. But it was Nashville the people watched. Carefully, painstakingly, Thomas got ready for battle. An excited Washington urged him to move. There were fears that he might be another McClellan. Hood realized he could not leave Nashville behind him and march north, but could he take it? Retreat was unthinkable. Snow, ice, and the needs of the Union army delayed things. So much so that orders were given to replace Thomas with Maj. Gen. John A. Logan. But the horses became ready, the weather improved, and Logan didn't get his command. Dec. 15 Thomas slugged forward in a beautifully planned and executed two-day battle. The first day the Federal advance line broke in on Hood who retreated to the Brentwood Hills. On the 16th Schofield's infantry and James Harrison Wilson's cavalry broke the Confederate left. It was evening and the Army of Tennessee was in full flight, but there was little army left; it had been virtually destroyed by the ponderous Thomas. Forrest managed to hold the rear guard as the disheartened remnants, no longer homeward bound, crossed the Tennessee the day after Christmas. Nashville's cost—Union: 49,773 engaged, 387 killed, 2,562 wounded, and 112 missing; Confederates: 23,207 engaged, with no accurate reports of casualties, but 4,462 prisoners. Victory for the North in the West; victory in Georgia, but there was still Lee at Petersburg.

1865

S	M	T	W	T	F	S
1	2	3	4	5	6	7
8	9	10	11	12	13	14
15	16	17	18	19	20	21
22	23	24	25	26	27	28
29	30	31				

The fourth new year of the war and there were few who would not admit that it would be the last. There was only blind hope in the South now. Fort Fisher at Wilmington, N. C., fell Jan. 15 but the city managed to hold out a little longer. Sherman headed northward for the Carolinas. Hood left his beaten army at Tupelo, Miss., Jan. 14, with Gen. Richard Taylor taking command. Jefferson Davis said he was willing to open negotiations if they would bring peace to both countries. But to Lincoln there was one country. The United States House of Representatives Jan. 31 resolved to submit to the states an Amendment, the Thirteenth, which would prohibit slavery. The Confederate Congress Jan. 19 named General Lee Commander-in-Chief of all the Southern armies, a move many had proposed for years.

Davis formally appointed Lee Feb. 6. Lee suggested in January that slaves be used as soldiers by the Confederacy. The Confederate Congress also urged that Davis restore Joseph E. Johnston to command of the remaining forces in the southeast. Confederate offers to reopen exchange of prisoners, man for man, were accepted by the Federals late in the month. On Jan. 28, Davis named three commissioners to hold informal meetings with Lincoln. And there were still siege lines at Petersburg.

S	M	T	W	T	F	S
			1	2	3	4
5	6	7	8	9	10	11
12	13	14	15	16	17	18
19	20	21	22	23	24	25
26	27	28				

The late winter action was quiet; but in the quiet, time was running out for the South. The little probes continued at Petersburg and Sheridan mopped up Early again late in the month in the Shenandoah. Sherman destroyed his way across the Carolinas, aiming for a junction with Grant. On February 17 Columbia, capital of South Carolina, was taken and that night it burned. The South blamed Sherman and Sherman blamed the fleeing Confederates. Charleston, known to many as the birthplace of secession, was now completely cut off and occupied on the 18th without a fight. Schofield took Wilmington, N. C., Feb. 22. Lee named Joseph E. Johnston to gather in the tattered leftovers and try to stop Sherman. In Hampton Roads, Va., on Feb. 3, Lincoln and Secretary of State Seward conferred with Confederate Vice-President Alexander Stephens and his fellow commissioners. But the South still demanded independence as a nation before there could be peace. The meeting was futile. Reconstruction began its confused operation in many sections of the faltering South.

MARCH, 1865

S	M	T	W	T	F	S
			1	2	3	4
5	6	7	8	9	10	11
12	13	14	15	16	17	18
19	20	21	22	23	24	25
26	27	28	29	30	31	

Sheridan gave the reeling Valley one last blow and headed east to join Grant. There were many conferences in Richmond, but the fight was to continue at Petersburg. Sherman's easy march ahead paused briefly March 19 to 21 when Johnston, back in command but with few to lead, attacked at Bentonville, N. C. Sherman merely threw in more troops and Johnston retreated toward Raleigh. There was cleaning up to be done throughout the South. Wilson's Federal cavalry raided March 22 to April 24th from Nashville to Selma and Montgomery, Ala., and on to Macon, Ga. At Petersburg Gordon tried to break through from Fort Stedman and succeeded in his first rush March 25 only to be thrown back. After a conference with Lincoln March 27-28, Grant sent Sheridan eastward March 29, pushing past Dinwiddie Court House on the 31st toward the road junction at Five Forks. The Congress of the United States was busy with Reconstruction and established a Freedman's Bureau to handle and mishandle the Negro problem. Congress also disowned any debts of the Confederacy; and made wives of Negro soldiers free. States began ratifying the Thirteenth Amendment during March but New Jersey rejected it. On March 4 Abraham Lincoln was inaugurated for a second term. Fully recognizing that the task of reconstruction might be more difficult even than winning the war he said "With malice toward none, with charity for all; with firmness in the right, as God gives us to see the right, let us strive to finish the work we are in; to bind up the nation's wounds; to care for him who shall have borne the battle, and for his widow, and his orphan—to do all which may achieve and cherish a just and lasting peace, among ourselves, and with all nations." Andrew Johnson of Tennessee was inaugurated Vice-President amidst charges that he was intoxicated while being sworn in. On that same March 4 the Confederate Congress adopted a new flag, authorized the use of slaves in the army on the 13th, and adjourned for the last time March 18.

Genl. Bragg,

The despatch of Genl. F. Lee would indicate the propriety of looking for Sheridan on the lower Chickahominy rather than at the White House.

We cannot start troops now if the report be correct with any prospect finding the Enemy where Genl. Hampton left him.

If we have force enough to expel the party at and near "deep bottom" so as to destroy the Bridge, it will then be easier to combine on Sheridan's corps so as to destroy it. Unless this can be done there will be hazard in going far down the Chickahominy.

Every practicable combination and effort should be made to prevent Sheridan's cavalry from returning to Grant's army.

The telegram of Genl. R. E. Lee in relation to the movement against the So. Side R. R. renders it more necessary than before that Genl. Kemper should go up to supervise the assembling & distribution of the "Reserves."

very respectfully yrs
Jeffn. Davis

President Jefferson Davis writes his military adviser Braxton Bragg concerning means of stopping Sheridan from joining his army with Grant's. Davis regarded himself as the over-all strategist of the war and took a major role in the direction of military action.

COLUMBIA, SOUTH CAROLINA

After capturing Savannah, Sherman turned North and cut a swath through South Carolina. On Feb. 17, 1865, his army captured and burned Columbia, the capital of South Carolina. This view, seen from the capitol, shows the devastation which the Union army brought to the Southern city.

RUINS OF COLUMBIA

Another view of the havoc which Sherman's army wrought on the South Carolina capital. The town was virtually leveled.

IN WAR'S WAKE

These ruins had once been Charleston's railroad station. Despite a full-scale Union attack in Aug.-Oct., 1863, the city withstood the enemy. Charleston did not fall to the Union until evacuated Feb. 17, 1865, the same date that Sherman captured and burned the South Carolina capital, Columbia. This view shows the condition the Southern city was in when Federal troops took it over.

APRIL, 1865

S	M	T	W	T	F	S
						1
2	3	4	5	6	7	8
9	10	11	12	13	14	15
16	17	18	19	20	21	22
23	24	25	26	27	28	29
30						

There was little left and Lee knew it. Sheridan was heading out to cut off any retreat west and south of Petersburg. On April 1 Sheridan attacked George E. Pickett at Five Forks and overwhelmed him. Assault on Petersburg itself was ordered for April 2 and amidst the fighting A. P. Hill, who had done so much so often for the South, was killed. In St. Paul's Church in Richmond, President Davis was attending services. A messenger came down the aisle and Davis quietly left to begin preparation for leaving his capital. As the government, some civilians, and a small garrison fled the falling city, Lee's army pulled out of the Petersburg defenses toward the west. April 3 and after almost four years of war the Confederate capital, symbol of so much, had fallen. The next day Abraham Lincoln walked the streets of Richmond. Lee's nearly starving army was to get supplies April 4th at Amelia Court House, but the supplies were not there. The Federals swarmed around the edges of the retreating Army of Northern Virginia and Ewell's corps was cut up and captured April 6 at Saylor's Creek. There was a delaying action April 7 near Farmville. The same night correspondence began between Grant and Lee. The general of a fading army asked for terms and proposed to treat for peace. But Grant had no authority nor wish to do so. He could only accept surrender. Early April 9 Lee attacked Sheridan's cavalry to no avail, and sent a flag of truce for an interview with Grant at Appomattox Court House. It was 3:45 p.m. in the McLean farm house and Ulysses S. Grant was tendered the care of 28,356 men of the great army of the Confederacy. Yes, they could retain their horses and side arms, and they could have food, but they also had defeat. The arms were stacked, the flags were furled, and a proud army with its proud commander was gone. The Confederate government fled to Greensboro, N. C., by the 12th and to Charlotte by the 18th. April 14 and Joseph E. Johnston asked for terms from Sherman. The general signed a memorandum of peace April 18 which was not accepted in Washington, and finally April 26 near Durham Station, N. C., Johnston and 37,-047 men received the same terms as the Army of Northern Virginia. On April 12 the city of Mobile, last major Confederate center, fell. April 14 and the Stars and Stripes were raised over Fort Sumter in the harbor at Charleston. Morning of April 15 and the Stars and Stripes were lowered in Washington. For Abraham Lincoln, shot by actor John Wilkes Booth in Ford's Theatre on Good Friday evening, died. The North mourned and the South mourned and it was a time of victory and defeat and sorrow.

AN END AND A BEGINNING

The United States had a new President, Andrew Johnson of Tennessee, and the South had old memories and new problems. John Wilkes Booth was shot in a blazing barn near Bowling Green, Va., April 26. The conspirators were tried and executed or imprisoned. Gen. Richard Taylor surrendered all remaining Confederate troops east of the Mississippi at Citronelle, near Mobile, May 4 and the same day Lincoln was buried at Springfield, Ill. Wilson's Federal cavalry found Jefferson Davis and Postmaster General Reagan May 10 near Irwinville, Ga. Davis was taken to Fort Monroe to await trial. Surrenders in Florida May 17; at Chalk Bluff, Ark., May 11. President Johnson proclaimed the end of armed resistance May 10. Sunset of May 13 at Palmetto Ranch near Brownsville, Tex., the last shots of the war were said to have been fired as Confederates under Brig. Gen. James E. Slaughter defeated Federal Col. T. H. Barrett, a final "victory" for the South. On May 25 Sabine Pass, Tex., was evacuated by the Confederates and on the 26th E. Kirby Smith surrendered the Trans-Mississippi to E. R. S. Canby. President Johnson May 29 proclaimed amnesty to all citizens of the South who would pledge allegiance to the United States. Only Confederate officers and a few others were withheld the pardon of peace. On the Rio Grande, horsemen of the South dipped their colors in the muddy waters and under Jo Shelby rode into Mexico. At Liverpool, England, on November 6 the *C.S.S. Shenandoah*, the last of the Confederate States of America, surrendered.

What was the cost? In dollars there is no estimate. In dead, 360,222 Federals, including 110,000 dying from wounds. Another 275,175 were wounded. Confederacy: 258,000 dead, 94,000 of them falling in battle. The wounded—unknown. Total manpower? By the end of April 1865 there were about a million Federals in the field, while possibly two million to 2,300,000 actually served during the war. Confederate totals are often put at 600,000 to 700,000, but no one knows the real figure.

It was over, and yet it was only begun. So much had changed, so much had been lost. What had been won?

[131]

HAVEN FROM WAR

The country near this house, on Weldon Railroad (near Petersburg) in Virginia, was the scene of heavy fighting during Grant's drive on Richmond in February, 1865. The surrounding country was as rough as the Wilderness, with woods of heavy pines, a dense growth of underbrush, and malaria-infested swamps. Headquarters for the operation were pitched close to Aiken House, to the gratification of members of the staff, for no less than seven young women were living in the house. Inside the railing was the tent of the safeguard, posted to protect the house and its inhabitants. Often the safeguard was left behind when the army advanced or retreated. If the place was taken by the enemy, the safeguard was given safe conduct under a flag of truce to his own lines.

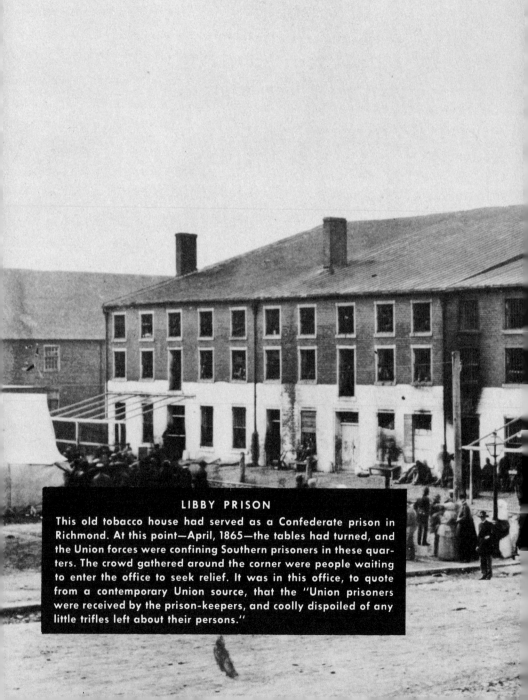

LIBBY PRISON

This old tobacco house had served as a Confederate prison in Richmond. At this point—April, 1865—the tables had turned, and the Union forces were confining Southern prisoners in these quarters. The crowd gathered around the corner were people waiting to enter the office to seek relief. It was in this office, to quote from a contemporary Union source, that the "Union prisoners were received by the prison-keepers, and coolly dispoiled of any little trifles left about their persons."

"FORT HELL"

ıere are the "bomb-proof" quarters occupied by both officers and men at Fort Sedgwick near Petersburg. After the excavation was made, the ground was covered with heavy pieces of timber, over which a layer of earth several feet thick was thrown. Fort Sedgwick was one of the advance positions in the Union Army's siege of Petersburg. Almost daily for many grim months it was the scene of heavy artillery duels, hence the name "Fort Hell."

PATRIOTS
FALL IN! FALL IN!!

HEAD QUARTERS, PENNA. 543rd REGIMENT,
Philadelphia, August 20th, 1861.

A Regiment for the War, will be raised at Philadelphia, on a plan which enables the projectors of the enterprise to offer the

GREATEST INDUCEMENTS

To those anxious to serve the country, and at the same time secure

FAT SNAPS!

IT IS PROPOSED TO HAVE THIS REGIMENT COMPOSED

ENTIRELY OF OFFICERS!

as follows:—25 Brigadier Generals, 73 Colonels, 118 Lieutenant Colonels, 243½ Majors, 58 Quarter-masters, 93 Captains, 156 First Lieutenants, and the balance to be filled up with Second Lieutenants, which will be the lowest position in the Regiment. In order to secure at once the services of so invaluable a Regiment, the Government will pay each man on enlistment, a

BOUNTY OF $681,18,

and furnish clothing, all covered with buttons and gold lace, also Rations, Tobacco and **WHISKEY,** and at the close of the War the men will receive land warrants for 14 farms apiece, to comprise not less than 3000 acres each, with the privilege of locating them in any part of the United States, Jersey, or any other place.

APPLY AT ONCE AT HEAD QUARTERS, TO

Brevet Maj. Gen. J. H. WILLBEE,

J. M. CANBEE, 1st Assistant Adj. General.

This is a lampoon of the recruiting efforts on behalf of the Union Army.

THE LINEUP

THE MAJOR ARMIES NORTH AND SOUTH

In no war in American history did the outfit a man belonged to mean as much as in the Civil War. There was his squad, company, and primarily his regiment made up of men in many cases from his own home community, often led by officers of his own election. There was a comradeship in victory and defeat that, despite the independence in some ways of the American soldier, was a necessary ingredient in making him the fighting man he was. And this feeling went beyond the regiment to the brigade, division, corps and even to the army level. Spirit, elan, pride, and even affection for a unit or a commander were vital elements in the creation of a successful fighting force.

As organizations, the armies were extremely complex, North and South. As the war went on units were changed, commanders replaced, plans disrupted, and units reorganized time and again by necessity or desire. It is valuable for the student of the period to study the twistings and turnings of an individual corps or minor army, who commanded what, what the various names and dates were, and where it fought. But for the general reader we have tried to clarify and simplify the picture of the lineup of the several major armies on both sides, where they fought, who led them, and to give a brief summary of their operations. There are forces not mentioned. Some of these existed for the duration in far-off places, some blazed to success or failure in a few days, some were merely garrisons or departmental commands. In addition there were the nearly unattached cavalry and raiding forces, the home guard or militia units, and of course the naval commands. This entire subject is worthy of special and detailed treatment, which neither space nor the general reader's interest will permit in a work of this type.

The larger armies often had their bulk broken into army corps, corps were divided into divisions, divisions into brigades and brigades into regiments. The number of men in such units varied greatly due to time and circumstances. Early in the war a Confederate division nearly equalled a Federal corps in size. It took many elements, many groups, and many men to make a war. Here then is the lineup for that war featuring the major actors.

THE UNITED STATES OF AMERICA

President and Commander-in-Chief
ABRAHAM LINCOLN, March 4, 1861-April 15, 1865
ANDREW JOHNSON, April 15, 1865-March 4, 1869

Secretary of War
SIMON CAMERON, March 4, 1861-January 14, 1862
EDWIN M. STANTON, January 15, 1862-May 28. 1868

General-in-Chief of the Armies
[Brevet] Lieutenant General WINFIELD SCOTT, June 1841-November 5, 1861
Major General GEORGE B. McCLELLAN, November 6, 1861-March 11, 1862

(No general commander between March 11, 1862-
July 11, 1862)
Major General HENRY WAGER HALLECK, July 11, 1862-March 12, 1864

(Chief of Staff, March 12, 1864-April 19, 1865)
Lieutenant General ULYSSES S. GRANT, March 12, 1864-March 4, 1869

(Promoted to the newly created grade of General
July 25, 1866)

At the beginning of the Civil War, aged Lieutenant General Winfield Scott was General-in-Chief of the United States Army under the Constitutional Commander-in-Chief, Abraham Lincoln. The veteran of over fifty years of active duty ably prepared the hastily improvised forces for war, but because of age and infirmities, was replaced by youthful Major General George Brinton McClellan. In March, 1862, McClellan was relieved of his over-all command although he still led the Army of the Potomac. After four months without a General-in-Chief, Major General Henry Wager Halleck was given the post in July, 1862, and continued in command until the appointment of Ulysses S. Grant as General-in-Chief. Halleck continued as Chief of Staff and military advisor to the President, but subordinate to Grant, until the end of the war. Grant served as General-in-Chief of the Armies until March 4, 1869, when he became the 18th President of the United States.

ARMY OF THE POTOMAC
(Union)

The principal Northern army in Virginia, the Army of the Potomac, was actually established August 20, 1861, growing out of the Military District of the Potomac. Units of the Military District of the Potomac under the command of Major General Irvin McDowell fought at First Bull Run (or First Manassas) July 21, 1861. Major General George B. McClellan commanded the army from August 20, 1861, to November 9, 1862. During his leadership the army was capably organized into a unit, taken to the Virginia Peninsula near Richmond to fight the campaign up to the Confederate capital and in the Seven Days Battles near Richmond in which it was pushed back to the James River. In November, 1861, McClellan also was made General-in-Chief of the Armies, a post he held until March 11, 1862. After the failure in front of Richmond he maintained nominal command of the Army of the Potomac but was in a secondary position until the defeat of the Federal Army of Virginia under Major General John Pope at Second Bull Run (or Second Manassas). Following this loss, McClellan reorganized his Army of the Potomac and halted Lee's northern advance into Maryland at Antietam or Sharpsburg in the fall of 1862. President Lincoln removed McClellan from army command for his failure to follow up after Antietam, and named Major General Ambrose E. Burnside as commander, November 9, 1862. Burnside served ineffectively, leading the army in the tragic charge at Fredericksburg. Due to great dissatisfaction in the army itself, poor strategy and obvious inability, Burnside was replaced January 26, 1863, by Major General Joseph Hooker, who overconfidently led the Army of the Potomac into the battle at Chancellorsville in the spring of 1863 and was badly beaten. As Lee advanced north across the Potomac River again towards Gettysburg, Lincoln replaced Hooker on June 28, 1863, with Major General George Gordon Meade. Forced to take over just before a major battle, Meade withstood the Confederate assaults at Gettysburg and continued to command the army for the remainder of the war. But when Lieutenant General U. S. Grant was named General-in-Chief of the Armies he decided to make his headquarters with the

Army of the Potomac and actually directed the advance of the army to Richmond, at the siege of Petersburg and in the final Appomattox campaign, issuing orders through Meade. The Army of the Potomac had loved with deep affection George B. McClellan, disliked Burnside, lacked confidence in Hooker, was respectful of Meade, and was intensely proud of Grant. As an army it had taken it on the chin time and time again but had never disintegrated. It could suffer defeat and tremendous physical losses but remained a fighting force that grew in experience and strength until it became by the war's end the mightiest army on earth at the time.

ARMY OF VIRGINIA
(*Union*)

The unhappy Federal Army of Virginia was organized from various elements around Washington, June 26, 1862, for the purpose of defending the capital while McClellan was on the Peninsula of Virginia near Richmond with the Army of the Potomac. Major General John Pope, victorious in western fighting, was given command. A vainglorious man, he tried unsuccessfully to create a new army almost overnight. He led the Army of Virginia in the Battle of Second Bull Run (or Second Manassas) and led it badly. Thoroughly whipped late in August, 1862, the army fell back to Washington. Some units of the Army of the Potomac which were brought back from Richmond had fought with Pope. On September 12, 1862, the Army of Virginia was discontinued and its elements largely merged with the Army of the Potomac. Few of the units of the Army of Virginia had ever served or fought together as an integrated force. Its commander was beyond his depth and its history was brief and unfortunate.

ARMY OF THE TENNESSEE
(*Union*)

The Army of the Tennessee grew out of the force that had fought at Shiloh or Pittsburg Landing, Tennessee, under General Grant, which was then known as the Army of West Tennessee. On October 16, 1862, it became the Army of the Tennessee under Grant and fought in the Vicksburg campaign, battles around Chattanooga, the Atlanta campaign, and Sherman's march through Georgia and the Carolinas. When Grant took over the entire western command Major General William T. Sherman was named commander of the

Army of the Tennessee, October 24, 1863. When Sherman in turn assumed western command, Major General James B. McPherson took over the army, March 26, 1864. Upon the death of McPherson, July 22, and after a few days under Major General John A. Logan, Major General Oliver Otis Howard was put in command, July 27, 1864. But in some ways the Army of the Tennessee could be said to have been Sherman's army. It was Sherman who fused it into a real fighting unit and Sherman who used it so well in the advance to Atlanta and to the sea. The Army of the Tennessee was a rough and ready outfit without even the limited military polish of the Army of the Potomac. It had a devil-may-care attitude about it, a sloppiness, and in the end a rugged strength equal to its assignments in the West. Its story as a formal army is largely one of victory, of great ability to move fast, to slug it out when necessary. It early demonstrated the value of strategic movement and, under Sherman and McPherson especially, used that movement to great advantage.

ARMY OF THE CUMBERLAND
(Union)

On November 15, 1861, Major General Don Carlos Buell took over command of the Department of the Ohio and his troops became known as the Army of the Ohio. After relieving Grant at Shiloh, Buell's army took Nashville and was badly outmarched in the Confederate invasion of Kentucky in the fall of 1862, although successful in the Battle of Perryville in October. Buell, a stiff, rather formal soldier, was replaced for his ineffectiveness in the Kentucky campaign by Major General William S. Rosecrans, October 30, 1862, and the army became known as the Army of the Cumberland. It was as the Army of the Cumberland that it fought at Stone's River (or Murfreesboro) December 31, 1862, and January 2, 1863, and moved toward Chattanooga in the brilliant Tullahoma campaign later in the year. But Rosecrans was nearly routed in the Battle of Chickamauga near Chattanooga in September, 1863, and retreated into Chattanooga itself where he was besieged. Major General George H. Thomas was appointed to replace Rosecrans, October 20, 1863. Thomas, who had fought so well at Chickamauga, led the army in the charge on Missionary Ridge. In the advance to Atlanta it was a part of Sherman's force. Detached from Sherman after Atlanta, the Army of the Cumberland was sent back to Nashville under Thomas to defend against Confederate General John Bell Hood's invasion of Tennessee. And it was the Army of the Cumberland that broke the back of the Confederate Army of Tennessee in the fateful battles of Franklin and Nashville late in 1864. Under its two main commanders, Rosecrans and Thomas, it had become an efficient fighting force, able to take such blows as the Kentucky campaign, Stone's River and Chickamauga. It did not have quite the free and easy ways of Sherman's old Army of the Tennessee. Its commanders were somewhat more formal soldiers but it had a tradition running deep and firm, growing out of adversity into victory at Missionary Ridge, the Atlanta Campaign and at Nashville. It reflected the character of Thomas, "The Rock," and as an army it stood hard and struck hard when needed.

OTHER UNION ARMIES

In addition to the four main Union armies—Army of the Potomac, Army of the Tennessee, Army of the Cumberland, and Army of Virginia—there were a number of other important fighting forces. The second Federal Army of the Ohio grew out of a new department formed when the old Army of the Ohio became the Army of the Cumberland in the fall of 1862. It was not until March 25, 1863, that the widely scattered troops of the Department of the Ohio became known as the Army of the Ohio commanded by Major General Ambrose E. Burnside, although it was in reality largely a single army corps, the 23rd. After fighting at Knoxville in the fall of 1863, the Army of the Ohio, commanded after February 9, 1864, by Major General John M. Schofield, took part in the campaign to Atlanta and fought well against Hood at Franklin, Tennessee, and again with the Army of the Cumberland at the battle of Nashville.

The Federal Army of the Mississippi was organized in February, 1862, and fought under Major General John Pope at Island No. 10, until he went east June 26. It was then commanded by Major General William S. Rosecrans until it was discontinued October 26, 1862, following the battles of Iuka and Corinth.

In the Trans-Mississippi area there was the Army of Southwest Missouri, created in December of 1861, and lasting for a year before being merged into a department. The Army of Southwest Missouri fought at many places in Missouri and Arkansas, including Pea Ridge.

The Army of the James grew out of troops from the Department of Virginia and the combined Department of Virginia and North Carolina. In April, 1864, the troops became known as the Army of the James and under Major General Benjamin F. Butler fought in the ill-fated attacks on Petersburg early in the summer of 1864 when the army was actually bottled up and rendered almost useless.

In February, 1862, forces in the Gulf States occupying various points were known as the Army and Department of the Gulf. At first it was commanded by Major General Benjamin F. Butler, later by Major Generals N. P. Banks, S. A. Hurlbut and E. R. S. Canby. Its operations included the unsuccessful Red River expedition in 1864 and fighting around Mobile late in the war. The Army of Georgia consisted of two corps during the march from Atlanta to the sea and through the Carolinas under the command of Major General Henry W. Slocum and was a part of Sherman's general command.

During Early's invasion into the Shenandoah, an Army of the Shenandoah was created to fight him in August, 1864, and was commanded until February 28, 1865, by Major General Philip H. Sheridan. Troops from the Department of West Virginia, known as the Army of West Virginia, operated with it. Both groups were active in laying waste the Shenandoah Valley and bringing the war to a virtual end in that region late in 1864. In March, 1862, the Army of the Mountain Department was organized under Major General John C. Frémont and operated against Stonewall Jackson unsuccessfully at McDowell and Cross Keys. In June, the army was discontinued.

In addition to the formal armies the Union was divided into various divisions, departments and districts, all of which had troops for garrison duty and for fighting in lesser battles. This organization underwent numerous changes throughout the war.

THE CONFEDERATE STATES OF AMERICA

President and Commander-in-Chief
JEFFERSON DAVIS, February 18, 1861-May 10, 1865
Secretary of War
LEROY P. WALKER, February 21, 1861-September 16, 1861
JUDAH P. BENJAMIN, September 17, 1861-March 22, 1862
GEORGE W. RANDOLPH, March 22, 1862-November 17, 1862
Major General GUSTAVUS W. SMITH, November 17, 1862-
November 20, 1862 (acting)
JAMES A. SEDDON, November 21, 1862-February 4, 1865
Major General JOHN C. BRECKINRIDGE, February 4, 1865 to end
General-in-Chief
General ROBERT E. LEE, February 6, 1865-April 9, 1865
(post created by Confederate Congress for Lee)

MY FELLOW-CITIZENS,
TO ARMS!

I have just received a message direct from the highest authority in the Confederacy, to call upon the Militia Organizations to come forth, and upon all other Citizens to organize Companies for the defence of this City against immediate attack of the enemy. They are approaching, and you may have to meet them before Monday morning. I can do no more than give you this warning of their near approach.

REMEMBER NEW ORLEANS!

Richmond is now in your hands. Let it not fall under the rule of another BUTLER. Rally, then, to your Officers to-morrow morning at 10 o'clock, on BROAD STREET, in front of the CITY HALL.

JOSEPH MAYO,
Mayor of Richmond.

Saturday Afternoon, June 27, 1863.

In a desperate plea for the defense of Richmond, Mayor Mayo reminds his citizens of Butler's notorious rule of New Orleans.

THE LINEUP

The Constitution of the Confederate States of America, like that of the United States, conferred upon President Jefferson Davis the post of Commander-in-Chief of the Army and Navy. Davis literally assumed these duties and consequently the Confederacy did not have a General-in-Chief until a few months prior to the end of the war when its Congress created the post of General-in-Chief and Robert E. Lee was appointed on February 6, 1865. However, Davis did have military advisors. While the highest rank in the Union army was that of Lieutenant General, the Confederacy had long before instituted the rank of full general. Shortly after the beginning of the war this rank was conferred upon Samuel Cooper, who was to serve as both adjutant-general and inspector-general; upon Albert Sidney Johnston; Robert E. Lee; Joseph E. Johnston; and P. G. T. Beauregard. Before taking over command of the Army of Northern Virginia, Lee served as military advisor to President Davis. Later in the war, in December, 1863, General Braxton Bragg was relieved of command of the Army of Tennessee and was brought to Richmond to serve as military advisor to the Confederate President, after which time and until his supersedence by Lee, he was the acting commander-in-chief, under Davis, of the Confederate armies.

ARMY OF NORTHERN VIRGINIA
(Confederate)

One of the most famous of all American armies, the Army of Northern Virginia as such had only one commander, General Robert E. Lee. He assumed command during the battles in front of Richmond, June 1, 1862, and actually gave the army its formal name. The force had been known generally as the Army of the Potomac during the fighting at First Bull Run (or First Manassas) and during the early days of the Peninsula campaign under General Joseph E. Johnston. As the Army of Northern Virginia, its battles were many: the Seven Days, Second Bull Run (or Second Manassas), Antietam (or Sharpsburg), Fredericksburg, Chancellorsville, Gettysburg, the Wilderness, Spotsylvania, Cold Harbor, the siege of Petersburg and the Appomattox Campaign. Its history ended with its surrender, April 9, 1865. As a unit it was Lee's army and fought entirely in the east except for the use of one corps under Longstreet at Chickamauga in the fall of 1863. It was an army of great personality—that of its commander. It was an army undoubtedly blessed with many outstanding leaders, perhaps more than any other single army in the Civil War. Among those who marched and fought along the road to glory with this great army were such military immortals as "Stonewall" Jackson, "Jeb" Stuart, James Longstreet, A. P. Hill, Jubal A. Early and Richard S. Ewell. The Army of Northern Virginia gained such a reputation for brilliance in movement and in fighting that a legend of invincibility rose around its name. But it was able to take its blows as well at Antietam, Gettysburg and in the campaign at Richmond. Perhaps no army in American history has possessed a spirit as strong, a love and faith as embodied in its commander, and a tradition of victory as well-earned as did the Army of Northern Virginia. When this army surrendered, to all intent and purpose the war was over both militarily and spiritually.

ARMY OF TENNESSEE
(Confederate)

The Army of Tennessee ranks, along with the Army of Northern Virginia, as one of the principal armies of the Confederacy and the primary one in the western theater of war. On November 20, 1862, the Army of Kentucky and the Army of the Mississippi were joined to form the Army of Tennessee under General Braxton Bragg, who commanded the army at the Battle of Murfreesboro (or Stone's River), the Tullahoma campaign, Chickamauga, and Chattanooga. It was not generally a contented army as both soldiers and officers had little faith in Bragg. But adversity had created cohesion and despite much grumbling over defeat, and lost opportunities such as at Chickamauga, the army was a strong unit until pushed off Missionary Ridge in the siege of Chattanooga in late fall of 1863. A complete overhaul was provided when General Joseph E. Johnston replaced Bragg December 27, 1863. A revitalized force, the Army of Tennessee contended brilliantly with Sherman in the campaign of retreat and fighting to the outskirts of Atlanta. It had belief in Johnston's ability and the withdrawal almost made it a stronger force rather than weakening it. However, President Davis saw it otherwise and replaced Johnston July 18, 1864. The new commander, General John Bell Hood, was known as a fighter and the army fought often and with great loss in the battles at Peachtree Creek, Atlanta, Ezra Church, and Jonesboro only to lose Atlanta itself. In a calculated gamble Hood led his army northward, striking Sherman's supply line and eventually plunging into Tennessee to charge uselessly at Franklin and then to be overwhelmed at Nashville, December 15-16, 1864. A remnant of the decimated Army of Tennessee again fought in 1865, once more under Joseph Johnston. But it was far too late for it to do more than offer token resistance until Johnston surrendered to Sherman at Durham Station April 26, 1865. Under its three major commanders and subordinates, including William J. Hardee, Leonidas Polk, Patrick R. Cleburne, B. F. Cheatham, A. P. Stewart, Joseph Wheeler and the often detached cavalry under General Nathan Bedford Forrest, the Army of Tennessee suffered much from the disunity of its officers and mediocre command under Bragg and Hood, while Johnston was unable to be more effective because of little support from the Confederate government. Generally lacking, except for Johnston, the brilliancy of leadership given the Army of Northern Virginia, the Army of Tennessee was blessed with great fighting soldiers who often fought and lost, but until the final heavy blows continued to exist as a battered but fighting army.

OTHER CONFEDERATE ARMIES

The Confederacy also had numerous forces of varying sizes which existed at different times as armies and it also had the usual department commands. There was the Army of the Kanawha which fought in what was to be West Virginia, under Brigadier General John B. Floyd in the fall of 1861. The Army of Eastern Kentucky had a brief existence in late 1861 and early 1862 in the eastern counties of Kentucky. The Army of New Mexico was formed in December, 1861, under Brigadier General H. H. Sibley with the aim of conquering New Mexico and Arizona. But after the capture of Santa Fe the Army of New Mexico was beaten at the battle of Glorietta and forced to retreat into Texas. Louisiana State troops were known briefly as the Army of Louisiana, as were troops near Pensacola, Florida, called the Army of Pensacola from October, 1861, until March, 1862.

Early in the war the troops in the Shenandoah Valley commanded by General Joseph E. Johnston were known as the Army of Shenandoah until this army moved to Manassas to aid in the Battle of First Bull Run (or First Manassas). Forces on the Peninsula east of Richmond were known as the Army of the Peninsula from November, 1861, until April, 1862, when they became merged with the main Army of Northern Virginia. The Army of the Northwest consisted of forces in northwestern Virginia from June, 1861, until February, 1862, when the army was disbanded following the loss of much of the new state of West Virginia to the Federals.

Troops around Mobile constituted the Army of Mobile from January, 1862, until late June of the same year. The Central Army of Kentucky was organized in September, 1861, but was merged with the Army of the Mississippi in March, 1862. Troops known until November, 1862, as the Army of East Tennessee and the Army of Kentucky were attached as a corps to the Army of Tennessee in November, 1862. Small forces near Murfreesboro, Tennessee, in October, 1862, were briefly known as the Army of Middle Tennessee. Other Confederate armies were the Army of the West that fought in the Trans-Mississippi at Pea Ridge and later moved east of the river to fight at Corinth and Iuka before being merged with other Confederate forces. There was also the Army of the Southwest or Army of the Trans-Mississippi which was active in Arkansas and Louisiana. The Army of Missouri consisted of forces under Major General Sterling Price that operated into Missouri in August, 1864. The Army of the West and other units in September, 1862, formed the Army of West Tennessee which was later known as the Army of Mississippi, commanded by Lieutenant General John C. Pemberton. It was this force that surrendered at Vicksburg, July 4, 1863. However, the title "Army of Mississippi" was applied after Vicksburg to troops under Lieutenant General Leonidas Polk which was organized in mid-summer, 1863, but by May, 1864, it had joined the Army of Tennessee.

Still another army known as the Army of the Mississippi was formed in March, 1862, under General P. G. T. Beauregard and was taken over by General Albert Sidney Johnston. As a major army of the Confederacy for a short time, the Army of the Mississippi fought at Shiloh (or Pittsburg Landing) April 6-7, 1862. Upon the death of Johnston, Beauregard assumed command but was relieved June 27 and shortly thereafter General Braxton Bragg took over the army which in November, 1862, became the Army of Tennessee.

Headquarters, United States Forces,
Athens, Ga., May 9th, 1865.

$360,000 REWARD !

THE PRESIDENT OF THE UNITED STATES

HAS ISSUED HIS PROCLAMATION announcing that the Bureaus of Military Justice
have reported upon indubitable evidence, that

JEFFERSON DAVIS,

Clement Clay. Jacob Thompson.

GEORGE N. SAUNDERS:

BEVERLEY TUCKER AND W. C. CLEARY,

incited and concerted the assassination of Mr. Lincoln and the attempt on Mr. Seward.
He therefore offers for the arrest of Davis, Clay and Thompson, One Hundred Thousand Dollars
each; for that of Saunders and Tucker, Twenty-Five Thousand Dollars each, and for that of
Cleary, Ten Thousand Dollars.
By command of

Br'v't Brig Gen. WM. J PALMER, Com'd'g.

Henry McAllister, Jr., Capt. & A. A.A. G.

*This political effort to involve top Confederate leaders in the
plot to murder Lincoln did not get far.*

Lieutenant General Grant   March 3. 1865

The President directs me to say to you that he wishes you to have no conference with General Lee unless it be for the capitulation of Gen. Lee's army, or on some minor, and purely, military matter, He instructs me to say that you are not to decide, discuss, or confer upon any political question. Such questions the President holds in his own hands; and will submit them to no military conferences or conventions. Meantime you are to press to the utmost, your military advantages,

Edwin M. Stanton
Secretary of War

LINCOLN DIRECTS PEACE

With the Confederate cause sinking rapidly by spring of 1865 General Lee wrote to General Grant for an interview to plan a possible peace. Grant immediately wired Secretary of War Stanton. It was the night of March 3, 1865, the evening before Lincoln's second inauguration and he was at the Capitol signing last minute bills passed by Congress. The President read Grant's message in silence, took a pen and slowly wrote out his reply. Lincoln showed it to Secretary of State Seward, and then handed it to Stanton who addressed, dated and signed it. Thus the President himself made it clear that Grant had no authority to confer with the Confederates on anything except the actual surrender of Lee's army or upon minor problems. In this momentous document, Lincoln showed that he alone as President had the authority to make peace and that any effort to compromise or arrive at conditional terms of surrender with a Confederate commander would not be tolerated. The war went on until Lee surrendered his army more than a month later.

MEN WHO MADE WAR

WHEN war came to the United States in 1861 it came to a nation that had not fought a major conflict in eight decades—since the Revolution. While the country had a military history which included some notable and not so notable adventures in the War of 1812, in Florida, in Mexico and on the frontier, it did not possess a fire-hardened corps of commanding officers. None of the officers in the small regular army, nor any of those who had once been in the army, had commanded forces of any size in the field, with the exception of superannuated Winfield S. Scott. They had not been forced to think in terms of strategy on anything more than small unit tactics.

It is remarkable that with such a limited background both the United States and the Confederate States produced some commanders of rare military genius and many more who were eminently capable of command. These men had to learn, and they learned in the hardest possible way. Thrown suddenly into an all-inclusive and sometimes almost total war, the great and near great on both sides left a record that is a credit to the native ability of the American people.

In any such biographical selection as this there are obvious limitations of space that affect both those figures who are included and, of course, the many worthy and interesting commanders who have to be eliminated. An attempt has been made here to present a selection that does justice to the men in the ranks, who were the indispensable element of the conflict. An effort has been made to give an objective summation of each leader's ability and characteristics, but the authors fully realize that some students may differ with these opinions. Other writers would undoubtedly make other choices, including many of the worthy women, cabinet members, and political figures of the war. But this is a story of conflict and of fighting, and it is to soldiers that our major attention must be paid—soldiers of whom all Americans had and still have a right to be proud.

NOTE. The rank of an officer in the Civil War armies is often very confusing. There were ranks among the militia, or state troops, the volunteers and the regular army. When a man became a general he was most often a brigadier general of the volunteers officially but was known as a general. However, at the same time he might hold the rank of captain in the regular permanent army or perhaps no rank at all. Many officers with rank of brigadier or major general of volunteers reverted to their old army ranks after the war. Generally speaking, a regular army rank was considered superior to that of volunteer. In addition there was great use of "brevet" or what was really an honorary grade and applied both to volunteer and regular ranks. This might make a man a brevet brigadier general of volunteers or a brevet brigadier general of regulars when his actual rank was colonel.

As a result of this difficult nomenclature, the authors of the following biographies have generally avoided the question of whether a promotion or rank was volunteer, regular or brevet, except where it is of importance to the man's career. For instance, Ulysses S. Grant became a brigadier and major general of volunteers but was promoted to lieutenant general and finally full general of the regular United States army.

ADAMS, CHARLES FRANCIS.
1807-1886. Union.

Born in Boston, the son of President John Quincy Adams, Charles Francis Adams received much of his early education abroad and graduated from Harvard in 1825. In 1858 he was elected to Congress after an active political and writing career in Massachusetts. He was appointed by Lincoln and Secretary of State Seward as Minister to Great Britain and arrived in London in May, 1861. Through his understanding of the British people and his firmness in diplomacy he gained a large share of the credit in keeping Britain from recognizing the Confederacy as a separate nation, and in halting the building of Confederate cruisers in British ports. After serving seven years, he returned home to continue his writing and his public career. Direct and sincere in approach, Adams added much to the stature of the United States abroad.

ALEXANDER, EDWARD PORTER.
1835-1910. Confederate.

Born in Washington, Ga., Alexander was graduated from West Point in 1857 and served in the Mormon difficulties of 1858. Later, he taught at West Point. He helped develop the "wig-wag" signal-flag system. At the outbreak of the war Alexander resigned his U. S. commission and became a captain of engineers in the Confederate forces in March, 1861. With the rank of major, he became chief of ordnance in the Army of Northern Virginia and later commanded artillery at Fredericksburg, Chancellorsville, and Gettysburg. In February, 1864, he was named brigadier general and chief of artillery in Longstreet's corps, participating in the Virginia campaign against Grant. And he was with Lee in the retreat to Appomattox. Following the war he was active in business, particularly railroads. Author of a number of works, he is best known for his *Military Memoirs of a Confederate*, published in 1907. As a military man he ranks high among the more capable in the Confederacy.

ANDERSON, RICHARD HERON.
1821-1879. Confederate.

Born at Statesburg, S. C., Anderson was graduated from West Point in 1842, and served with the Dragoons in the Mexican War and on the frontier. At the outbreak of the Civil War he resigned from the U. S. Army and became colonel of a South Carolina regiment at Fort Sumter. Anderson was made a brigadier general in July, 1861, and led brigades during the Peninsula Campaign. He received command of a division, with rank of major general, in July, 1862. With Longstreet at Second Bull Run or Manassas, he held off Federals at Crampton's Gap. He fought at the "Bloody Lane" at Antietam or Sharpsburg, where he was wounded. He also served at Fredericks-Chancellorsville, and Gettysburg. After Longstreet was wounded in the battle of the Wilderness in May, 1864, Anderson took over Longstreet's corps and fought ably at Spotsylvania. Made a lieutenant general in May, 1864, he commanded one or more divisions for the rest of the war. Anderson was somewhat colorless, but he showed considerable ability in subordinate command.

ANDERSON, ROBERT. *1805-1871. Union.*

Born near Louisville, Ky., Anderson was graduated from West Point in 1825 and served in the Black Hawk, Florida, and Mexican wars. With the rank of major he commanded the forts in Charleston Harbor in 1860-61. When the threat of war became real Anderson moved his garrison from indefensible Fort Moultrie Dec. 26, 1860, to Fort Sumter, on a shoal in the harbor. He was in command during the attack that began the Civil War April 12-13, 1861. He refused several demands of surrender before he was forced to give up the battered fort.

Named a brigadier general, he commanded in Kentucky from May, 1861, until his health failed in October. He saw little further duty. He was a sincere Union man, and a generally competent officer.

while with the rear guard near Harrisonburg June 6, 1862. An amateur at war, he won the respect of Jackson and his own troops and became one of the colorful early heroes of the Confederacy.

ASHBY, TURNER. *1828-1862. Confederate.*

Born in Fauquier County, Va., Ashby was a Virginia farmer and businessman before the Civil War. He organized an independent company of horsemen, and in June, 1861, it was taken into the Confederate Cavalry. He succeeded to command of his regiment late in 1861. By March, 1862, he was a colonel and served with Jackson in the battle of Kernstown. He was active in the fight at Winchester, May 25, and in the pursuit of Federals toward Harpers Ferry, being promoted to brigadier general in May. Ashby, with his cavalry brigade, covered the retreat of Jackson in the Shenandoah Valley. He was killed

BANKS, NATHANIEL PRENTISS. *1816-1894. Union.*

Born in Waltham, Mass., Banks had little formal education. Almost completely self-taught, he became a lawyer, actor, editor, and politician. He first entered Congress in 1853 as a Democrat but later became a Know Nothing and Freesoiler and; in 1856 on the 133rd ballot he was elected Speaker of the House. He was elected governor of Massachusetts and served from 1858-1860. In May, 1861, he was commissioned a major general of volunteers. Commanding in the Shenandoah he was badly beaten by Jackson in 1862. He fought at Cedar Mountain and succeeded Butler in command at New Orleans in the fall of 1862.

He commanded the capture of Port Hudson in July, 1863, and failed in the Red River expedition in May, 1864. Following the war he served again in Congress. Always considered a political general, Banks proved incapable of high military command.

BEAUREGARD, PIERRE GUSTAVE TOUTANT. *1818-1893. Confederate.*

Born near New Orleans, Beauregard was graduated from West Point in 1838 and served well in Mexico. He was appointed a brigadier general of the Confederate Army at the outbreak of war and took command in the attack on Fort Sumter. Later, with Joseph E. Johnston, he was in command at First Bull Run or Manassas, and was made a full general. Sent west, he succeeded to command at Shiloh on the death of Albert Sidney Johnston. However, he was relieved from his post because of illness and politics and was put in charge of the defense of the South Atlantic coast, until taking over the defense of Petersburg in 1864. Here, with very inferior forces, he bottled up Butler at Bermuda Hundred and held Petersburg against Grant until Lee could come up in June. After the war Beauregard entered business and became associated with the Louisiana lottery. Known as the "Great Creole" and the "Napoleon in Gray," he was a dashing, argumentative figure who failed to get along with President Davis, but who proved his ability in the defensive fighting at Petersburg.

BENJAMIN, JUDAH PHILIP. *1811-1884. Confederate.*

Born on St. Thomas Island in the British West Indies, Benjamin was reared in Charleston and attended Yale. A successful lawyer and businessman in New Orleans, he served in the Senate first as a Whig but became a Democrat and advocated secession after Lincoln's election. He was appointed Attorney General by Davis and in September, 1861, shifted to the Confederate War Department where he received some undeserved blame for Confederate failures. Davis moved him to Secretary of State in March, 1862, which post he held until the end of the war. Fleeing to England, Benjamin began a new and very successful law career. An extremely able and intelligent lawyer, Benjamin stands out as one of the few major and forthright figures of the Confederate cabinet.

Civil War he was granted permission to take pictures with the armies. Brady hired a number of other photographers to work with him, and they toured battlefields and followed marches with their clumsy portable photographic equipment and darkroom wagons. It is estimated that about 3,500 pictures were taken, making the war the first in history to be extensively photographed. But financially Brady lost heavily. Although barely able to write, Brady, with his advances in technique and artistry, left an imperishable and invaluable record of the war and pointed the way for future photographers.

BRADY, MATHEW B. *1823-1896.*
Union.

Born in Warren County, N. Y., Brady received little formal education. He was encouraged to take up art, and in New York became interested in photography, which was in its early stages of development. Around 1842 Brady set up his own daguerreotype studio in New York, won several awards for his work, and built up an extensive business with a branch in Washington. At the outbreak of the

BRAGG, BRAXTON. *1817-1876.*
Confederate.

Born at Warrenton, N. C., Bragg was graduated from West Point in 1837 and served in the Seminole War before making an outstanding record as an artillery officer in the Mexican War. He resigned from the army in 1856 and became a Louisiana planter.

In February, 1861, he was made a brigadier general of the Confederacy, and soon major general. He commanded a corps at Shiloh. Promoted to full general in April, 1862, he took command of the Army of Tennessee in June and invaded Kentucky after holding Chattanooga, only to be beaten in the Battle of Perryville, October 8, 1862. He commanded at Murfreesboro or Stone's River and during the Tullahoma and Chattanooga campaigns. He defeated the Federals at Chickamauga but was in turn beaten at Missionary Ridge and turned over his command to Joseph E. Johnston in December, 1863. Despite his failure and unpopularity he was made military adviser to Jefferson Davis. Stern, uncompromising, and a rigid disciplinarian, he made enemies readily among his officers and men. His main fault lay in failure to follow up what successes he achieved.

☆

BRECKINRIDGE, JOHN CABELL.
1821-1875. Confederate.

Born near Lexington, Ky., of a distinguished family he graduated from Centre College in 1839. Entering law practice in Kentucky, Breckinridge fought in the Mexican war, and then turned to politics. In 1851 he was elected to Congress as a Democrat, and soon established his leadership in the House, as well as in Kentucky. He was nominated for vice-president by the Democrats in 1856 and was elected as running-mate to James Buchanan. Breckinridge was nominated for President by the Southern Democrats in 1860 after the breakup of the Democratic Party, but lost to Lincoln in the four-way race. Returning to the Senate, he worked for a compromise

to avoid war, but in October, 1861, resigned to serve in the Confederate Army at Shiloh, Murfreesboro or Stone's River, Chickamauga, Missionary Ridge, in the Shenandoah Valley, and at Cold Harbor, rising to major general. He was appointed Secretary of War of the Confederacy, Feb. 4, 1865. Following the end of hostilities he escaped to Cuba and went on to Europe where he stayed until 1868. Returning to Lexington, Ky., he became immensely popular. He resumed his practice of law and was active in the development of railroads. Breckinridge believed in the right of secession as an abstract principle but did

not believe that it should be applied in 1860. On the other hand he was strongly against coercion of a state and favored non-interference by Congress with slavery in the territories. Highly respected, he was a competent military commander, but better qualified for political activities.

BUCHANAN, FRANKLIN. *1800-1874. Confederate.*

Born in Baltimore, Buchanan became a naval midshipman in 1815 and began a long career. He was the first superintendent of the Annapolis Naval Academy, which he helped found in 1845. He returned to active duty in the Mexican War and was with Commodore Perry in the 1853 expedition to Japan. When it appeared that Maryland might secede, Buchanan hastily resigned his commission and became a captain in the Confederate Navy in September, 1861. In February, 1862, he commanded the *C.S.S. Virginia*, the revolutionary ironclad constructed from the old *U.S.S. Merrimac.* With this vessel he destroyed two Union vessels in Hampton Roads on March 8, 1862, but was wounded and turned his command over to Lieutenant Catesby ap Roger Jones who fought the drawn duel with the *Monitor.* Promoted to admiral, he commanded the Confederate squadron at Mobile Bay and in

the ram *Tennessee* challenged the Union fleet. An able commander, Buchanan was a naval officer of the older style, but an advocate of the new ironclad steam navy.

BUCKNER, SIMON BOLIVAR. *1823-1914. Confederate.*

Born near Munfordville, Ky., Buckner graduated from West Point in 1844 and was active in the war with Mexico. He resigned from the army in 1855 and successfully entered busi-

ness. At first he refused commissions in either army, but with the final abandonment of Kentucky neutrality Buckner joined the Confederate forces. He was at Fort Donelson as third in command when Grant attacked, and surrendered the fort when his superiors fled. After some months in prison he was exchanged and commanded in Bragg's invasion of Kentucky and later in East Tennessee, at Chickamauga, and in Louisiana rising to lieutenant general. He had another business career after the war and served as governor of Kentucky. One of the last important Confederate generals to die, he acted as a pallbearer at the funeral of Grant. A competent officer, he was highly respected.

BUELL, DON CARLOS. *1818-1898. Union.*

Born of Welsh descent near Marietta, Ohio, Buell grew up in Lawrenceburg, Ind., and was graduated from West Point in 1841. He served in the Seminole and Mexican wars and was a lieutenant colonel in the Adjutant General's Department by the start of the Civil War. Appointed a brigadier general in May, 1861, Buell took over command of the Army of the Ohio˙ in November that same year. In February, 1862, he moved south in support of Grant and occupied Nashville, February 24. His army arrived at Pittsburg Landing during the battle of Shiloh and was partially responsible

for the defeat of the Confederates. Promoted to major general, Buell moved toward Chattanooga but never got there, for he had to follow Confederate Bragg who was invading Kentucky. Buell managed to get into Louisville September 25 and then turned south to defeat Bragg at Perryville, October 8, 1862, but was removed from command for not more effectively opposing Bragg. A good organizer, he lacked aggressiveness in field command.

BURNSIDE, AMBROSE EVERETT. *1824-1881. Union.*

Born in Liberty, Ind., Burnside was graduated from West Point in 1847, but saw little service in Mexico and resigned from the army in 1853. He entered business as a gun manufacturer and later became a railroad executive. He organized the 1st Rhode Island Regiment in April, 1861, and rushed to Washington. After fighting at First Bull Run or Manassas he was commissioned brigadier general and in January, 1862, captured Roanoke Island. He became a major general in March, 1862, and had a command in the attack on South Mountain and later in the assault on the Stone Bridge, on the Union left at Antietam or Sharpsburg. In October Burnside was named to succeed McClellan as commander of the Army of the Potomac, a post he was unfitted for and he admitted it. On December 13 his army made the tragic assault at Fredericksburg and failed. Relieved from command of the army in January, 1863, he later defended Knoxville and commanded the 9th corps in the Wilderness, Spotsylvania, Cold Harbor and Petersburg campaigns. He held important business positions after the war and was elected governor of Rhode Island and U.S. Senator. A likable personality, Burnside had great integrity but little ability as an army commander.

BUTLER, BENJAMIN FRANKLIN.
1818-1893. Union.

Born at Deerfield, N. H., Butler went to Waterbury College and later studied law, which he practiced with great success. In the course of his career, he built up a fortune through investment and entered politics. Although he backed the southern Democrats in 1860, he nevertheless was named brigadier general of Massachusetts militia. Throughout the war he was a subject of great controversy. He helped in relieving Washington in 1861 and commanded at Fort Monroe. But he gained his notorious reputation as commander at New Orleans in 1862. Removed from this post, he next commanded the Army of the James but failed at Petersburg and Fort Fish-

er, N. C., and was again removed. He became a Radical Republican and after the war served in Congress with various other parties. He was elected Governor of Massachusetts in 1882. He was presidential candidate of the Anti-Monopoly and Greenback parties in 1884. Known in the South as "Beast" for his extreme harshness toward the people of New Orleans, Butler was an inferior military leader, a brilliant lawyer, and above all a consummate political manipulator.

CHASE, SALMON PORTLAND.
1808-1873. Union.

Born in Cornish, N. H., Chase lost his father at the age of nine, and was reared by an uncle in Ohio. Graduated from Dartmouth in 1826, he began practicing law in Cincinnati and took part in anti-slavery activities, often defending fugitive slaves. He was active in the Free Soil party and

CLEBURNE, PATRICK RONAYNE.
1828-1864. Confederate.

Born in the county of Cork, Ireland, Cleburne served in the British army and came to the United States in 1849. As a druggist he settled in Helena, Ark.; and in 1856 he became a lawyer. He organized the Yell Rifles in 1860; and upon the secession of Arkansas, Cleburne was made a captain and later colonel of the infantry. By early 1862 Cleburne was a brigadier general and served at Shiloh, Richmond, Ky., and Perryville. In December of 1862 he was appointed a major general and distinguished himself in fighting at Murfreesboro, Chicamauga, and in repulsing Sherman at Missionary Ridge. Cleburne urged that slaves be freed and used in the army, an opinion that may have kept him from higher army command. He was with Johnston in the retreat to Atlanta and with Hood in the fights for Atlanta. He was killed at the Battle of Franklin, while with Hood's advancing Army of Tennes-

was elected to the Senate in 1849, where he continued his anti-slavery fight. In 1855 and 1857 he was elected governor of Ohio and became a Republican. In 1856 and 1860 he was a declared candidate for the Republican presidential nomination. Defeated by Lincoln in the convention of 1860, he was appointed Lincoln's Secretary of the Treasury, serving capably from March, 1861, until July, 1864. Finally, after receiving several resignations from Chase which he refused to accept, Lincoln felt that further association was impossible, and he allowed Chase to resign. In October, 1864, Lincoln appointed Chase Chief Justice to succeed the deceased Roger Taney. His term was stormy, with many difficult problems of Reconstruction to face. Strong-willed, Chase was extremely ambitious for the Presidency, and this ambition materially reduced his value in other offices.

see. Cleburne was sometimes known as the "Stonewall Jackson of the West," so strongly did he hold the affection and respect of his men and other officers.

COOPER, SAMUEL. *1798-1876. Confederate.*

Born at Hackensack, N. J., Cooper was graduated from West Point in 1815 and began a long career as a regular army officer. In 1852 he was named colonel and Adjutant General of the army, following efficient staff work in the Mexican war. Despite his Northern birth, Cooper had many friends in the South and had married a Virginia woman. At the outbreak of the Civil War he resigned and offered his services to Jefferson Davis, a close friend. He was appointed Adjutant and Inspector General of the Confederate Army with the rank of full general, outranking all other officers by seniority. Despite his high rank he made little impression on Confederate military history, but performed moderately well in staff duty.

CUSTER, GEORGE ARMSTRONG. *1839-1876. Union.*

Born in New Rumley, Ohio, Custer was graduated from West Point in June, 1861, at the bottom of his class of 34. He was assigned to the 5th U. S. Cavalry, served at First Bull Run, and in June, 1862, became aide on McClellan's staff with the rank of captain. In June, 1863, after a distinguished record in several cavalry fights, Custer was named brigadier general. He served through the Gettysburg and Virginia campaigns and fought under Sheridan, particularly distinguishing himself in the pursuit of Lee from Richmond. He ended the war a major general of volunteers, commanded a

division of cavalry in Texas until March, 1866, and in July, 1866, was made lieutenant colonel in the new 7th Cavalry. He served actively in the West until his death in the Battle of the Little Big Horn (more popularly known as "Custer's Last Stand"), June

25, 1876. There have been few figures in American history as controversial as Custer, who is often considered mainly a "glory hunter," but on the other hand he showed courageous, although often rash, ability in command.

DANA, CHARLES ANDERSON. *1819-1897. Union.*

Born in Hinsdale, N. H., Dana had little or no formal primary education, but was largely self-taught. He did manage to attend Harvard for three years and became a teacher at the Brook Farm socialist enterprise for five years. Writing for the farm publications led him to journalism. In 1846 he became city editor of the New York *Tribune* and soon was second only to its editor, Horace Greeley. At the time of the Civil War he was managing editor of the *Tribune* and was responsible for the war cry "On to Richmond!" Breaking with Greeley, Dana resigned in March, 1862, and

entered the War Department, serving as the ears and eyes of Secretary Stanton, particularly in the Western campaigns. In mid-1863 he became Assistant Secretary of War. After the war he continued his journalistic career as owner of the New York *Sun*. He broke with his old friend Grant and was a political independent throughout his entire career. An intellectually curious man, Dana was responsible for many developments in newspaper and editorial operations.

DAVIS, JEFFERSON FINIS. *1808-1889. Confederate.*

Born in Christian (now Todd) County, Ky., he was the son of a middle class farm family. Despite some legends, he was not related to Lincoln. Reared in Wilkinson County, Miss., he attended Transylvania University in 1821 and was graduated from West Point in 1828 with a spotty conduct record. For about seven years he was at army posts in Wisconsin and Illinois and served during the Black Hawk War. He married Sarah Knox Taylor, daughter of then Col. Zachary Taylor, and resigned from the army. His wife died in September, 1835, and for about ten years he was in semi-seclusion as a slave-holding planter at Brierfield, near the home of his older brother, Joseph, in Mississippi. Joseph Davis was an extremely important influence in his life. At this time he studied a great deal and developed his political ideas. In 1845 he married Varina Howell and was elected to Congress as a State Rights Democrat. He resigned in June of 1846 to serve with distinction in the Mexican War. It was here he learned, perhaps, to over-evaluate himself as a

military commander. After that war he served in the Senate from 1847 to 1851, but upon losing an election for the governorship of Mississippi in 1851, became Secretary of War under Franklin Pierce from 1853 to 1857. He is considered one of the most capable administrators the office has ever had. He was again in the Senate from 1857 until January of 1861. He was prominent in debate and defended slavery and the right of a state to secede. He announced the withdrawal of Mississippi from the Union following Lincoln's election. Hoping for the command of the Southern armies, Davis, tired and in ill health, was elected provisional President of the Confederacy February 9, 1861, and President by popular vote in November, 1861. He faced the simultaneous and overwhelming tasks of creating a new nation and fighting a bitter war. He is greatly criticized for interfering with his generals and favoring incompetents in the army and in the govern-

ment. On the other hand, this apparently cold and austere personality can be credited with keeping his nation in the fight for four years. He never publicly gave up until captured May 10, 1865, near Irwinville, Ga. After two years in prison in Fort Monroe, he was released in May, 1867, and became a rather unsuccessful businessman. He retired in 1879 to Beauvoir near Biloxi, Miss., and wrote his defense of the South and the Confederacy. Beneath the stubborn, aristocratic and at times overbearing personality there was a sensitive, warm person who believed deeply in his cause and was more than willing to share in the responsibility for the war years, although he resented the criticism heaped upon him.

DOUBLEDAY, ABNER. *1819-1893. Union.*

Born at Ballston Spa, N. Y., Doubleday was educated as a civil engineer. While at school in Cooperstown he aided in the development of the game of baseball, but cannot be considered its inventor. He was graduated from West Point in 1842 and served in Mexico, in Florida, and in garrison posts. As a captain at Fort Sumter he took part in its defense in April, 1861. After serving around Washington, he was appointed brigadier general of volunteers in February, 1862, and commanded a brigade at Second Bull Run or Manassas and a division at South Mountain, Antietam, and Fredericksburg. Named major general in November, 1862, Doubleday was at Chancellorsville and at Gettysburg, where he temporarily took over the corps of General Reynolds, who was killed. He spent the rest of the war in

Washington and later served as a lieutenant colonel and colonel of the regular army. Distinguished in appearance, he was a calm and methodical soldier of reasonable capabilities.

EARLY, JUBAL ANDERSON. *1816-1894. Confederate.*

Born in Franklin County, Va., Early was graduated from West Point in 1837 and served in the Seminole war. In 1838 he resigned from the army to practice law at Rocky Mount, Va., and later was in the Virginia legislature. He served on garrison duty as a volunteer officer in the Mexican War. Opposing secession, he nevertheless entered the Confederate army and served at Bull Run or Manassas as a colonel. Early became a division commander in 1862 and led a corps in 1864. He was named major general in January of 1863 and promoted to lieutenant general in May of 1864. He served well as a subordinate, but his

main operation was as independent commander in the Shenandoah Valley dating from June, 1864. His small force entered the suburbs of Washington itself July 11 and 12, but retreated into Virginia where he was beaten by Sheridan at Winchester and Fisher's Hill. He attacked Sheridan's forces at

Cedar Creek October 19, 1864, but Sheridan arrived in time to turn the tide. Early was extremely bitter toward the North after the war and he was never popular, despite his able military operations against usually terrific odds.

EWELL, RICHARD STODDERT. *1817-1872. Confederate.*

A native of Georgetown, D. C., Ewell was graduated from West Point in 1840 and fought in the Mexican War and in the Southwest. He resigned from the U. S. Army in May, 1861. As a brigadier general in the Confederate forces he participated in First Bull Run or Manassas. By January, 1862, he was

duty under Porter in 1811 on the *Essex* as a midshipman. He thus began a long career of sea duty, becoming lieutenant in 1825. In 1841 he was made commander and served briefly in the Mexican War. In the 1850's he was on ordnance duty. He became a captain in 1855 and established the Mare Island, Calif., Navy Yard. With 49 years of service at the outbreak of the Civil War, he commanded at the capture of New Orleans and on the Mississippi during the Vicksburg campaign. Farragut was commissioned rear admiral in July, 1862. In August, 1864, he captured Mobile Bay and is said to have cried, "Damn the torpedoes!" as his ship, the *Hartford*, led the fleet. In December, 1864, the rank of vice admiral was created for Farragut as was the rank of full admiral in July,

a major general and commanded a division under Jackson in the Shenandoah and fought in the Seven Days campaign. During Second Bull Run or Manassas he was wounded at Groveton and lost a leg. Returning to duty in May, 1863, as lieutenant general, he commanded a corps and led the advance of Lee's army into Pennsylvania. Ewell was criticized for his failure on the Confederate left at Gettysburg. He led his corps in some of the heaviest fighting at the Wilderness and at Spotsylvania. He commanded later at Richmond and the remnant of his force surrendered at Sayler's Creek. Eccentric and nervous, Ewell believed in fighting hard and often.

FARRAGUT, DAVID GLASGOW,
1801-1870. Union.

Born near Knoxville, Tenn., he was taken to New Orleans as a boy and, sponsored by the elder David Porter, entered the Navy. He first saw sea

1866. Completely absorbed in his profession, Farragut was painstaking in his work and independent in action and thought. He was undoubtedly the most successful naval figure of the Civil War.

FORREST, NATHAN BEDFORD.
1821-1877. Confederate.

A native of Bedford County, Tenn., Forrest had little education, having to care for a large family. He became wealthy through land purchases and later as a slave dealer in Memphis. Beginning as a private in the Confederate Army, Forrest equipped a mounted battalion at his own expense and as lieutenant colonel made good his escape from surrounded Fort Donelson. As a colonel he fought at Shiloh and in July, 1862, as brigadier general began his daring career of cavalry raids that made him unparalleled in that type of warfare. For most of the rest of the war Union forces sought Forrest and when they found him were defeated. As a major general he normally held independent command. He was accused of slaughtering Negroes at Fort Pillow in April, 1864. One of his most brilliant victories was at Brice's Cross Roads, Mississippi. In February of 1865, after the Nashville campaign, he became lieutenant general. After the war he was allegedly active in the Ku Klux Klan for a time. Often violent in temper, Forrest showed great courage in personally leading his men, and his native military ability bordered on genius. He is credited with originating the phrase that the one who "gets there first with the most" is victorious.

FOX, GUSTAVUS VASA. *1821-1883. Union.*

Born in Saugus, Mass., Fox graduated from Annapolis in 1841 and served in many assignments including the handling of troop transportation to Vera Cruz during the Mexican War. He resigned in 1856 and entered business. Consulted regarding possible relief of Fort Sumter in February, 1861, Fox began his new career and became chief clerk of the Navy Department in Washington in May, 1861; in August he became Assistant Secretary of the Navy, an office created for him. After the war Fox resigned and was sent to Russia on a diplomatic mission. He then again entered business. Fox worked well with Navy Secretary Gideon Welles. He is credited with aiding in developing the Civil War Navy to a high degree of efficiency, promoting such developments as the *Monitor*, making vital changes in personnel and management, and earning a reputation as one of the top administrators in U. S. naval history.

FREMONT, JOHN CHARLES. *1813-1890. Union.*

Born in Richmond, Va., and educated in Charleston, S. C., Frémont served briefly in the Navy and then in the Topographical Corps. This began his long career of western exploration, which became his major claim to fame. In 1841 he married Jessie Benton, daughter of Missouri Senator Thomas Hart Benton, and she became a most important asset to his career.

His first two important expeditions were in 1842 and 1843. In his third expedition, in 1845, he entered California and became involved in the conquest of that state. Found guilty of mutiny and other charges, Frémont resigned from the service and continued his explorations. He was elected U. S. Senator from California in December, 1850. In 1856 he was the first Republican candidate for President but lost the election to Buchanan. Taking command in July, 1861, at St. Louis as major general, he issued what was really an emancipation proclamation, but it was not supported by the government, and Frémont was removed. He later served in western Virginia and the Shenandoah, largely unsuccessfully. Nominated by radical Republicans in 1864 for President, he withdrew before the election, and entered business. An outstanding success as an explorer, Frémont made important contributions to the development of the West. But in other fields of endeavor his lack of judgment, his high temper and his wont to become the storm center of controversy hampered him greatly. He is generally considered to have been a failure both as a military commander and as a politician.

GIBBON, JOHN. *1827-1896. Union.*

Born near Holmesburg, Pa., but reared in North Carolina, Gibbon graduated from West Point in 1847 and served in Florida and the West as well as teaching at West Point. He remained loyal to the Union and was in the artillery under McDowell, but his main ability was in molding the volunteer into a fighting soldier. In May, 1862, he became brigadier gen-

and later practiced law and entered business. Completely without military experience, he served in lower commands until named brigadier general in November, 1862. In May of 1864 he was made major general and later lieutenant general. He served in the Seven Days, Chancellorsville, Gettysburg, Wilderness, Spotsylvania, and commanded a corps in the Petersburg-Appomattox campaign. His post-war

eral of volunteers and led what was to be the famous "Iron Brigade." He fought at Second Bull Run or Manassas, South Mountain, Antietam, and commanded a division at Fredericksburg until wounded. He temporarily commanded the II Corps at Gettysburg and was wounded again. Returning early in 1864, he commanded a division in the Wilderness and at Spotsylvania, and was made major general in June, 1864. He fought throughout the final campaigns, heading the new XXIV Corps. A brilliant organizer, Gibbon showed his major development as a soldier in the West after the war, and was active in the Little Big Horn campaign and the defeat of the Nez Percé Indians in 1877 in the Northwest.

GORDON, JOHN BROWN. *1832-1904. Confederate.*

Born in Upson County, Ga., Gordon studied at the University of Georgia,

career included election once as governor of Georgia and three times as U.S. Senator. He was commander of the United Confederate Veterans from its start in 1890 until his death. As a youthful officer he showed great development and earned the love and respect of those under and over him. Vitally interested in reconstruction of his state, Gordon was one of Georgia's most honored citizens, although greatly criticized for some of his official actions while in office. He denied charges of bargaining and of political corruption.

GRANT, ULYSSES SIMPSON. *1822-1885. Union.*

Born Hiram Ulysses Grant at Point Pleasant, Ohio, the future general grew up at Georgetown, Ohio, in a middle-class family. He was graduated from West Point with an undistinguished record in 1843, noted only for his riding ability and his change in name. However, he did serve meritoriously in the Mexican War. He married Julia Dent in 1848, and resigned from the army with the rank of captain in 1854 in California. His resignation has been attributed by some to drinking and homesickness. The following years Grant was unsuccessful in business near St. Louis, and he joined his brothers in his father's leather goods store in Galena, Ill., in 1860. After drilling local troops and seeking a commission, he was named colonel of the 21st Illinois in June, 1861. In August he was appointed brigadier general and took charge at Cairo, Ill. After the raid on Belmont, Mo., in November, Grant led the expedition which captured Forts Henry and Donelson, and leaped to fame overnight after demanding and receiving the "unconditional surrender" of Fort Donelson. Named major general, Grant defeated the Confederates at Shiloh or Pittsburg Landing, Tenn., but his reputation was somewhat tarnished and he remained under a cloud until the start of the brilliant Vicksburg campaign. In one of the most tenacious and masterful campaigns of military history, Grant made repeated attempts on the fortress, and deserted his supply lines to lay siege to the city, which surrendered on July 4, 1863. Named commander in the West, he defeated Bragg at Missionary Ridge in November, 1863. He was called to Washington to command all the armies in March of 1864, with the rank of lieutenant general. Grant led the Army of the Potomac to victory in Virginia in 1864-65, but only after terrific loss of life in the Wilderness, at Spotsylvania, Cold Harbor and in the siege of Petersburg. He accepted the surrender of Lee at Appomattox Court House, April 9, 1865. After the war he became involved in the controversy between President Johnson and Secretary of War Stanton. In July, 1866, he was made a full general. He emerged from the fray the almost unanimous choice for the Republican presidential nomination in 1868 and was easily elected for two terms. His record as President is generally considered to have been poor. Leaving office in 1877, he toured the world, failed in business, and turned to writing to earn a living. He finished his monumental *Personal Memoirs* shortly before his death from cancer. Grant may be said to have failed in his pre-war career and as President but he succeeded as a soldier and writer. As a commander he saw the war as a whole and knew it would take the loss of many lives to win. Although called a butcher by some, later historians have seen that this simple, deep-feeling man, with his admitted faults, came to the national scene at a time when a great military leader was needed and he met that challenge victoriously.

GREELEY, HORACE. *1811-1872. Union.*

Born in Amherst, N. H., Greeley had little schooling and at 14 entered printing and journalism. He edited many publications in New York City and was active in Whig politics. He started the New York *Tribune* in 1841 and soon built it into one of the country's most influential papers. With an outstanding staff it set new patterns in journalism. Gradually Greeley adopted a stronger and stronger anti-slavery policy. During the Civil War

he opposed compromise with the South, although he believed in letting the "erring sisters" go. He opposed Lincoln's policy of conciliation and soon was listed with the Radical Republicans. In 1864 he opposed Lincoln's re-election at first, and in 1864-65 attempted to make peace by private negotiations. A Radical in Reconstruction days, he gradually broke with Grant. He was nominated for the presidency in 1872 by the Liberal Republicans and Democrats, but was badly beaten by Grant. Exhausted by a difficult campaign, stunned by the death of his wife, deeply affected by his overwhelming defeat, and virtually losing control of the *Tribune*, Greeley died a broken man a few weeks after the election. One of the nation's greatest editors and popular educators, he was controversial in character, often shifting in his viewpoints.

GRIERSON, BENJAMIN HENRY. *1826-1911. Union.*

Born in Pittsburgh, Pa., Grierson was educated in Youngstown, Ohio. He taught school in Jacksonville, Ill., and was a merchant in Meredosia, Ill. He entered the army April, 1861, and soon became major and then colonel. By spring of 1862 he had been engaged in several small cavalry raids. Commanding a cavalry brigade, Grierson was ordered by Grant to leave La Grange, Tenn., April 17, 1863, on his famous raid. With about 1,700 men he moved into enemy country in Mississippi for 16 days, destroying railroads and public property. He reached Baton Rouge, La., May 2, having greatly aided Grant in the Vicksburg campaign. Promoted to brigadier general of volunteers, he made other lesser

raids in 1864. By summer, 1865, he was a major general in the West and commanded various departments. A cavalry leader who disliked horses, Grierson is known primarily for his one great raid in the Civil War, but he was considered a valuable and competent officer in the post-war army.

HALLECK, HENRY WAGER. *1815-1872. Union.*

Born in Westernville, N. Y., he was graduated from West Point in 1839 with a high scholastic standing. As an engineer he studied and wrote on military science and earned a reputation as a student. He fought the Mexican War in California but resigned from the army in 1854 to enter law. Active in mining, he wrote extensively on mining law. In August, 1861, Halleck was commissioned a major general in the regulars and succeeded Frémont in command at St. Louis. He ably reorganized the department. During his command Grant captured Forts Henry and Donelson, Pope won at Island No. 10 and there were other successful battles. In March, 1862, he was given command of the entire West and after Shiloh took command in person in the field for the only time in his career. An extremely overcautious march to Corinth showed his inability in field operations. In July, 1862, Halleck was made general-in-chief by Lincoln, who recognized his administrative abilities. His operations of the office resulted in unhappy relations with many generals and a reluctance to act speedily. Halleck is charged with failure to follow up victories and with delaying offensive action. His somewhat uncertain position was changed in March, 1864, and Halleck became chief-of-staff of the army,

a post he was much better fitted for. Often criticized, Halleck made many mistakes and tried to fight the war "by the book," but certainly his mastery of administrative detail, his continuing energy and devotion to duty were of great value to the North.

tenant general in February, 1865, and spent the final months of the war in the Carolinas. After the war he was governor of South Carolina and U.S. Senator. Hampton had natural abilities of leadership, both militarily and politically.

HANCOCK, WINFIELD SCOTT.
1824-1886. *Union.*

Named for Winfield Scott, he was born at Montgomery Square, Pa., and was graduated from West Point in 1844. He served well in Mexico, in Florida, and in the West. Experienced in handling troops, Hancock was made brigadier general of volunteers in September, 1861, and worked at organizing and training. He served in the Peninsula campaign, at South Mountain and Antietam. Promoted to major general in November, 1862, he headed a division at Fredericksburg, and at Chancellorsville, and then took over the II Corps. At Gettysburg he was at his best defending against the

HAMPTON, WADE. *1818-1902.*
Confederate.

Born of a distinguished South Carolina family at Charleston, Wade Hampton, III, was graduated from South Carolina College (now the University of South Carolina) in 1836 and became a planter. He served in the state legislature, opposing secession in 1860. But at the start of war he organized what was known as "Hampton's Legion" at his own expense. Hampton fought at Manassas or Bull Run, and commanded a brigade on the Peninsula after becoming a brigadier general in May, 1862. As commander of a cavalry brigade he took part in most of the movements of Stuart, but led some raids of his own. In August, 1863, he was made major general and commanded the cavalry corps of the Army of Northern Virginia after Stuart's death in May, 1864. With insufficient horses he often sent his men into battle dismounted. He was promoted lieu-

Confederate attacks of the second and third days. He continued in high command through 1864 and through Appomattox. After the war he led expeditions in the West and held many other commands. In 1880 he was Democratic nominee for President and was barely defeated by Garfield. A careful though aggressive man, he inspired his men, and was extremely steady and capable under fire.

Kentucky and fought at Shiloh, Perryville, Murfreesboro, Missionary Ridge, and in the Atlanta campaign. He became a lieutenant general in October, 1862, and after the fall of Atlanta commanded vastly inadequate forces in the Department of South Carolina, Georgia, and Florida against Sherman. A cool, courageous officer, Hardee was admired by commanders in both armies.

HARDEE, WILLIAM JOSEPH. *1815-1873. Confederate.*

Born on the family estate in Camden County, Ga., Hardee was graduated from West Point in 1838 and was a captain in 1844. He served in the war with Mexico and wrote the influential *Rifle and Light Infantry Tactics* known as "Hardee's Tactics," in 1855. A lieutenant colonel at the outbreak of the Civil War, by June, 1861, he was a Confederate brigadier general and stationed in Arkansas. Promoted to major general in the fall, he shifted to

HILL, AMBROSE POWELL. *1825-1865. Confederate.*

Born in Culpeper, Va., he was graduated from West Point in 1847 and served in Mexico and on the frontier. Hill was named colonel of infantry at the outbreak of the Civil War and in February, 1862, brigadier general. Made major general in May, 1862, he commanded the left of the Confederate lines in the opening of the Seven Days. His division won the title "Hill's Light Division" in this campaign. He fought at Second Manassas or Bull Run and then brought his division into the fight at Antietam in time to stem the Federal advance, one of his most brilliant actions. He served at Fredericksburg and at Chancellorsville and as lieutenant general from May, 1863, commanded a corps. He fought at Gettysburg, and the Wilderness, as well as in the siege of Petersburg. He was killed in the retreat from Petersburg, April 2, 1865. Although he had difficulties in his associations with other officers, he was courageous and dashing in action. He was one of the most brilliant commanders.

1861, and major general in March, 1862. He led a division during the Seven Days and commanded at South Mountain. In the spring of 1863 he defended Richmond, and by July was made lieutenant general and sent to the Army of Tennessee. After difficulty with Bragg and Davis, he saw no further ·duty until he commanded a small division at Bentonville. After the war he was a writer and educator. Deeply religious, Hill was a strong believer in discipline, but his difficulties with his superiors held back his military career.

HILL, DANIEL HARVEY. *1821-1889. Confederate.*

He was born in York District, S. C. of a family unrelated to A. P. Hill. He was graduated from West Point in 1842. After fighting in Mexico he resigned from the army to teach. Entering the Civil War as a colonel, he was promoted to brigadier general in July,

HOOD, JOHN BELL. *1831-1879 Confederate.*

A native of Owingsville, Ky., Hood was graduated from West Point in 1853 and fought against the Indians. Resigning in April, 1861, Hood became a Confederate lieutenant but rose rapidly and was brigadier general by March, 1862, taking command of the "Texas Brigade." He led them at Gaines' Mill, Second Bull Run or Manassas, and Antietam. Promoted to major-general in October, 1862, he led a division at Gettysburg, and was wounded in the arm. At Chickamauga he was again wounded and lost his right leg. Made lieutenant general in February, 1864, Hood commanded a corps under Johnston in the fighting before Atlanta, and replaced Johnston in July, 1864, as commander of the Army of Tennessee with the temporary rank of full general. Failing in the fighting around Atlanta, Hood led his army back into Tennessee to be outmarched at Spring Hill, and to be beaten at Franklin and Nashville. Hood assumed full responsibility for the near destruction of his army. After the war he entered business. He had considerable ability and was able to inspire his men, but he was rash—a general who fought too much and too often.

☆

HOOKER, JOSEPH. *1814-1879. Union.*

Born in Hadley, Mass., Hooker graduated from West Point in 1837 and fought in the Mexican War. He resigned from the army in 1853 and became a farmer in California. In May, 1861, he was named brigadier general of volunteers and led a division in the Peninsula fighting, where he earned the rank of major general. Known as "Fighting Joe," he was at Second Bull Run or Manassas, at South Mountain and Antietam. After the defeat at Fredericksburg, Hooker violently protested Burnside's action. In January, 1863, Lincoln, with some misgivings, named Hooker commander of the Army of the Potomac, replacing Burnside In a famous letter Lincoln cautioned Hooker against rashness.

Hooker showed great optimism and audacity at the start of the Chancellorsville campaign in early May, 1863, but was badly beaten by Lee and Jackson. He seemed to lose his normal

drive. Hooker followed Lee's army north toward Pennsylvania, and on June 28, 1863, Meade took command of the army. Taking two corps to the West, Hooker fought well at Lookout Mountain and in the fighting to Atlanta. But he was overlooked for army command by Sherman on the death of McPherson, and asked to be retired. After the war he commanded various army departments. An intensely ambitious and at times very able man, his temperament aroused distrust in his superiors, which was often justified.

☆

HOWARD, OLIVER OTIS. *1830-1909. Union.*

Born at Leeds, Me., and graduated from West Point in 1854, Howard held various army posts before becoming colonel of a Maine regiment at the start of the war. He was made briga-

dier general of volunteers in September, 1861, and major general in 1862. He fought at First Bull Run or Manassas, and lost an arm at Fair Oaks, but was still active at Second Bull Run, South Mountain, Antietam, Fredericksburg, Chancellorsville, and Gettysburg. He was strongly criticized for being surprised by Jackson at Chancellorsville while in command of a corps, and also received censure for the first day at Gettysburg. Shifted to the West in September, 1863, Howard fought around Chattanooga and commanded a corps in the march to Atlanta. In July, 1864, he succeeded to command of the Army of the Tennessee. After the war he headed the Freedmen's Bureau, and later was notable in negotiations with Indians in the West. Working in behalf of the Negro, he established Howard University and was active in religious and educational work. He did considerable writing and helped found Lincoln Memorial University. Howard was a man of only moderate military abilities.

JACKSON, THOMAS JONATHAN.
1824-1863. Confederate.

Born at Clarksburg, then Va., now W. Va., he was reared by an uncle and was graduated from West Point in 1846 in time to serve well in the Mexican War. He left the army in 1851 to teach none too successfully at Virginia Military Institute. He was opposed to the idea of civil war. Sent to Harpers Ferry at the start of the conflict, Jackson became a brigadier general in June, 1861, and fought at First Bull Run or Manassas, where his troops stood firm against attack and General Bee said, "There is Jackson standing like a stone wall." And it was as "Stonewall" that he marched to fame. Promoted major general in October, 1861, he made his reputation in the Shenandoah Valley in the summer of 1862, fighting, advancing and retreating in one of the most brilliant campaigns of the war. Called to Richmond during the Peninsula fighting, the rapidly moving Jackson slowed up considerably at Beaver Dam Creek and White Oak Swamp, dimming his reputation somewhat. But he showed his ability again in the march to and in the battle of Second Bull Run and at Antietam. Promoted to lieutenant general in October, 1862, he fought well at Fredericksburg and then, detached from Lee, swung around the Union army to deliver the crushing blow at Chancellorsville. During the fighting in the dusk he was shot by his own men, was severely wounded and died of pneumonia May 10, 1863. The Confederacy lost much with his death; how much, no one knows. In any evaluation of the great soldiers of this country, Jackson must stand high. He was at his best in independent command where in his secretive way he could move freely and rapidly, striking hard when he chose to strike. Despite eccentricities of manner, Jackson and his "foot cavalry" entered American legend, and Lee rightly said, "I know not how to replace him."

JOHNSON, ANDREW. *1808-1875. Union.*

Born in very modest surroundings in Raleigh, N. C., Johnson finally settled at Greeneville, Tennessee, as a tailor, with no formal education. Aided greatly by his wife, he taught himself, and became successful in business. In 1835 he was elected to the Tennessee legislature and in 1843 to Congress. He was elected governor of Tennessee in 1853 and 1855 and to the Senate in 1857, as a Democrat. He was an advocate of the "homestead" law and generally supported measures favoring the small farmer, laborer, and settler, as well as strict, conservative interpretation of the Constitution. He remained loyal to the Union at the beginning of the Civil War, and was denounced by extremists. He declared that the purpose of the war was to maintain the Constitution and the Union, and not to interfere with the Southern states. In March, 1862, Johnson was appointed military governor of Tennessee by Lincoln. When Lin-

coln was nominated for a second term by the National Union Convention, Johnson was chosen Vice-Presidential candidate, in recognition of the Democrats and Southern unionists. Succeeding to the Presidency upon the death of Lincoln, April 15, 1865, Johnson at first was considered the tool of the Radical Republicans but soon broke with them in a long quarrel which resulted in his impeachment by the House of Representatives in February, 1868. But in May the Senate failed by one vote to convict him of high crimes and misdemeanors. He was not a candidate for re-election. In 1874 he was elected again to the Senate from Tennessee. Johnson was a man of great personal courage and considerable ability, but often intemperate and unable to control other men or earn their respect. He made a supreme effort to carry on the reconstruction plans generally laid down by Lincoln, but failed, partly through his own fault and partly because of the temper of the times.

JOHNSTON, ALBERT SIDNEY. *1803-1862. Confederate.*

Born in Washington, Ky., he graduated from West Point in 1826 and began a distinguished pre-Civil War military career, which included a period with the Texas army and as Secretary of War for Texas. He served in the Mexican War and in the West, and also farmed in Texas. In command of the Department of the Pacific as brevet brigadier general at the start of the Civil War, he traveled overland to join the Confederate Army and was named a full general with command in the West. He set up the Kentucky defense line, which was too long and thinly held to stand, and when troops under his general command were defeated at Mill Springs, Fort Henry, and Fort Donelson, he withdrew to Corinth, Mississippi, in the spring of 1862. Johnston struck Grant at Pittsburg Landing or Shiloh on April 6, 1862. The Confederates nearly routed the Federals at first, and while leading some of his troops, Johnston was wounded in the leg and needlessly bled to death, his army retreating from Shiloh the next day. Entering the Confederate army with a somewhat overblown reputation and the strong support of Davis, Johnston may have been overestimated as a strategist, as some of his mistakes indicate. But with his death the South lost its brightest hope in the West.

JOHNSTON, JOSEPH EGGLESTON. *1807-1891. Confederate.*

Born in Prince Edward County, Va., Johnston was graduated from West Point in 1829 and resigned from the army eight years later to become a civil engineer, but rejoined the topographical engineers and fought in Mexico. By 1860 he was quartermaster-general and a brigadier general. He was named brigadier general of the Confederacy in May, 1861, and with Beauregard was victorious at First Bull Run or Manassas. In August he was made a full general and commanded in northern Virginia, and in the retreat up the Virginia Peninsula until wounded at Seven Pines or Fair Oaks in front of Richmond. Placed in nominal command in the West in November, 1862, he continued his disputes with Jefferson Davis, which were

detrimental to his career. In the late spring and summer of 1863 he was ineffective in attempting to relieve Pemberton at Vicksburg. He took command of the Army of Tennessee in December, 1863, south of Chattanooga and began his masterful retreat toward Atlanta, seeking to draw Sherman into a trap. On July 17, 1864, he was relieved from command in front of Atlanta for having failed to attack or halt Sherman. In February, 1865, with all Southern hope gone, he reassummed command of the Army of Tennessee, and surrendered to Sherman April 26. After the war he served in Congress and entered business. A pessimistic commander, he was unable to get along with his superiors, particularly Davis. Johnston showed great ability to keep his often outnumbered army intact. He was known mainly for the use of the strategic retreat.

KIRBY SMITH, EDMUND, see Smith, Edmund Kirby.

LEE, FITZHUGH. *1835-1905. Confederate.*

Born in Fairfax County, Va., Fitzhugh was a nephew of Robert E. Lee. He was graduated from West Point in 1856 and saw duty in the West. In May, 1861, he entered the Confederate service and served as a staff officer and lieutenant-colonel of cavalry. Promoted to brigadier general in July, 1862, he conducted a number of raids, and commanded at Kelly's Ford and fought at Chancellorsville. He was made a major general in August, 1863, and was often engaged during the 1864 Virginia campaign, and later served briefly with Early in the Shenandoah. Near the end of the war, he commanded the cavalry of the Army of Northern Virginia. After the war, he was governor of Virginia and returned to the blue uniform to command a corps in the Spanish American War. Although a hard hitting cavalry fighter, Lee was better known for his post-war political career.

LEE, ROBERT EDWARD. *1807-1870. Confederate.*

The outstanding hero of the Confederacy was born at Stratford, Westmoreland County, Va., son of "Light-Horse Harry" Lee, and was reared in Alexandria, Va. He was graduated from West Point in 1829, number two in his class scholastically, and with the amazing record of no demerits. For the next 17 years he served in various commands and carried on the active social life of a Virginia gentleman. In 1831 he married Mary Ann Randolph Custis, great-granddaughter of Martha Washington, at the family home of "Arlington" and entered into the traditions of the Washington family. They had seven children. Serving in various engineering capacities, he had a distinguished record as a captain in the Mexican War. Later, he worked on construction of forts and was superintendent at West Point. As lieutenant colonel he joined the Second Cavalry in 1855, but was with the

regiment in Texas only occasionally. While in Washington in 1859 he commanded troops during John Brown's raid on Harpers Ferry. Lee professed little agreement with secession and the Southern extremists, and had freed what slaves he owned. In early 1861 Lee, then a colonel, declined the command of the United States Army. Upon the secession of Virginia, he was forced to make a decision as to his course and submitted his resignation April 20. At first he served as commander of the Virginia forces and as adviser to Davis, with the rank of general. Late in July he was sent to western Virginia, where he largely failed in halting the Federal invasion, due to mistakes, bad weather, and jealousies among officers. From November until March, 1862, Lee organized defenses on the Atlantic coast and then again assisted Davis. With the wounding of Joseph E. Johnston on May 31, 1862, Lee took command of what soon was to become the Army of Northern Virginia, and never relinquished the command until Appomattox. Taking over in the midst of a campaign, he successfully defended Richmond, pushing back McClellan during the Seven Days. Learning much from his experience, and earning the high regard of his army, he moved rapidly north to victory at Second Manassas or Bull Run, and then into Maryland, where his invasion was halted at Antietam or Sharpsburg. Retreating into Virginia, he halted and defeated Burnside at Fredericksburg and, greatly aided by Jackson, crushed Hooker in May, 1863, at Chancellorsville. Carrying out the idea of an offensive-defensive, he invaded Pennsylvania only to be beaten July 1-3, 1863, at Gettysburg. Retreating again to Virginia, Lee was engaged the rest of 1863 in operations toward Bristoe Station and the Mine Run campaign. On May 4, 1864, Grant began his move into the Wilderness, and although held again and again by Lee in individual actions in the Wilderness fighting—at Spotsylvania, the North Anna and Cold Harbor—Grant evaded Lee by sliding eastward and crossing the James to attack Petersburg. Lee was caught off-guard by Grant's move across the James, but due mainly to inept Union attacks and Beauregard's defense, managed to get to Petersburg in time to hold off the Union attack and set up siege lines. From then until the end of the war it was largely a holding of the lines around Petersburg. In February, 1865, Lee was made General-in-Chief of all Confederate armies, but the move, opposed by Davis, had come too late to be effective. Forced to evacuate Petersburg on April 2-3, Lee retreated toward Appomattox and a possible junction with Joseph E. Johnston. Lack of supplies and a piecemeal cutting up of his army resulted in the surrender at Appomattox Court House, April 9. Following the war Lee accepted the presidency of Washington College at Lexington, Va. (since renamed Washington and Lee University), and largely submitted to the decisions of the war. Lee, like Lincoln, has become a legend. He was admittedly a splendid gentleman and a great soldier. His grasp of strategy in Virginia, and his handling of logistics, and perhaps above all, his ability to judge his enemy, led to his victories which were generally won with inferior numbers. He is sometimes charged with planning a battle and then leaving the fighting to his subordinates. Lee has become a symbol not only in the South,

but in the North as well, for what was best in Southern life. His ability to inspire men has led to his enshrinement as a great hero of the war.

LEE, STEPHEN DILL. *1833-1908. Confederate.*

Born at Charleston, S. C., he was graduated from West Point in 1854 and served in Florida and in the West. Lee rose rapidly in the Confederate ranks, beginning with Fort Sumter. In 1862 he was in the Peninsula campaign, at Second Bull Run or Manassas and Antietam, mainly with artillery commands. Named brigadier general, Lee fought in the Vicksburg campaign,

was promoted to major general and in June, 1864, was made a lieutenant general, youngest in the Confederacy. He fought at Tupelo and in the Atlanta and Nashville campaigns, rising to corps command. Lee had an active postwar career as a planter, public figure, and writer. As an officer, he proved very capable and often heroic.

LINCOLN, ABRAHAM. *1809-1865. Union.*

The facts of Lincoln's life are well known, but what kind of man he really was, the reasons for his greatness, are still subjects for discussion. Today, all the world recognizes his stature, but it was not always so. Part of that respect and hero worship has come in retrospect—from understanding of his background, his character, and the tragedies of his life and times. Born near Hodgenville, Ky., in a primitive cabin, of undistinguished parents, he lived in Kentucky for seven years until his father moved to Spencer County, Ind. In the frontier life there he received little education and used his hands to help carve out an existence. In 1830 the family went to Illinois, near Decatur, and Lincoln at 22 was on his own. Working in a store and in other jobs in the frontier village of

New Salem from 1831 to 1837, Lincoln spent some of his most important and formative years. He served briefly in the Black Hawk War, was postmaster, learned surveying, studied law, and after one unsuccessful try was elected to the state legislature in 1834, and re-elected three times, becoming a leading member of the assembly. He began his practice of law at Springfield in 1837, and in 1842 married Mary Todd, daughter of a prominent Kentucky family. As a Whig he was elected to the national House of Representatives in 1846 and served one rather inauspicious term. He gained considerable reputation as a lawyer, and in 1854 re-entered politics with great speeches, given at Springfield and Peoria, opposing the spread of slavery but not the institution itself where it already existed. In 1856 he joined the new Republican party, and received 110 votes for vice-president in the party's first national convention. Opposing Stephen A. Douglas of Illinois for the Senate in 1858, he was defeated but added greatly to his reputation through their famous debates (known to history as the Lincoln-Douglas debates) over the expansion of slavery and the theory of popular sovereignty. Important addresses outside Illinois gave him some national recognition, but he was not considered a prominent contender for the Republican nomination in 1860, although he was mentioned by some. However, he received the nomination at the Chicago convention, due largely to his availability on grounds that he had few enemies and appeared more moderate than other candidates, and because of the shrewd political promises of his friends. He did not campaign personally, but was elected November 6 as a minority President, receiving less than half the total vote in a four-way election. The election of Lincoln, or of any Republican, was sure to lead to secession of some states, and did. Lincoln remained silent, and apparently had no policy except an intense desire to maintain the Union. Inaugurated March 4, 1861, his aim was to avoid any inflammatory act which might set off the fuse of conflict. But the war began at Fort Sumter on April 12, 1861. Lincoln acted promptly, and sometimes without Congressional authority, to defend and preserve the Union. As Commander-in-Chief of the Union forces, he searched long for a general who could win, and after numerous tries, he found the man in Grant. Throughout the war his main task was to hold various elements of opposition in control, and to prosecute the conflict as it developed. Following the battle of Antietam or Sharpsburg, Lincoln announced his Emancipation Proclamation, to become effective Jan. 1, 1863, which freed no slaves actually, but declared that slaves in sections still in rebellion would be freed. Its main purpose was to halt possible recognition of the Confederacy abroad, to placate anti-slavery forces in the North, and to set a pattern for future abolition of slavery. One of his major public actions in 1863 was his address dedicating the Gettysburg National Cemetery, in which he called for "a new birth of freedom." In June, 1864, he was renominated for the Presidency, but not without opposition, and he himself despaired of re-election. But victories around Atlanta, the valuable soldier vote, and shrewd politics gave him the election over Democrat George B. McClellan. By the time of his second inaugural, Lincoln had

formulated basic ideas regarding reconstruction of the South, including a desire to "bind up the nation's wounds," to form new state governments, to pardon the vast majority of Confederates, and to adopt a generally lenient policy which included the constitutional abolition of slavery, and reunification of the nation. With the surrender of Lee on April 9, 1865, it was apparent that the war was nearing an end, and the problems of reconstruction loomed large. But on April 14, Lincoln was assassinated by John Wilkes Booth at Ford's Theater, and he died the following day. Assassination confirmed his place in history and folklore. His humble beginnings, his self-made career, a now discredited legend of romance at New Salem with Ann Rutledge, his over-emphasized difficulties with his wife, his coming to the national scene at the time of extreme crisis, his personal characteristics and appearance, and finally his martyrdom, all added to the picture. Over the years, as his stature has increased to gigantic proportions, some of his human failings have been forgotten. Lincoln was ambitious, inclined to despondency and moodiness; he desired office, and won it with consummate political skill by doing the right thing and saying the right thing at the correct time, and by not bucking public opinion any more than absolutely necessary. His ability to run with the tide and yet seem almost to direct it, his use of other men and ability to make them work for him, his deep insight into human nature, and the tenacity of his feeling for the Union, are part of his real greatness. Violently attacked during the war by abolitionists on one side and anti-war Democrats on the other, he managed the affairs of the nation to insure victory. What the reconstruction years would have done to him we do not know. But stripping away the legends, Lincoln becomes a much more human, a truly greater man, not perfect, but one in whom there dwelt the seeds of something, intangible even today, that grew and blossomed during the greatest trial of our nation.

LOGAN, JOHN ALEXANDER. *1826-1886. Union.*

Born in Jackson County, Ill., Logan received some education, particularly in law, and fought in the Mexican War. After holding a number of local and state offices and practicing as a lawyer, Logan was elected to Congress in 1858 as a Democrat. He gained a large following with his now old fashioned oratory and persuasive spirit. Although faced with charges of Southern sympathy, Logan actually was a strong Union man and raised a regiment in Illinois, becoming its colonel. He

fought at Belmont, Fort Donelson, and in the Vicksburg campaign. He was made a brigadier general after Fort Donelson and a major general after Vicksburg. He commanded a corps in the Atlanta fighting and briefly commanded the Army of the Tennessee, but was relieved because Sherman mistrusted his political activities, although praising his military abilities. After the war he helped organize the Grand Army of the Republic, and served in the House and Senate as a Republican. Logan was probably the most capable of the so-called "political" generals.

LONGSTREET, JAMES. *1821-1904. Confederate.*

Born in Edgefield District, S. C., Longstreet was reared near Augusta, Ga., and Somerville, Ala. He was graduated from West Point in 1842, served in the Mexican War, and by the outbreak of the Civil War was a major in the paymaster's office. Commissioned a Confederate brigadier general

in June, 1861, he fought at First Bull Run or Manassas, and was promoted to major general in October. Longstreet fought throughout the Peninsula campaign, and commanded about half of the Army of Northern Virginia at Second Bull Run. Serving at Antietam or Sharpsburg, he became lieutenant general October, 1862. His corps participated in a main part of the defense at Fredericksburg, and then he was in semi-independent command against Suffolk, Va. Following the death of Jackson, Longstreet was Lee's principal lieutenant. At Gettysburg on July 2, he was charged with disagreeing with Lee's plans and delay in carrying them out, a criticism still much debated. Sent to Georgia, he ably served Bragg at Chickamauga in September, 1863, but was unable to capture Knoxville in an independent campaign. Back in Virginia, he was severely wounded in the Wilderness on May 6, 1864. He returned to duty in November and fought until the end of the war. After the war, Longstreet became a Republican and turned to business and politics, earning the dislike of many Southerners. An excellent officer in combat, he was inclined to be slow in advancing, but was an able corps commander.

organizing Federal forces in Missouri, he pushed the state troops out of Jefferson City and Boonville in June, and on August 10, 1861, fought the Confederates at Wilson's Creek, near Springfield. A possible Northern victory was defeated by the rout of Franz Sigel and the death of Lyon. He had done much to hold Missouri in the Union, had shown great energy and fire in command, and the North lost what might well have been a leading commander in the West.

McCLELLAN, GEORGE BRINTON. *1826-1885. Union.*

Born in Philadelphia, McClellan was graduated second in his West Point class in 1846 and participated in the military action in Mexico. After serving as an engineer, he went to the Crimea to study military affairs during the Crimean War. After this experience, he developed a cavalry saddle known to this day as the "McClellan saddle." In 1857 he resigned from the

LYON, NATHANIEL. *1818-1861. Union.*

Born in Ashford, Conn., Lyon was graduated from West Point in 1841 and fought in Florida and in Mexico. After serving in Kansas, Lyon, with the rank of captain, was at the St. Louis Arsenal in 1861 and was largely responsible, with Francis P. Blair, for seizing Camp Jackson from the pro-Confederates. Enlisting volunteers and

army, became chief engineer and later vice-president of the Illinois Central Railway, and in 1860 was president of the Ohio and Mississippi Railroad. Given command of all Ohio forces at the outbreak of the Civil War, in May, 1861 he was made major general in the regular army, commanding the Department of the Ohio. He was successful in the West Virginia campaign, and after the Union defeat at First Bull Run or Manassas, was given command of the Division of the Potomac and at once began organizing what was to become the Army of the Potomac. In November, 1861, McClellan succeeded Scott as general-in-chief. By this time the public was demanding action from the army, but McClellan failed to heed, claiming he was not ready. The President and many others became impatient, and tried to rouse McClellan to action. He was removed as general-in-chief in March, 1862, but left in command of the Army of the Potomac. Finally, Lincoln agreed to

McClellan's plan to take the army to the Virginia peninsula, provided the city of Washington was protected. McClellan moved to the peninsula and began an extremely cautious advance on Richmond, continually overestimating the size of the enemy force. McDowell's corps, which was to join him overland, was held back to aid in protecting Washington from Jackson, and McClellan kept claiming he had insufficient men, although a number of forces joined him and his men far outnumbered the Confederates. A portion of his army held off the enemy at Seven Pines or Fair Oaks, but the entire army was forced to retreat to the James River during the Seven Days when Lee, joined by Jackson, attacked. McClellan bitterly blamed Washington for alleged failure to support him. In August, 1862, the army was removed from the James, and a portion of it fought with Pope at Second Manassas or Bull Run. After Pope's failure, McClellan was given command of the entire army in Virginia and reorganized it. Following Lee north, McClellan fought at Antietam or Sharpsburg, but failed to put in his reserves and allowed Lee a full day to recuperate and move south. Late in October, 1862, McClellan followed, and on Nov. 7 was removed from command. He was nominated as Democratic candidate for the Presidency in 1864 and lost to Lincoln. After the war he entered business, and served as governor of New Jersey. Still a controversial figure, McClellan must be given credit as a great organizer who lacked the will or the ability to fight. His intense egotism hurt him in dealing with his superiors, but he never lost the loyalty and affection of his men.

McCLERNAND, JOHN ALEXANDER. *1812-1900. Union.*

Born near Hardinsburg, Ky., he was admitted to law practice in 1832, and soon entered politics in Illinois as a Jackson Democrat. Stepping up from state politics, he served in the House of Representatives from 1843 to 1851, and 1859 to 1861. He left Congress to become a brigadier general and fought at Belmont, Fort Henry, and Fort Donelson. Made a major general in March, 1862, he served at Shiloh. After the battle he strongly criticized Grant. In October, 1862, he was authorized by Lincoln to gather a force to attack Vicksburg. Intensely ambitious, McClernand attempted to use this assignment to set aside Grant, but this attempt was defeated and McClernand commanded a corps in the Vicksburg campaign, but was removed by Grant in June, 1863, for issuing unauthorized orders. In February, 1864, he again commanded a corps in the West, but resigned in November. Definitely a "political" general, he showed more interest in self-advancement than in successful military command.

McDOWELL, IRVIN. *1818-1885. Union.*

Born at Columbus, Ohio, he graduated from West Point in 1838 and fought in Mexico, after which he was largely assigned staff duties, being promoted to major in 1856. At the outbreak of war, as a brigadier general he organized the army in front of Washington. Although not ready, pressure forced the army to move toward Manassas Junction, where McDowell was defeated at First Bull Run on July 21, 1861. Replaced by McClellan, he continued as major general to lead a division in defense of Washington and commanded a corps at Second Manassas or Bull Run, Aug. 29-30, 1862. Severely criticized, he was again re-

lieved and left the field of major fighting, serving in various smaller commands for the rest of the war and afterward. A capable staff officer without field experience, McDowell was a serious, devoted soldier who perhaps was rushed into major command when he was not ready, and at a time when it is possible no one could have succeeded completely.

McPHERSON, JAMES BIRDSEYE.
1828-1864. Union.

A native of Sandusky County, Ohio, McPherson was graduated from West Point in 1853 at the head of his class. He was a first lieutenant at the outbreak of the war, and in August, 1861, as a captain in the regular amy, served as an aide to Halleck. After the Fort Donelson campaign he was a field officer, becoming brigadier general of volunteers in May, 1862. After reinforcing Rosecrans at Corinth, he became major general commanding a division,

and in January, 1863, headed a corps. Active in the Vicksburg campaign, McPherson was given command of the Army of the Tennessee in March, 1864, when Sherman moved up to command the western forces. Fighting ably at Kenesaw Mountain, McPherson was killed July 22, 1864, in the fighting around Atlanta. Considered one of the most capable generals of the entire army by his superiors, his loss was keenly felt. Both Grant and Sherman recognized his ability as a commander who was known as "the whiplash of the army."

MAGRUDER, JOHN BANKHEAD.
1810-1871. Confederate.

A native of Port Royal, Va., Magruder was graduated from West Point in 1830, and served in Texas, Florida, and Mexico. A captain and brevet lieutenant colonel at the start of the Civil War, he became a colonel in the Confederate army in May, 1861,

and commanded on the Peninsula in Virginia. After Big Bethel in May, he was promoted brigadier general in June, and in the fall, major general. Magruder defended Yorktown in the spring of 1862 with 12,000 men, completely fooling McClellan and his huge force. After some mistakes in the Seven Days, Magruder had difficulties with Lee and was sent to command the District of Texas, and in January, 1863, captured Galveston. A very socially minded man, Magruder was known as "Prince John." He had a rather hasty temper, and while not possessing great command ability, did show dash and willingness to fight, but he disappointed Lee.

MAHONE, WILLIAM. *1826-1895.* *Confederate.*

Born in Southampton County, Va., Mahone graduated from Virginia Military Institute in 1847 and entered the railroad business as an engineer. In the

Civil War he commanded in the Norfolk District as colonel and then joined the Army of Northern Virginia, becoming a brigadier general on November 16, 1861. He served with that army to the end of the war. After his capable fighting in defending the crater at Petersburg, he was made a major general. By the war's end, Mahone had shown great promise and had won the affection of his men. In his postwar career he was a railroad executive, U.S. Senator, and built a powerful Republican political machine in Virginia.

MALLORY, STEPHEN RUSSELL. *1813-1873. Confederate.*

Born in Trinidad, where his father was working, Mallory grew up in Key West, Fla. Despite modest education, he studied law, was elected to the U. S. Senate in 1851, re-elected in 1857, and was Chairman of the Naval Affairs Committee. He left the Senate upon the secession of Florida, and in February, 1861, was appointed Secretary of the Navy of the Confederacy. He held this office for the entire war. Lacking a navy of any kind, Mallory set out to make one, developing ironclads, obtaining vessels in England, and utilizing substitutes in order to oppose the Union blockade with a few strong ships and the commerce raiders. One of the few Confederate leaders to avoid trouble with Davis, Mallory showed ingenuity and administrative ability in a difficult task.

MEADE, GEORGE GORDON. *1815-1872. Union.*

His father was a U. S. naval agent, and Meade was born in Cadiz, Spain. He was graduated from West Point in 1835, fought in Florida, did considerable engineering work, and served in the Mexican War. A captain of topographical engineers at the outbreak of the war, Meade was appointed a brigadier general of volunteers in August, 1861, commanded a bri-

gade in the Seven Days, and was badly wounded. But he was able to fight at Second Bull Run or Manassas, South Mountain, and Antietam. In November, 1862, Meade was promoted to major general and commanded a corps at Fredericksburg and at Chancellorsville. On June 28, 1863, he replaced Hooker as commander of the Army of the Potomac. He protested his appointment, but concentrated his army to stop Lee's invasion, although the meeting of the opposing forces at Gettysburg was accidental. While victorious at Gettysburg, he was criticized for not counter-attacking and for not following up the Confederates. He took his army into the Rapidan and Mine Run campaigns, and continued in nominal command of the army until the end of the war, although Grant accompanied the Army of the Potomac and actually directed operations. Despite the difficulties of this arrangement, Meade worked well with Grant, and was made a major general in the regular army in August, 1864. Following the war, he commanded several departments. Certainly not a brilliant soldier, and because of his stubborn convictions not extremely popular, his high character and admittedly outstanding abilities as a commander have been overshadowed by his superiors.

MORGAN, JOHN HUNT. *1825-1864. Confederate.*

Morgan—"Morgan the Raider"—was born at Huntsville, Ala., and received his education at Lexington, Ky. He enlisted in the Mexican War and later was a successful businessman. He joined the Confederacy as a scout in

September, 1861, became a captain, and in 1862 began his series of famous raids. In April, 1862, he became a colonel and continued his raiding in Tennessee and Kentucky. As a reward for capturing a Federal force at Hartsville, Tenn., he was appointed brigadier general in December, 1862. On July 2, 1863, he crossed the Ohio and rode through southern Indiana to beyond Cincinnati until, his men exhausted, he finally surrendered July 26, near New Lisbon, Ohio. Morgan escaped from the Ohio Penitentiary at Columbus in November and was given a command in southwest Virginia. On Sept. 3, 1864, he was killed by Federals at Greeneville, Tenn. A man of great energy and driving spirit and devotion to the cause of the South, "Morgan and his terrible men" were a source of considerable annoyance to the North.

MOSBY, JOHN SINGLETON. *1833-1916. Confederate.*

Born in Edgemont, Va., he practiced law, and at the outbreak of the war, enlisted in the cavalry. By February, 1862, he had been commissioned a lieutenant and began to operate as a scout. He was on Stuart's staff during the Peninsula campaign, Second Bull Run or Manassas, and Antietam. By early 1863, Mosby began independent operations as a ranger in Loudoun County, Va., with only a few men. Partisan law permitted division of captured property, and his actions against Federal outposts were very successful. Mosby's operations grew, and the highly informal outfit seemed to appear and disappear at will. On March 9, 1863, he captured Federal General Stoughton in bed at Fairfax Court House. For this he was promoted to captain and soon to major. In 1864, named lieutenant colonel and later colonel, he refused command and con-

tinued to lead his Partisan Rangers, duly mustered units of the Confederate army. After the war he practiced law and joined the Republican Party. He was an admirer of Grant and held several government posts. He became, in short, truly reconstructed.

PELHAM, JOHN. *1838-1863. Confederate.*

Born on a plantation in Benton County, Ala., Pelham resigned from West Point in April, 1861, to enter the Confederate army. As a captain he formed a battery of horse artillery under Stuart. In the Seven Days the Stuart Horse Artillery won its fame, and Pelham was promoted to major, and held important points at Second Manassas or Bull Run, and at Antietam. Pelham was idolized by his men and continued his brief, heroic career in Stuart's raid in Loudoun County and at Fredericksburg, where he held a vital position against heavy odds. He was fatally wounded at Kelly's Ford, Va., March 17, 1863. Known as the

"boy major" and "the gallant Pelham," he showed great military ability and promise, and his winning personality endeared him to the leaders and citizens of the South.

PEMBERTON, JOHN CLIFFORD. *1814-1881. Confederate.*

Born in Philadelphia, Pemberton was graduated from West Point in 1837, fought in Florida, in Mexico, and in the West. He was married to a Virginia woman, and despite his Northern birth, at the outbreak of war he joined the Confederacy. He served in organizational duties in Virginia, and by February, 1862, was a major general commanding in South Carolina, Georgia, and Florida. In October he was promoted to lieutenant general and commanded the department along the Mississippi and was ordered by President Davis to hold Vicksburg at all costs. Joseph E. Johnston, on the other hand, eventually told him to evacuate Vicksburg. Faced with conflicting orders and an impossible situ-

ation, he was forced by Grant to retreat to the city itself, which was besieged. With defeat inevitable, Pemberton surrendered July 4, 1863. Resigning his general's commission, he held the rank of lieutenant colonel of artillery during the rest of the war. Southerners charged him with disloyalty, but he had the full confidence of President Davis, and fought as well as limited opportunities and a desperate position allowed him.

PICKETT, GEORGE EDWARD. *1825-1875. Confederate.*

A native of Richmond, Va., Pickett was graduated from West Point in 1846, last in his class. He went immediately to Mexico, and then served in the Northwest. Resigning at the outbreak of the Civil War, he was first a colonel in the Confederate army, and was promoted to brigadier in January, 1862. He won notice for his daring in the Seven Days, during which he was wounded. A major general in October, 1862, he commanded a division at Fredericksburg and was in the Suffolk campaign. His most important day in the war was July 3, 1863, when, with other divisions his men fearlessly stormed the center of the Union line, only to be thrown back in bloody defeat, ending the battle of Gettysburg. He later commanded the Department of Virginia and North Carolina and bore the main attack in the hopeless fight at Five Forks, near Richmond, April 1, 1865. He entered business after the war. Relieved of his command for alleged dereliction of duty at Five Forks, Pickett nevertheless was a fighting soldier upon whom fate perhaps played unkind tricks.

PINKERTON, ALLAN. *1819-1884. Union.*

A native of Glasgow, Scotland, Pinkerton had little education. He came to America in 1842 and settled at Dundee, Ill., near Chicago. After capturing a group of counterfeiters, Pinkerton became a local detective,

and as an abolitionist operated an underground railroad station. Moving to Chicago, he was the city's first and only detective in 1850, and at the same time set up one of the first private detective agencies. Solving several railroad express robberies, he gained a national reputation, and in 1861 he guarded Lincoln's trip to Washington. Under his friend McClellan, he organized a secret service bureau and gave such erroneous overestimates of Confederate strength that they seriously affected the Peninsular campaign. With McClellan's removal he resigned from the service, continued his detective business, and wrote several books. Despite his success as a detective, his work in the Civil War generally was inaccurate and productive of little but trouble.

POLK, LEONIDAS. *1806-1864. Confederate.*

Born in Raleigh, N. C., Polk was graduated from West Point in 1827, where, under the influence of a chaplain, he became interested in the church and resigned his army commission to study theology. In 1831 he be-

came a Protestant Episcopal priest, and in 1838 was a missionary bishop of the Southwest. In 1841 he was made Bishop of Louisiana. In 1860 he founded the University of the South at Sewanee, Tenn. Offered the rank of major general in the Confederate army by Davis, Polk accepted in June, 1861. He fortified Columbus, Ky., and under Johnston defended the Mississippi, fighting at Belmont. He fought at Shiloh, in the invasion of Kentucky, at Perryville, and at Murfreesboro as a corps commander. Promoted to lieutenant general in October, 1862, he was somewhat slow in attacking at Chickamauga, and had difficulties with Bragg. He was killed in the fight at Pine Mountain near Marietta, Ga., June, 1864, during the Atlanta campaign. Polk was a competent though not great commander. His religious convictions had great influence on the army.

POPE, JOHN. *1822-1892. Union.*

Born in Louisville, Ky., Pope was graduated from West Point in 1842 and worked with the topographical engineers before serving in Mexico and in the West. A captain at the outbreak of the Civil War, he was named brigadier general of volunteers, and in command of the Army of the Mississippi captured New Madrid, Mo., and Island No. 10. Named a major general in March, 1862, he was given command of scattered forces near Washington, which were formed into the Army of Virginia while McClellan was still on the Peninsula after the Seven Days. In a flamboyant, ill-advised order, Pope bade his army to fight, saying his "headquarters were in the saddle." Fight they did at Second Manassas or Bull Run, but not well. Pope mangled

and in various naval posts with the rank of lieutenant until the Civil War. After some early activities, Porter commanded a mortar flotilla at the attack on New Orleans and captured the forts below the city. In October, 1862, with the rank of acting rear admiral, he commanded the Mississippi River Squadron during the Vicksburg campaign, in which the Navy was very effective in its cooperation with Grant. Commissioned rear admiral in July, 1863, he continued to command on the Mississippi and led the naval arm in the unsuccessful Red River campaign. He organized the North Atlantic Blockading Squadron and, aided by troops, captured Fort Fisher on the North Carolina coast. After the war he was superintendent at Annapolis and did much to reorganize the academy. In 1870 he succeeded Farragut as admiral. Porter was a man of great energy and excellent administrative abilities.

the campaign, had difficulty with some of McClellan's troops which joined him, and retreated to Washington. His army was dissolved and he was relieved of command in September, 1862. He spent the rest of the war capably handling Indian troubles in the Northwest until 1865, when he commanded in Missouri. He held important western commands following the war. Of definitely limited capacity, Pope was overconfident at Second Manassas and directed a difficult situation badly, but he did show ability in the West.

☆

PORTER, DAVID DIXON. *1813-1891. Union.*

Son of naval officer David Porter, David Dixon Porter was born in Chester, Pa. He received little formal education and followed his father to sea. In 1829 he was a midshipman in the American Navy. Later he served in the Coast Survey, in the Mexican War,

PORTER, FITZ JOHN. *1822-1901.*
Union.

A native of Portsmouth, N. H., he was graduated from West Point in 1845 and, like so many others, served in Mexico and in various capacities. At the outbreak of the Civil War he became a colonel of infantry, and in May, 1861, brigadier general of volunteers in the Shenandoah. On the Peninsula he commanded a division and later a corps, defending ably at Mechanicsville and Gaines' Mill. Sent north to aid Pope in defending Washington, Porter had orders to attack Jackson at Second Manassas or Bull Run, August 29, 1862, but running into Longstreet's arriving corps, either failed to attack or was unable to do so. Following the defeat of Pope, Porter led a corps at Antietam, but was not engaged. Relieved of his command in November, 1862, he faced charges of disobedience, disloyalty and misconduct brought by Pope, was found guilty and turned out of the army. He began a long effort to clear himself, and in 1882, after a successful hearing, he was allowed to rejoin the army, but was put on the retired list. Historians generally agree that Porter was treated unduly severely. His friendship for and support of McClellan hindered him, but he was a man of considerable talent and a victim of circumstances.

PRICE, STERLING. *1809-1867. Confederate.*

Born in Prince Edward County, Va., he studied law and in 1831 went to Missouri. After state legislative posts, Price was elected to Congress in 1844, resigned to serve in the Mexican War first as a colonel and then a brigadier general of volunteers. He was governor of Missouri 1852-1856. Price conditionally favored the Union at the outbreak of war, but he became so angered by local Unionists that he joined the Confederates. Serving with the Missouri State Guard under the com-

mand of McCulloch, Price was instrumental in the victory at Wilson's Creek, he captured Lexington, Mo., and retreated into Arkansas, fighting at Pea Ridge or Elkhorn Tavern, after which he was made a major general in the Confederate service. He fought at Iuka and Corinth, Miss., and beat Federals aiming at the Red River in 1864. His last Missouri raid was in 1864, after which he retreated to Texas. One of the leading figures in the Southern field west of the Mississippi, Price had great influence, and generally did well militarily with what he had.

QUANTRILL, WILLIAM CLARKE.
1837-1865. Confederate.
    A native of Canal Dover, Ohio, he taught school and then went to Kansas in 1857 and worked on western wagon trains. Going under the name of Charley Hart, he later lived near Lawrence, Kan., where he was known as a gambler and possible murderer and horse thief. At the outbreak of the Civil War he was connected irregularly with the Confederates and organized a group of guerrillas who robbed and pillaged Missouri and Kansas. He and his band were declared outlaws in 1862 by the North. In August, 1862, his troops joined the regular Confederate service, and Quantrill became a captain. On August 21, 1863, he sacked Lawrence, Kan., killing possibly over 150 persons, all of them men, and burned part of the town. During 1864 his band broke up from dissension, and Quantrill was fatally wounded in May, 1865, by Federal troops near Taylorsville, Ky., while on a robbing and foraging expedition. A very unsavory character, Quantrill added greatly to the horrors of war in Missouri. He was little short of a common bandit who took advantage of the conflict.

RAWLINS, JOHN AARON. *1831-1869. Union.*
    Born in Galena, Ill., Rawlins studied and practiced law in his home town. A locally prominent pro-Union Democrat, Rawlins was asked by U. S. Grant

to be his aide in August, 1861. For the rest of the war he was Grant's closest friend and staff officer, exercising great influence over him. Rising with Grant, he became brigadier general and chief-of-staff of the army in March, 1865, and brevet major general of the regular army in April, 1865. Grant appointed him Secretary of War in 1869, but he died five months later. Rawlins was a man of strong moral fibre and was often known as Grant's conscience, particularly in regard to Grant's occasional drinking. He had a keen, penetrating mind, was not afraid to give his opinions, and made himself an almost indispensable companion to Grant.

ROSECRANS, WILLIAM STARKE.
1819-1898. Union.

A native of Delaware County, Ohio, Rosecrans was graduated from West Point in 1842. He resigned his commission in 1854 to practice engineering and enter business. Shortly after the outbreak of the Civil War, he was made a regular brigadier general and served with McClellan in West Virginia, winning at Rich Mountain. By summer, 1862, he was in Mississippi under Grant. Rosecrans successfully attacked Confederates at Iuka, and then defended the attack on Corinth in October, 1862. Promoted major general of volunteers, Rosecrans succeeded Buell in Kentucky. At the end of 1862 he fought at Murfreesboro or Stone's River, one of the bloodiest battles of the war, which forced the Confederates to retreat. In the summer of 1863, he conducted a skillful campaign of movement near Tullahoma, forcing Bragg back into Chattanooga. He then maneuvered Bragg out of the city, but the Confederates attacked the overextended Union lines at Chickamauga in September, 1863. Rosecrans was personally defeated and much of the Federal army was crushed. Relieved of his command, Rosecrans saw little more duty and resigned in March, 1867. He was active in business and politics after the war. He was often in conflict with his superiors, but was a capable military commander until he went to pieces completely at the time of his greatest crisis.

SCHOFIELD, JOHN McALLISTER.
1831-1906. Union.

Born in Chautauqua County, N. Y., he was graduated from West Point in 1853. In addition to army duties, he taught physics at Washington University in St. Louis. At the outbreak of war he was chief of staff to Lyon, and in November, 1861, was made brigadier general of volunteers, with various commands. From October, 1862, to April, 1863, he headed the Army of

the Frontier in Missouri, becoming major general, and in May, 1863, commanded the Department of the Missouri. In February, 1864, he took over the Army of the Ohio, one of the three armies under Sherman in the campaign to Atlanta. Late in 1864, Schofield, with his corps and part of another, held off Hood's advance on Nashville at Franklin, and then fought in the Battle of Nashville under Thomas. He rejoined Sherman near the end of the war in North Carolina. He was Secretary of War 1868-69 and later became a regular major general. In 1888 he became Commanding General of the Army, gaining the rank of lieutenant general in 1895. Never brilliant, Schofield was considered an able career soldier.

☆

SCOTT, WINFIELD. *1786-1866. Union.*

Born near Petersburg, Va., Scott studied law, and joined the army in 1808. After early difficulties, he served during the War of 1812 at the battles of Queenstown, Fort George, Chippewa, and Lundy's Lane. At a time when heroes were few, his outstanding record won him a brevet rank of major general. He led the army in the Black Hawk War and in the 1835 Indian troubles in Florida. By 1839 he was prominently mentioned for the Whig presidential nomination, and in 1841 he was made general-in-chief of the army. The climax of his career was in the Mexican War, where he led the army personally from Vera Cruz to Mexico City in a generally skillful and successful operation. Scott was nominated by the Whigs for President in 1852, but was defeated by Pierce. In 1855 he was given the brevet rank of lieutenant general, first since Washington to have that office. At the outbreak of the Civil War, despite his age and near crippled condition, he resolutely recruited and supervised the training and building up of the Federal armies, ignoring efforts of the Confederates to lure him South. Practically pushed out of office by age and by youthful

George B. McClellan, Scott retired as commander in October, 1861. Scott had known all the Presidents from Jefferson to Lincoln and had given most of his long life to his country's service in many forms. Known as "Fuss and Feathers," he liked the trappings of the military and had ambitions for the presidency. He was a man of initiative and made full use of his high talents.

SEDDON, JAMES ALEXANDER.
1815-1880. Confederate.

Born in Fredericksburg, Va., he was graduated from the University of Virginia and practiced law in Richmond. He was in the U. S. House of Representatives, 1845-47, and in 1849-51. A successful lawyer, his country estate was the center of Virginia social life. He was elected to the Confederate Congress and in November, 1862, replaced George Randolph as Confederate Secretary of War. Though he lacked military experience, his skill as a politician and his general intelli-

gence gave him tact and administrative ability in a very difficult position. Despite President Davis' control of things military, Seddon had considerable influence. He resigned in early 1865, after several quarrels with the Confederate Congress. He retired to his estate after the war.

SEDGWICK, JOHN. *1813-1864. Union.*

A native of Cornwall Hollow, Conn., Sedgwick was graduated from West Point in 1837. He served in Florida, in the Canadian border disputes, and in the Mexican War. On the frontier as a lieutenant colonel before the Civil War, he was quickly promoted to brigadier general and commanded a division fighting on the Peninsula, where he was wounded. He became major general of volunteers in July, 1862, and was again wounded at Antietam. He commanded the forces operating against the city of Fredericksburg dur-

ing the Battle of Chancellorsville and served well at Gettysburg and at Mine Run. In the 1864 campaign into the Wilderness, Sedgwick led his old VI Corps and on May 9 was killed in the fighting at Spotsylvania. A strict but generous soldier of outstanding ability, he was known to his men as "Uncle John" and held the respect of his superiors.

SEMMES, RAPHAEL. *1809-1877. Confederate.*

A native of Charles County, Md., Semmes was appointed a midshipman in the U. S. Navy in 1826, served in various stations, and during leaves studied and practiced law in Maryland and Ohio. He served during the Mexican War and was a naval aide to the army during the campaign to Mexico City. He resigned from the Navy with the rank of commander and held the same rank in the Confederate Navy at first. In April, 1861, he took command of the *C.S.S. Sumter,* a commerce raider. Outfitting her, he successfully

harried Union commerce until his ship was blockaded in Gibraltar in April, 1862. Sent to England, he took command of the *Alabama,* which had been built in Britain, and began raiding again, sinking the *U.S.S. Hatteras* off Galveston in January, 1863. After extended cruising he was at Cherbourg, France, when the *U.S.S. Kearsarge* appeared, and in the two-ship duel June 19, 1864, the *Alabama* was destroyed. Promoted to rear admiral in February, 1865, Semmes commanded the James River Squadron until the end of the war. Semmes in his career captured 82 Union merchant vessels valued at over $6,000,000. He was considered almost a pirate in the North, but he held the admiration of naval men abroad and was one of the leading naval heroes of the South.

SEWARD, WILLIAM HENRY. *1801-1872. Union.*

A native of Florida, Orange County, N. Y., Seward graduated from Union College in 1820 and settled in Auburn, N. Y., to practice law. As a successful, rising lawyer he entered politics and began a long association with the political wire-puller Thurlow Weed. After several years in the state legislature, he was defeated as a Whig for governor but was elected in 1838 and 1840. A humanitarian, he gradually strengthened his stand against slavery, and in 1848 was elected to the U. S. Senate. He soon became famous for opposing all compromise on slavery. Always an able politician, he began to seek the Presidency and worked for the merger of the Whigs with the new Republican Party. By 1860 he was viewed as an extremist on the slavery question, and was the leading candidate for the Re-

publican presidential nomination in 1860, only to lose to Lincoln. Accepting the post of Secretary of State under Lincoln, he at first tried to set himself up as a sort of "prime minister" for the administration, but soon came to admire and respect Lincoln. His conduct of his office during the war was generally very successful. Despite a tendency to threaten England and even to urge a foreign war, Seward, aided by such diplomats as Charles Francis Adams, prevented recognition of the Confederacy abroad. In general he exercised a strong but not dominating influence upon Lincoln. Badly injured in a carriage accident early in 1865, Seward, while convalescing, was stabbed the night of the assassination of Lincoln, but recovered to serve successfully in the Johnson administration and negotiate the purchase of Alaska. A politician with presidential ambitions, Seward was also a man of convictions and great ability and materially aided the nation in time of crisis.

SHERIDAN, PHILIP HENRY. *1831-1888. Union.*

According to Sheridan himself, he was born in Albany, N. Y., though it has been said that he was born in Ireland or en route to the United States. He was graduated from West Point in 1853 after a tempestuous school career. He served in the West and was a captain at the start of the war. At first on staff duty, he became colonel of cavalry in May, 1862, and about a month later was made brigadier general after fighting at Boonville, Mo. One of the few successful commanders at Perryville and Stone's River, he was promoted major general of volunteers in December, 1862. Commanding a corps, he fought at Chickamauga and at Missionary Ridge, earning favor with Grant. When Grant went east, Sheridan was given command of the cavalry of the Army of the Potomac, which he made into a hard, fighting body, always in the scrap and making frequent raids. In August, 1864, he took com-

mand of the Army of the Shenandoah and drove the Confederates from the Valley in a campaign in which he earned the enmity of the people for laying waste the country with dreadful effectiveness. Arriving on the field at the darkest moment (his famous "20-mile ride"), he defeated Early at Cedar Creek on October 19—the last big battle in the Shenandoah. Made major general of the regular army in November, 1864, "Little Phil" moved from Winchester to Petersburg, destroying en route. In April, 1865, he turned the Confederate flank at Petersburg, winning at Five Forks. He participated in the final Appomattox campaign. After the war he administered various areas and was accused of taking retaliatory measures against the South. Later he fought in the West, and in 1883 succeeded Sherman as Commander-in-Chief of the army. Made lieutenant general in 1869, he became a full general in 1888. Sheridan was a soldier through and through and typified the newer type of army officer developed during the war—men with stern devotion to duty, come what may. Though considered over-rated by some authorities, he had natural aptitude for command, and while fortunate to rise to high rank near the end of the war when the enemy was less able, Sheridan won his reputation as an aggressive, hard-fighting, uncompromising soldier.

SHERMAN, WILLIAM TECUMSEH.
1820-1891. Union.

Born in Lancaster, Ohio, "Cump" was graduated from West Point in 1840 and served in the Mexican War. Following the war he resigned in 1853, only to fail in the banking business. He

then became superintendent of a military college that is now Louisiana State University. He refused high rank in the Confederacy and was president of a St. Louis street railway for a short time before entering the Federal Army as a colonel of regulars in May, 1861. He fought at First Bull Run or Manassas, was promoted to brigadier general, and then commanded in Kentucky, where he earned an unfounded reputation for being mentally odd, due to his weighty responsibilities and his nervous disposition. Relieved of command and later restored, Sherman fought at Shiloh. Promoted to major general, he commanded at Memphis in July, 1862. He failed in the attack on the Chickasaw Bluffs at Vicksburg and at first opposed Grant's plan of campaign to take the fortress, but later recognized its brilliance. He led a corps throughout the Vicksburg campaign. Sent to the relief of Chattanooga in the fall of 1863, he fought under Grant at Missionary Ridge and in the pursuit of the Confederates. In January, 1864, he led a march on Meridian, Miss., and when Grant was sent east, Sherman succeeded him as commander in the West. With three armies, Sherman advanced upon Atlanta and captured the city in a campaign mainly of maneuver. Sending part of his force back to Nashville to stop Hood's advance in November, 1864, Sherman, now a regular major general, led a force southeast from Atlanta. He was not heard from for a month until he appeared on the Atlantic coast at Savannah. This was his famous or infamous "March to the Sea." Sherman had no illusions about civil war and he was willing to destroy and commandeer property as he thought necessary. There were, however, excesses among some of his men. The march brought everlasting condemnation upon Sherman from the South. After the capture of Savannah he turned north into the Carolinas, an exploit that even outdid, in many ways, the march to the sea. Columbia, S. C., was burned, and Sherman moved into North Carolina, fighting one of the last battles of the war at Bentonville. On April 17, 1865, Joseph E. Johnston and Sherman met and made surrender arrangements which were not recognized at Washington until they were modified. In 1866 Sherman succeeded Grant as lieutenant general, and upon Grant's election as President, became a full general and General-in-Chief of the Army in 1869. He refused to allow his name to be mentioned for the presidency. He retired in 1883. A nervous, somewhat eccentric man, Sherman had an extremely quick mind, making decisions rapidly and spontaneously. His classic remark that "war is all hell" was typical of his thinking.

SICKLES, DANIEL EDGAR. *1825-1914. Union.*

Born in New York City, he attended the University of the City of New York and became a printer and lawyer. Entering politics, he served in the state legislature and was a Democrat in the U. S. House from 1857 to 1861. He shot and killed Philip Barton Key, son of Francis Scott Key, in 1859, because of Key's attentions to Sickles' wife. He was acquitted. At the start of the Civil War, Sickles raised troops and soon became a brigadier general in the Peninsular campaign. Promoted to major general commanding a corps in early 1863, he fought at Chancellorsville and headed the III corps at Gettysburg. It was here that he advanced his command to the Peach Orchard on July 2, without orders, and was badly beaten. Sickles was wounded, losing a leg. He was severely criticized for his action at Gettysburg. After the war, Sickles was military governor of the Carolinas, until dismissed for undue severity. In

1869 he was named Minister to Spain and later served again in Congress. One of the most cantankerous, irresponsible, rakishly colorful characters of his century, Sickles was far from being a great soldier and was more fitted for intrigue and romantic excursions, of which he had many.

SLIDELL, JOHN. *1793-1871. Confederate.*

Born in New York City, Slidell was graduated from Columbia College in 1810, failed in business in New York, and then practiced law in New Orleans. An active Democrat, he was Commissioner to Mexico in 1845 and served in the Senate from 1853 to 1861. He was a moderate Union man, but upon the election of Lincoln offered his services to the South and was named to represent the Confederacy in France. He and James M. Mason, Commissioner to England, were taken off the British steamer *Trent* by U. S. Captain Charles Wilkes and detained in Boston, but were released after the

tense situation almost resulted in a rupture between the United States and Britain. In France, Slidell worked toward recognition of the Confederacy by Napoleon III and arranged for ship construction and loans. He never returned home after the war. A powerful influence politically, particularly in the Buchanan administration, Slidell was a shrewd, ingenious controller of men, but somewhat distrusted in Europe.

SMITH, EDMUND KIRBY. *1824-1893. Confederate.*

Born in St. Augustine, Fla., E. Kirby Smith, as he styled himself, was graduated from West Point in 1845. He served in Mexico and on the frontier. He resigned with the rank of major to enter the Confederate army and was promoted to brigadier general in June, 1861, and was wounded at Manassas or Bull Run. Promoted to major general in October, 1861, he aided in com-

manding Bragg's 1862 invasion of Kentucky and was made lieutenant general in October, 1862. In February, 1863, he was put in command of the Trans-Mississippi Department, and the area, nearly cut off from the East, became known as "Kirby-Smithdom." Smith was made full general in February, 1864. In April, 1864, he repulsed the Red River campaign and on June 2, 1865, surrendered the last major force of the Confederacy. After the war he was chancellor of the University of Nashville for a time and held other teaching posts including the chair of mathematics at the University of the South (Sewanee). A man of great dash and capability as a military leader, he was a poor administrator.

STANTON, EDWIN McMASTERS.
1814-1869. Union.

Born at Steubenville, Ohio, Stanton was unable to finish at Kenyon College due to lack of funds, but in 1836 was admitted to the bar. He soon developed a prominent and lucrative prac-

tice, moving to Pittsburgh in 1847 and to Washington in 1856. In 1858 he was special counsel to the government in fighting land claims arising from the Mexican War. On Dec. 20, 1860, President Buchanan appointed Stanton Attorney General and he became one of the strongest supporters of the Union in the Cabinet. A Democrat, Stanton at first severely criticized Lincoln and mistrusted him, throwing his support to General McClellan. With the removal of Cameron from the War Department, Lincoln named Stanton as Secretary of War, Jan. 15, 1862. There was an immediate whirlwind overhaul of the department: personnel was changed, possibly fraudulent contracts investigated, and an entire new era of efficiency and force put into operation. As usual, Stanton applied tremendous energy and intelligence to his many problems, and while there were serious mistakes and many hurt feelings, things got done and the running of the war was put on a new basis. Stanton broke with McClellan over the latter's failure to move and fight and aided Lincoln in trying to find the right commanders. With great vigor he supplied the armies with materiel and men. He censored the press strongly, and made many enemies, but was able to take much of the pressure and blame off the President and place it on his own willing shoulders. His treatment of Sherman at the end of the war was extremely harsh, and he could never be said to have been subtle in working with others. Lincoln learned to know how to use Stanton and they had great respect for each other. At the time of the assassination, Stanton is reputed to have said of Lincoln, "Now he belongs to the ages." In the troubles with President Johnson, Stanton was deeply involved in intrigue with the "Black Republicans." It was over the removal of Stanton that much of Johnson's difficulties centered. When impeachment charges against Johnson failed, Stanton resigned in May, 1868. President Grant named him to the Supreme Court in December, 1869, but he died before taking the bench. Stanton is still a storm center of discussion among historians. His personality was not one to win friends and supporters. His ways were at times devious, and some of his actions reprehensible, but even most of his fiercest enemies give him credit for being a great "war minister."

STEPHENS, ALEXANDER HAMILTON. *1812-1883. Confederate.*

A slight, emaciated man with a shrill voice and feeble health, "Little Aleck" Stephens was born in Wilkes County, Ga. He was graduated from the University of Georgia in 1832, heading his class, and then taught school before beginning the practice of law in 1834. After earning a reputation as a lawyer and serving in the Georgia legislature, Stephens was elected to the House in 1843 as a Whig. During the pre-war troubles he upheld the right of a state to secede on principle and was against centralization of government. Strongly in favor of state's rights, he nevertheless favored compromise whenever possible. Shifting to the Democratic party in opposition to the Know Nothings, he supported Douglas in the Kansas-Nebraska Bill fight. At first not strongly in favor of slavery, he later defended the institution as being best for the Negroes. In 1859 he retired from Congress, and when the secession crisis broke in 1860, he urged moderation. At the Montgomery convention which set up the Confederate government, Stephens was named Vice-President on February 9, 1861. With his respect for constitutional principles, Stephens was generally unhappy in the Confederate government, and he soon came to oppose Davis and his appointees. Stephens led Georgia's Governor Brown in opposition to the Confederacy's power to conscript troops. In February, 1865, Stephens headed an official delegation which talked with Lincoln at Fortress Monroe, but found that armistice was not attainable. Stephens went home, and at war's end was arrested and held prisoner at Boston until released in October, 1865. In January of 1866 he was elected to the Senate, was not allowed to serve, but was elected to the House in 1872 where he did serve. He did considerable writing and counselled restraint in the reconstruction period. Possessed of a brilliant though somewhat unbending mind, he was a persuasive speaker and served his area with courage as he saw it. He was generally respected, both North and South.

STEWART, ALEXANDER PETER.
1821-1908. Confederate.

Born in Rogersville, Tenn., Stewart was graduated from West Point in 1842 and resigned from the army in 1845 to teach mathematics and philosophy at Cumberland and Nashville Universities in Tennessee. Despite the fact that he was a Whig and had opposed secession, he joined the Confederate Army, became a major, fought at the battle of Belmont, and was a brigadier general at Shiloh. In June, 1863, he was promoted to major general, commanding a division in Hardee's corps. After fighting at Chattanooga, Chickamauga, and in the Atlanta campaign, he became lieutenant general in June, 1864, and took over a corps. He was with the Army of Tennessee during the final days in North Carolina. His postwar career was notable for his work as chancellor of the University of Mississippi. He was a man of strong character and competent military ability. His personality is indicated in his nickname, "Old Straight."

STUART, JAMES EWELL BROWN.
1833-1864. Confederate.

Born on a Patrick County, Va., plantation, Stuart was graduated from West Point in 1854 and served with the cavalry in Texas and Kansas. He resigned in May, 1861, and almost immediately became a colonel of the 1st Virginia Cavalry. He served at First Bull Run or Manassas and was made brigadier general in September, 1861. Bringing his cavalry to high efficiency, Stuart led his men in a brilliant ride around McClellan's army on the Peninsula and fought at the Seven Days. In July, 1862, his reputation beginning to glow, Stuart became a major general. He won praise from Lee at Second Manassas or Bull Run, and again at Antietam or Sharpsburg. Following Antietam, he raided as far as Chambersburg, Pa., and once more rode around the Federal army. Intensely popular was this Southern cavalier with his plumed hat, his gallant manners, his pleasant camp. Lee considered him the eyes of his army. Stuart fought at Fredericksburg, and temporarily commanded Jackson's corps after the latter was wounded at Chancellorsville. Stuart commanded at Brandy Station, and in the Gettysburg campaign left Lee's army for another tour around the enemy, not rejoining until July 2. There was immediate controversy—had Stuart failed to keep Lee posted, and had the Army of Northern Virginia been working blind? After a hard riding winter in 1863-64, Stuart covered Lee's operations in the Wilderness. On May 9, 1864, Sheridan and the Union cavalry headed for Richmond. Stuart got between him and Richmond at Yellow Tavern, north of the Confederate capital. On May 11, 1864, "Jeb" Stuart was wounded and died the next day in Richmond. Fond of dramatic action, Stuart felt great loyalty to Lee, and possessed considerable though not original skill in battle tactics. But most of all, he was one of the gallant soldiers who epitomized the romantic spirit of the South.

Mississippi and Alabama, and on May 4, 1865, surrendered the last Confederate force east of the Mississippi. A man of high literary and cultural achievements, he served well, though never brilliantly as a commander, despite lack of military training.

TAYLOR, RICHARD. *1826-1879.*
Confederate.

Only son of Zachary Taylor, Richard was born near Louisville, Ky., and was graduated from Yale in 1845. He set up a plantation in Saint Charles Parish, La., but found time to become a widely read student. At first a colonel of Confederate infantry, he became a brigadier general in October, 1861, and served under Jackson in the Valley and during the Seven Days. A major general in July, 1862, Taylor commanded the district of West Louisiana, and in April, 1864, halted Bank's Red River campaign. Promoted lieutenant general for this service, he commanded the Department of East Louisiana,

THOMAS, GEORGE HENRY. *1816-1870. Union.*

A Southerner, Thomas was born in Southampton County, Va., and was graduated from West Point in 1840. He served in Florida, the Mexican War, and in the West. A major at the outbreak of the Civil War, he stayed with the Union despite his Southern birth, for which his family never forgave him. As a colonel he led a brigade in the Shenandoah, but in August, 1861, he became a brigadier general in Kentucky, winning the small but important battle of Mill Springs or Logan's Cross Roads, Jan. 19, 1862. With Buell's army, he became major general

of volunteers in April, 1862, and took part in the advance on Corinth, and fought throughout Buell's Kentucky campaign. Declining to supersede Buell, Thomas fought well under Rosecrans at Murfreesboro or Stone's River, commanding a corps. But it was at Chickamauga that he won his real fame, holding the vital Snodgrass Hill against the victorious Confederates, and earning the title "Rock of Chickamauga." Grant replaced Rosecrans with Thomas in command of the Army of the Cumberland, and his army carried Missionary Ridge. Thomas and his men moved with Sherman toward Atlanta, bearing the main drive of the Southern attack at Peachtree Creek. When Hood took over and Sherman decided to go to the sea, Thomas and his forces were sent back to defend Nashville against Hood. After the battle of Franklin, Hood moved to Nashville and Thomas was ordered to attack. But Thomas delayed until he was completely ready, and

moved out just as he was about to be relieved of command. On Dec. 15-16, 1864, Thomas completely routed and almost destroyed Hood's army in the battle of Nashville. For this he was promoted to major general in the regular army. After the war he served in various posts. A large, deliberate, slow-moving man, "Pap Thomas" has come to be regarded as one of the outstanding generals of the war, deserving to be ranked near the very top.

TOOMBS, ROBERT AUGUSTUS.
1810-1885. Confederate.

Born in Wilkes County, Ga., he attended the University of Georgia and Union College in New York, was admitted to practice law in 1830, and soon entered politics. Often serving in the state legislature, Toombs went to Congress in 1844 as a Whig. By 1850 he became a leading defender of the South. Elected to the Senate, he became a Democrat. With the election of

Lincoln, he felt that secession was almost imperative although he supported the compromise measures which failed. He left the Senate in January, 1861, and was disappointed at not being named President of the Confederacy. He did become its Secretary of State, but soon broke with Davis, and in July, 1861, commanded a Georgia brigade in Virginia. Toombs was a "political" general, often antagonizing his superiors. After Antietam he resigned, having failed to receive a promotion. Following the war he had strong influence on the South. A capable politician with strong opinions, he was a brave but none too able commander.

VAN DORN, EARL. *1820-1863. Confederate.*

Born near Port Gibson, Miss., he was graduated from West Point in 1842 and served in Mexico, Florida, and the West. Appointed colonel in the Con-

federate army, he served in Texas, and by September, 1861, was a major general. In January, 1862, he was commander of the Trans-Mississippi. Defeated at Pea Ridge or Elkhorn Tavern in March, he crossed the river and was beaten at Corinth, Miss., in October. He conducted a brilliant raid on the Federal supply depot at Holly Springs, Miss., in December. He was shot to death in May, 1863, at his headquarters at Spring Hill, Tenn., allegedly by a jealous husband. Although he suffered defeats, he was an outstanding cavalry officer.

WALLACE, LEWIS. *1827-1905. Union.*

A native of Brookville, Ind., "Lew" Wallace studied law, but early began a writing career. He served as a volunteer officer in the Mexican War and by 1853 was practicing law in Crawfordsville, Ind. At the start of the Civil War he became an adjutant-general of Indiana and fought in West Virginia. A

popular officer, he rose to major general in March, 1862, after Fort Donelson, but his force took little part in the desperate fighting at Shiloh when Wallace lost his way for reasons not yet entirely clear. In the Confederate campaign in Kentucky in 1862, Wallace strongly defended Cincinnati. He was then awarded a corps command at Baltimore. Gathering what troops he could, he was defeated, but temporarily held off Early in the battle of the Monocacy, possibly saving Washington from capture in July, 1864. After the war he was governor of New Mexico and minister to Turkey. He is well known for his writings, particularly the novel "Ben Hur."

WARREN, GOUVERNEUR KEMBLE. *1830-1882. Union.*

Born in Cold Spring, N. Y., Warren was graduated from West Point in 1850 and served with the topographical engineers in the West. After serving in the Peninsula and other early actions of the Civil War, Warren was at Second Bull Run or Manassas, and at Antietam. Named brigadier general in September, 1862, he was at Fredericksburg and as a major general of volunteers served as chief engineer of the Army of the Potomac from June to August, 1863. At Gettysburg he found that the vital position of Little Round Top was undefended and obtained troops at the critical moment to hold it. Commanding a corps, he fought in the 1864 campaign in Virginia and at Petersburg. At Five Forks in April, 1865, Warren was accused of slowness and removed from his command by Sheridan, an action still much discussed. After the war, Warren gave outstanding service with the Army Corps of Engineers. He was granted a hearing in 1879 and was exonerated for Five Forks after his death. Warren was a sensitive and extremely capable commander, though not a great one.

WELLES, GIDEON. *1802-1878. Union.*

Born in Glastenbury, Conn., Welles was well educated and had studied law, but he entered publishing and politics. After numerous positions, Welles, an anti-slavery Democrat, turned to the Republican party, and in 1856 established the *Hartford Evening Press.* Chosen as Secretary of the Navy by Lincoln, Welles held office from 1861 to 1869. Starting with a small and out-of-date navy, Welles almost overnight created a new force to fight the war and carry out the blockade. With invaluable assistance from Gustavus V. Fox, Welles made the Navy and his department one of the great instruments of victory. He worked well with Lincoln, ran an efficient and

He fought at Shiloh, rose to brigade command, and took over the cavalry of the Army of Mississippi in July, 1862. He rapidly rose to brigadier and then major general, and led the western cavalry ably through the Kentucky campaign, Murfreesboro, Chickamauga, and Chattanooga. He conducted a number of raids, particularly at Atlanta, and tried to oppose Sherman's march to the sea. He won the name of "Fighting Joe" and at war's end was a 28-year-old hero, often considered with Stuart and Forrest as one of the great Southern cavalry leaders. He became a merchant after the war,

largely honest department, and promoted many modern naval developments. Equally as important were his contributions to the administration in formulating policy and supporting the war. He usually opposed Secretary of War Stanton, but generally cooperated with the army. After the war Welles supported Johnson against the Radical Republicans. His diary is one of the most valuable records of Civil War days. Welles was devoted to duty and brought a methodical, calm approach to the business of running the war.

WHEELER, JOSEPH. *1836-1906. Confederate.*

A native of Augusta, Ga., Wheeler was graduated from West Point in 1859, served in the West, and joined the Confederate service as a lieutenant and soon became an infantry colonel.

served in Congress, and was a major general of volunteers in the Spanish-American War, fighting in Cuba and the Philippines. He retired as a brigadier general of the regular army of the United States. An outstanding soldier, Wheeler also did much to reunite North and South.

WILSON, JAMES HARRISON.
1837-1925. Union.

Born in Shawneetown, Ill., Wilson was graduated from West Point in 1860 and became a topographical engineer. Serving in the engineers in Virginia and with the Army of the Tennessee during Vicksburg, he was made brigadier general of volunteers in October, 1863. In the spring of 1864 he commanded a division in Sheridan's corps in the Army of the Potomac, fighting in the campaign to Petersburg. In October, as a brevet major general, he was given command of the cavalry of the Military Division of the Mississippi. He fought well against Forrest in the repulse of Hood from Nashville late in 1864, and led the advance into Alabama, capturing Selma in April, 1865. After the war he returned to engineering with the army, but resigned in 1870 to enter business. During the Spanish-American War he participated in the Puerto Rico campaign, and also fought in the Boxer Rebellion in China. A bold and capable cavalry leader, he was a fine organizer and undoubtedly was one of the outstanding commanders of horse troops, despite his youth at the time of the Civil War.

THE SOLDIER

THE CIVIL WAR SOLDIER was many things and one thing—all at once.
He was the commanding general with the responsibility of directing
thousands of men; he was the lower officer, the lieutenant, the captain,
the colonel with hundreds to think of and lead. He was the noncom-
missioned corporal and sergeant, not so very distinguished from that
common denominator—the private.

This was a civil war with civilian soldiers, and their differences
were those of environment and upbringing and development, rather
than differences North and South. "Johnny Reb" and "Billy Yank"
were of the same nation, the same language, though fighting on opposite sides. Even politics didn't mean too much—such beliefs melted
away under fire, leaving something else. They had to fight for survival
for themselves, their families, for their homes.

What was he like, this common soldier? In the dust of Federal
Army records, and undoubtedly it was about the same in the Confederate Army, we find figures which picture him as five feet eight
and a fourth inches tall on the average, weighing 143½ pounds.
Thirty per cent had brown hair, twenty-five per cent dark hair,
twenty-four per cent light hair; forty-five per cent were blue-eyed
and twenty-four per cent gray-eyed, while sixty per cent were
light in complexion. But there was much more to this average soldier
than height and weight and coloring, and he proved it.

Where did these soldiers come from? From everywhere—from
the slums of the cities, from countless small communities, from farms
and plantations. Forty-eight per cent of Union men were farmers,
twenty-four per cent mechanics, sixteen per cent laborers, five per
cent businessmen, three per cent professional men, and four per cent
from miscellaneous occupations. In the Confederate army the per-
centage of farmers ran more than half.

[219]

And they wanted to fight. On both sides, particularly at first, they just had to join the army. Anything else was unthinkable. Once in the army, once having seen a shot fired in anger or in necessity and once firing back, the soldier was a somewhat different man, but he still wanted to fight. Then, too, there was the former slave. He fought, too, mainly in the Northern army, and he fought well for the most part, considering his lack of training and his recent servitude. Later in the war when the draft on both sides began to drag in the reluctants and the thrill of war wore off, the army changed somewhat on the surface, but in the main, the Civil War soldier was a singing, cursing, frolicking personality, slightly disrespectful of his officers, but ready to be molded into an efficent, thinking, fighting force. But he needed something more. He needed a father, a leader, someone to look up to. In some cases he found a leader, actually to love with a deep, loyal affection. Lee, Jackson, McClellan and others filled those needs.

In material goods, the Northern soldier generally had much the better of it. His clothing, his food, his arms were superior. Of course, he often threw his overcoat away on a hot day, only to freeze at night, but at least he had an overcoat. Generally, too, except for the plantation boys, he expected more than the Southerner. It was a good thing, too, that the Confederate man at arms did not expect too much, for he didn't get it. His lot was often green corn and beans, butternut-dyed clothing, and as often as not former Union guns for weapons. But he was a self-reliant man and often picked up and found substitutes for what wasn't furnished him. The Southern soldier stood up a bit better under privation in many cases than his Northern counterpart. But it is everlasting glory to the American youth that on both sides they did so much with often so little.

And it was youth; for this was a young army, their ages averaging in the late teens and early twenties. Of course, there were the mere babes who lied about their ages, and the "old men" in their thirties who joined on principle.

The conduct of soldiers on both sides was not all creditable. There were the thousands who deserted and the thousands more who skulked and found convenient shelter in battle, but the average of courage was amazingly high.

For the soldier's body there was medical care which seems appallingly inadequate today, but for the times it was usually as good as could be furnished under the pressure and strain of war. For his soul, there was a haphazard chaplain service, but the soldier himself found time from his gambling, playing and foraging to undergo a religious revival largely brought on by himself and his pals.

There were the prison camps—no pleasure palaces North or South. There were executions occasionally for desertion or spying. There were other penalties, not too strictly enforced. There were the wounds, many fatal and many more disabling. And there were 500,000 dead in battle from wounds and disease. Five hundred thousand statistics, mere notations, mere records. But the muster rolls with their long lists of the killed in battle, the permanently wounded and maimed, record other things. The individualism of the American soldier even in death—a private kicked to death by a mule at Somerset, Ky., April 23, 1864; a lieutenant who died from amputation of right arm resulting from the bite of a man on thumb, December 11, 1861; a private killed by lightning near Gettysburg; a soldier who drowned on April 22, 1863, en route home on furlough; and a private killed April 17, 1863, by a shot from a house while filling his canteen at a well near Vermillion Bayou, La.

When it was all over those who went home made a new nation. For some it was hard to forget and forgive; others simply took up where they had left off, or tried to. But for all it was a bath of fire that left its deep scars upon the people of the nation.

TEXTS OF THE LETTERS

IN VIEW OF THE FACT that many of the leaders whose letters are reproduced in facsimile in this volume were better generals or statesmen than they were penmen, the full texts of the letters are reproduced here in the order that they appear in the book. The spelling, capitalization, and punctuation are retained as in the original.

Hd. Qrs. Army Northern Virginia/April 10th 1865

Gen'l Order/No. 9

After four years of arduous service marked by unsurpassed courage and fortitude the Army of Northern Virginia has been compelled to yield to overwhelming numbers and resources.

I need not tell the survivors of so many hard fought battles who have remained steadfast to the last that I have consented to this result from no distrust of them.

But feeling that valour and devotion could accomplish nothing that could compensate for the loss that would have attended the continuance of the contest I determined to avoid the useless sacrifice of those whose past services have endeared them to their country.

By the terms of the agreement officers and men can return to their homes and remain untill exchanged You will take with you the satisfaction that proceeds from the consciousness of duty faithfully performed, and I earnestly pray that a merciful God will extend to you his blessing and protection. With an unceasing admiration of your constancy and devotion to your country and a grateful remembrance of your kind and generous consideration for myself, I bid you an affectionate farwell

R E Lee/Genl

Head Quarters, Mil. Div. of the Miss./Chattanooga, Ten. Nov. 22d 1863

Maj. Gen. G. H. Thomas/Commdg. Army of the Cumb.d

General.

The bridge at Brown's Ferry being down to-day, and the excessively bad roads since the last rain, will render it impossible for Sherman to get up either of his two remaining Divisions in time for the attack to-morrow morning. With one of them up, and which would have been there now but for the accident to the bridge, I would still make the attack in the morning, regarding a day gained as of superior advantage to a single Division of troops.

You can make your arrangements for this delay.

Very respectfully/U. S. Grant/Maj. Gen. C

F. Ship Hartford/New Orleans, April 29th 1862

My dearest Wife,

We are now masters of the Mississippi River, the Forts Jackson and St. Phillips have surrendered. Mitchell & McIntosh & a host of others are my Prisoners. Of course the New Orleans papers abuse me but I am case hardened to all that. I dont read the papers except to gain information as to the War.

I find the Forts all along the coast are surrendering & we will have nothing to do but occupy them. I will be off for Mobile in a few days and put it to them there. I have done all I promised & all I was expected to do.

So thanks to God I hope I have acquitted myself to my friends as well as my country. I was recommended by others for the appointment, it was not sought & I hoped through Gods assistance not to disappoint either my friends or the country.

Your affection husband & father/D. G. Farragut

To/Mrs. D. G. Farragut

Corinth Miss May 23 1862

D. C. Trader

Sir your note of 21 ins is to hand I did not fully understand the contents and ask for information the amount you ask for is it for a publick contrabution or is it for my dues due the log [lodge] I wish you to give me the amt due the log from me as you did not State it in your notice or the amount asked for I had a small brush with the Enamy on yesterday I Suceded in gaining thir rear and got in to thir entrenchments 8 miles from hamburg and 5 behind farmington and Burned a portion of thir camp at that place they wair not looking for me I taken them by Surprise they run like Suns of Biches I captured the Rev Dr Warin from Ilanois and one fin Sorel Stud this army is at this time in front of our Entrenchments I look for a fite soon and a big one when it coms off Cant you come up and take a hand this fite wil do to hand down to your childrens children I feel confident of our success

your Respct/N. B. Forrest

To/D. C. Trader/Memphis Tenn

Near 3 P. M./May 2d, 1863

General,

The enemy has made a stand at Chancellor's which is about 2 miles from Chancellorsville. I hope as soon as practicable to attack.

I trust that an Ever Kind Providence will bless us with great success

Respectfully/T. J. Jackson/Lt. Genl.

Genl. R. E. Lee

The leading division is up & the next two appear to be well closed.   T. J. J.

United States Military Telegraph/War Department. Washington DC

"Cypher"   June 10, 1863. [6:40 P. M.]

Major General Hooker

Your long despatch of today is just received. If left to me, I would not go South of the Rappahannock, upon Lee's moving North of it. If you had Richmond invested to-day, you would not be able to take it in twenty days; meanwhile, your communications, and with them, your army would be ruined. I think Lee's Army, and not Richmond, is your true objective point. If he comes towards the Upper Potomac, follow on his flank, and on the inside track, shortening your lines, whilst he lengthens his. Fight him when opportunity offers. If he stays where he is, fret him, and fret him.

A. Lincoln

HEADQUARTERS, MILITARY DIVISION OF THE MISSISSIPPI

Genl Wilson.   In the Field.   Oct 27 1864

Your two dispatches are received. I am anxious to learn what Cavalry if any are left back towards Villa-Rica & the Chattahoochee.

Appearances are still at variance. A positive Report comes that Hardees Corps is in Mills Valley, and the Enemy Cavalry followed Garrard in from Turkey Town.

I have no doubt a large part if not the whole of Hoods Army has gone off towards Decatur. He would not venture up to Guntervill though he might fight all along the River from Decatur to Gunters. I hardly think he would give so much publicity to a movt into Tennessee. Still Hood is capable of undertaking anything.

Find out if you can if the Enemy has a Comm Line on the Road from Newman Georgia via Villa Rica, Cedartown Jacksonville, Gadsden, etc.

I would like you to hit some one body of the Cavalry a good lick if they will stand, for you can judge by that if they own anything like a depot of stores at Blue Mountain. I ordered Schofield to send a Brigade of Infantry out some 5 miles tomorrow morn'g.

Gen W. T. Sherman/Maj Gen. Comdg.

Genl. Bragg

The dispatch of Genl. F. Lee would indicate the propriety of looking for Sheridan on the lower Chickahominy rather than at the White House.

We cannot start troops now if the report be correct with any prospect finding the Enemy where Genl. Hampton left him.

If we have force enough to expel the party at and near "deep bottom" so as to destroy the Bridge, it will then be easier to combine on Sheridan's corps so as to destroy it. Unless this can be done there will be hazard in going far down the Chickahominy.

Every practicable combination and effort should be made to prevent Sheridan's cavalry from returning to Grant's army.

The telegram of Genl. R. E. Lee in relation to the movement against the So. side R.R. renders it more necessary than before that Genl. Kemper should go up to supervise the assembling & distribution of the "Reserves."

very respectfully yrs/Jeffer Davis

March 3d, 1865

Lieutenant General Grant

The President directs me to say to you that he wishes you to have no conference with General Lee unless it be for the capitulation of Gen. Lee's Army, or on some minor, and purely military matter. He instructs me to say that you are not to decide, discuss, or confer upon any political question. Such questions the President holds in his own hands; and will submit them to no military conferences or conventions. Meantime you are to press to the utmost, your military advantages.

Edwin M. Stanton/Secretary of War

(The text of the letter is in Lincoln's hand. Only the heading and closing was written by Stanton.)

THE WAR IN BOOKS

A BASIC CIVIL WAR LIBRARY

DOUGLAS SOUTHALL FREEMAN pointed out almost twenty years ago that most of us who work in what we believe to be the fascinating field of Civil War history receive many inquiries from comparative newcomers to the literary adventure of this period that could be summarized in five words, "What shall I read next?" Dr. Freeman tried in part to answer this oft-repeated query with his excellent volume, *The South to Posterity*, and one of the authors of this volume attempted to explore the problems of a Union book shelf in a series of articles appearing in the quarterly publication *Civil War History*. The job, however, remained to be done and both authors of this volume discussed the problem with Dr. Freeman shortly before his death in 1953.

It has been estimated that over 100,000 volumes and pamphlets exist relating in some manner or other to the Civil War. This figure includes books on military, naval, and political subjects, as well as biographies of the major and minor figures of the time, fiction, poetry and drama. While collectors of an earlier generation might have attempted to build an all-inclusive library of every book relating to the dramatic 1861-65 period of our history, and men like John Page Nicholson actually did attempt this herculean task, today problems of finance and space and above all the scarcity of the early titles make it unlikely that any individual will try to scale this literary Mount Everest.

This list is an attempt to put together a basic Civil War library—the essential titles necessary to give an individual (or for that matter an institution) a sound foundation with which to explore with some degree of scholarly exactness that most exciting, yet most confusing, period of American history. Perhaps the most difficult problem encountered by the compilers of this list was to keep it down to reasonable space. It is also the bibliography for this volume.

The books appear under ten classifications. Narratives and special studies appear in their respective groups—the reader today is much more interested in what happened than he is in whether the viewpoint is Northern or Southern, though this should by no means be overlooked. Only those titles referring specifically to the Confederate States as a government are listed under that heading; all other titles with Confederate emphasis appear in their more specific category. Space limitations made it impossible to include fiction, poetry or drama, though we will be the first to concede the great influence of books like *The Red Badge of Courage, John Brown's Body* and *Abe Lincoln in Illinois*.

The omissions are many, and yet we feel we have listed the major titles. Inevitably, the favorite books of some readers will be missing—it had to be so. Occasionally a title is listed because it is the only one available or the best of several mediocre works on a particular subject. This only happens when the subject could not be overlooked, and we hope that a better book in every such field will be written. In some cases we record a representative sampling. We expect the reader will want to continue and expand the list himself.

The list is divided into the following categories:

I. SOURCE COLLECTIONS, BASIC REFERENCE BOOKS
II. GENERAL HISTORIES
III. PHOTOGRAPHIC COLLECTIONS, PICTURE BOOKS
IV. BIBLIOGRAPHICAL AND LITERARY STUDIES
V. THE CONFEDERACY
VI. MILITARY STUDIES, BATTLES AND CAMPAIGNS
VII. NAVAL OPERATIONS
VIII. PERSONAL NARRATIVES, DIARIES, LETTERS AND SPEECHES
IX. BIOGRAPHIES OF OUTSTANDING CIVIL WAR FIGURES
X. SPECIAL STUDIES, MONOGRAPHS, MISCELLANEOUS WORKS

In using this selective list the reader is advised that all titles appear in standard form as to punctuation and capitalization. Dates appear in Arabic numerals though they may appear on the title page of the book in Roman numerals. Brackets [ ] are used to indicate material supplied by the compilers of this bibliography which does not appear on the title page of the book being described, but which may have been obtained from another portion of the book or from other sources. Within the main broad classifications most arrangements are alphabetical according to the authors' surnames, except in certain cases where the title is more important than the name of the editor or in the biographical section where the arrangement is according to subject, with a few obvious and understandable exceptions. Parentheses ( ) are used to indicate comments by the authors on the content of the volume or the edition. The title and edition listed will be the earliest appearance of the book, unless the work has been superseded by a better edition, in which case both editions will be recorded. Where possible, we have listed the latest edition in print.

I. SOURCE COLLECTIONS, BASIC REFERENCE WORKS

[Appleton's] *American Annual Cyclopaedia and Register of Important Events* ...14 volumes, 1861-74. New York: D. Appleton and Company, 1862-75.

(The 6 volumes, 1861-66, are of particular significance to students of the Civil War.)

Battles and Leaders of the Civil War... being for the most part contributions by Union and Confederate Officers. Based upon "The Century War Series." Edited by Robert Underwood Johnson and Clarence Clough Buel. 4 volumes. New York: The Century Company, 1887-88.

(Issued originally in serial form in *The Century* magazine and reissued in many forms including an eight volume, *Grant-Lee Edition*, but with identical text, and a one volume, *People's Pictorial Edition*, New York: [c1894]. Occasionally referred to as "The Century War Book." New and revised, one volume edition, edited by Ned G. Bradford, New York: Appleton-Century-Crofts, 1956.)

Dictionary of American Biography. Edited by Allen Johnson, Dumas Malone and Harris E. Starr. 20 volumes and supplement. New York: Charles Scribner's Sons, 1928-1944. *Centenary Edition,* [11 volumes on thin paper], 1946.

DYER, FREDERICK HENRY, *A Compendium of the War of the Rebellion*...Des Moines: The Dyer Publishing Company, 1908.

EVANS, CLEMENT ANSELM, editor, *Confederate Military History: A Library of Confederate States History* . . . 12 volumes, Atlanta: Confederate Publishing Company, 1899.

Fox, WILLIAM FREEMAN, *Regimental Losses in the American Civil War, 1861-1865* ... Albany: Albany Publishing Company, 1889.

HEITMAN, FRANCIS BERNARD, *Historical Register of the United States Army, from its organization, September 29, 1789 to September 29, 1889.* Washington: The National Tribune, 1890. New and enlarged edition, with a slightly altered title, *to March 2, 1903.* 2 volumes, Washington: Government Printing Office, 1903.

LIVERMORE, THOMAS L., *Numbers and Losses in the Civil War in America, 1861-1865.* Boston: Houghton, Mifflin and Company, 1900.

MOORE, FRANK, editor, *The Rebellion Record; A Diary of American Events* ... [Introduction by] Edward Everett. 11 volumes and supplement, New York; G. P. Putnam, 1861-63; D. Van Nostrand, 1864-1868.

RHODES, JAMES FORD, *History of the United States from the Compromise of 1850 to the Final Restoration of Home Rule at the South in 1877.* 7 volumes, New York: The Macmillan Company, 1892-1906.

STEELE, MATTHEW FORNEY, *American Campaigns.* 2 volumes [text and atlas]. Washington: B. S. Adams, 1909. [Reprinted] Washington: United States Infantry Association, 1935. [New edition in larger format], *Volume I, Text,* Washington: Combat Forces Press, [1951]. [Volume II], *Atlas to accompany Steele's American Campaigns.* Edited by Colonel Vincent J. Esposito. [Foreword by Colonel T. Dodson Stamps], West Point: United States Military Academy, 1953.

The Union Army: A History of Military Affairs in the Loyal States, 1861-1865 ... 8 volumes, Madison, Wisconsin: Federal Publishing Company, 1908.

U. S. War Department. *War of the Rebellion ... Atlas to Accompany the Official Records of the Union and Confederate Armies.* Compiled by Calvin D. Cowles. 175 plates, Washington: Government Printing Office, 1891-95.

(Issued in 35 parts and also bound in both a two volume and a three volume edition.)

U. S. War Department. *War of the Rebellion ... Official Records of the Union and Confederate Armies.* 70 volumes in 128 parts, Washington: Government Printing Office, 1880-1901.

II. GENERAL WORKS

CATTON, BRUCE, *This Hallowed Ground.* Garden City: Doubleday & Company, 1956. (A one volume history of the Civil War from the Northern viewpoint.)

COMMAGER, HENRY STEELE, editor, *The Blue and the Gray; The Story of the Civil War as Told by Participants.* [With a preface by Douglas Southall Freeman], 2 volumes, Indianapolis: The Bobbs-Merrill Company, [1950]. (Reprinted in a one volume edition, [1954]).

HENRY, ROBERT SELPH, *The Story of the Confederacy.* Indianapolis, The Bobbs-Merrill Company, [c1931]. *New and Revised Edition.* With a Foreword by Douglas Southall Freeman, New York: Grosset & Dunlap, [1954].

MILTON, GEORGE FORT, *Conflict; The American Civil War.* New York: Coward-McCann, [1941].

NEVINS, ALLAN, *The Ordeal of the Union.* 2 volumes, *Volume I—Fruits of Manifest Destiny, 1847-1852. Volume II—A House Dividing, 1852-1857.* New York: Charles Scribner's Sons, 1947.

NEVINS, ALLAN, *The Emergence of Lincoln.* 2 volumes, *Volume I — Douglas, Buchanan, and Party Chaos, 1857-1859. Volume II — Prologue to Civil War, 1859-1861.* New York: Charles Scribner's Sons, 1950.

(The four volumes by Dr. Nevins form the beginning of a larger work which will cover the Civil War and Reconstruction periods.)

PRATT, FLETCHER, *Ordeal by Fire, An Informal History of the Civil War.* New York: H. Smith & R. Haas, 1935. [Revised edition,] Maps by Rafael Palacios, [1948]. (Published under the title,) *An Informal History of the Civil War.* With, a Preface by D. W. Brogan, London: John Lane, [1950].

(Reprinted in two editions by Pocket Books, Inc.)

[227]

RANDALL, JAMES GARFIELD, *The Civil War and Reconstruction.* Boston: D. C. Heath and Company, [1937]. [Revised Edition] *With Supplementary Bibliography,* [1953].

STEPHENS, ALEXANDER HAMILTON, *A Constitutional View of the Late War Between the States.* 2 volumes, Philadelphia: National Publishing Company, 1868-70.

III. PHOTOGRAPHIC COLLECTIONS, PICTURE BOOKS

BARNARD, GEORGE N., *Photographic Views of Sherman's Campaign, from Negatives taken in the Field by George N. Barnard, Official Photographer of the Military Division of the Mississippi.* New York: [Privately printed], 1866.

BUCHANAN, LAMONT, *Pictorial History of the Confederacy.* New York: Crown Publishers, [1951].

DONALD, DAVID, HIRST D. MILHOLLEN, MILTON KAPLAN and HULEN STUART, editors, *Divided We Fought: A Pictorial History of the War, 1861-1865.* New York: The Macmillan Company, 1952.

GARDNER, ALEXANDER, *Gardner's Photographic Sketch Book of the War.* 2 volumes, Washington: Philp & Solomons, Publishers, [1865].

MEREDITH, ROY, *Mr. Lincoln's Camera Man, Mathew B. Brady.* New York: Charles Scribner's Sons, 1946.

MEREDITH ROY, *The Face of Robert E. Lee in Life and Legend.* New York: Charles Scribner's Sons, 1947.

MESERVE, FREDERICK HILL and CARL SANDBURG, *The Photographs of Abraham Lincoln.* New York: Harcourt, Brace and Company, [1944].

MILLER, FRANCIS TREVELYAN and ROBERT S. LANIER, editors, *The Photographic History of The Civil War.* 10 volumes, New York: The Review of Reviews Co., 1911.

(Often called "Miller-Brady," this is the great photographic source work of the war. The Barnard and Gardner volumes are so excessively rare that few collectors or institutions have copies, but this work was widely distributed. The text has many errors, but the photographs are superb.)

PRATT, FLETCHER, *Civil War in Pictures.* New York: Henry Holt and Company, [1955].

(This work is illustrated with drawings and other illustrative material from the files of *Harper's Weekly* and *Frank Leslie's Illustrated Newspaper.*)

The Soldier in Our Civil War: A Pictorial History of the Conflict, 1861-1865, Illustrating the Valor of the Soldier as Displayed on the Battle-field, From Sketches drawn by Forbes, Waud, Taylor, Hillen, Becker, Lovie, Schell, Crane . . . and other Eye-witnesses. Edited by Paul F. Mottelay and T. Campbell-Copeland, Assisted by the most Notable Generals and Commanders of both sides. 2 volumes, New York: J. H. Brown Pub. Co., 1884-85.

(A fine reference work containing, in addition to the effective illustrative material, an excellent chronological history of the war and other useful reference data.)

IV. BIBLIOGRAPHICAL AND LITERARY STUDIES

ANGLE, PAUL M., *A Shelf of Lincoln Books: A Critical, Selective Bibliography.* New Brunswick: Rutgers University Press, 1946.

BARTLETT, JOHN RUSSELL, *The Literature of the Rebellion: A Catalogue of Books and Pamphlets relating to the Civil War in the United States . . .* Providence: Sidney S. Rider and Bro., 1866.

(The first Civil War bibliography. 250 copies were printed in octavo and 60 copies printed in quarto. It is interesting to note that within a year of the

end of the war, this work listed 6,073 titles including pamphlets and periodical articles.)

COULTER, E. MERTON, *Travels in the Confederacy: A Bibliography.* Norman: University of Oklahoma Press, 1948.

CRANDALL, MARJORIE LYLE, *Confederate Imprints; A Check List Based Principally on the Collection of the Boston Athenaeum.* With an Introduction by Walter Muir Whitehill. 2 volumes, [Boston:] The Boston Athenaeum, 1955.

FREEMAN, DOUGLAS SOUTHALL, *The South*

to Posterity; An Introduction to the Writing of Confederate History. New York: Charles Scribner's Sons, 1939.

HARWELL, RICHARD BARKSDALE, *Cornerstones of Confederate Collecting.* Charlottesville: Bibliographical Society of the University of Virginia, 1952. *Second Edition, with Facsimiles* and an Introduction by Clifford Dowdey, Charlottesville: The University of Virginia Press, for the Bibliographical Society of the University of Virginia, 1953.

NICHOLSON, JOHN PAGE, *Catalogue of Library of Brevet Lieutenant-Colonel John Page Nicholson, U.S. Vols. . . . Relating to the War of the Rebellion 1861-1866.* Philadelphia: [Privately printed]. 1914.

(Issued in a limited edition of 300 copies, this is one of the most useful Civil War bibliographical tools. Though it possesses all of the imperfections of the work of an amateur, the Nicholson Collection was so great that the mere listing of the titles in any order is of great use to students and collectors, and Colonel Nicholson did much more than that. He indicated the number of copies printed, whenever the information was available to him and many variant printings are listed in this catalogue which comprises a volume of 1,022 pages.)

U.S. War Department. Library. *Bibliography of State Participation in the Civil War, 1861-66.* [3rd edition]. Washington: Government Printing Office, 1913. [At head of title]: *War Department. Office of the Chief of Staff. War College Division, General Staff, No. 19.* [On verso of title page]: War Department, Document no. 432. "Office of the Chief of Staff."

(One of the great reference works for the Civil War student. It was preceded by two earlier editions and a supplement. These were: U. S. War Department. Library. *Military Literature in the War Department library relating chiefly to the participation of the individual states in the war for the union.* [Subject Catalog no. 6.] G.P.O., 1897; G.P.O. [2nd edition] 1899, and *Appendix to Subject catalog no. 6,* G.P.O. 1904.

This 3rd edition of subject catalog no. 6 is an attempt to compile a definitive list of regimental and special unit histories, as well as all material relating to local participation not embraced in separate histories. It is sincerely hoped that this work will be reissued, with additions, for the Civil War Centennial.)

V. THE CONFEDERACY

COULTER, E. MERTON, *The Confederate States of America 1861-1865.* [Baton Rouge]: Louisiana State University Press, 1950. [Volume VII, *A History of the South.*]

DAVIS, JEFFERSON, *The Rise and Fall of the Confederate Government.* 2 volumes, New York: D. Appleton and Company, 1881. *Memorial Edition,* Richmond: Garrett & Massie, [1938].

DOWDEY, CLIFFORD, *Experiment in Rebellion.* Garden City: Doubleday & Company, 1946.

DOWDEY, CLIFFORD, *The Land They Fought For; The Story of the South as the Confederacy, 1832-1865.* Garden City: Doubleday & Company, 1955.

EATON, CLEMENT, *A History of the Southern Confederacy.* New York: The Macmillan Company, 1954.

JONES, KATHERINE M., editor, *Heroines of Dixie: Confederate Women Tell Their Story of the War.* Introduction by Robert Selph Henry. Indianapolis: The Bobbs-Merrill Company, [1955].

OLMSTED, FREDERICK LAW, *The Cotton Kingdom: A Traveller's Observations on Cotton and Slavery in the American Slave States.* Based upon three former volumes of journeys and investigations . . . 2 volumes, New York: Mason Brothers, 1861. [New edition], Edited, with an Introduction, by Arthur M. Schlesinger, New York: Alfred A. Knopf, 1953.

OWSLEY, FRANK LAWRENCE, *King Cotton Diplomacy: Foreign Relations of the Confederate States of America.* Chicago: The University of Chicago Press, [c1931].

VI. MILITARY STUDIES, BATTLES AND CAMPAIGNS

BALLARD, COLIN R., *The Military Genius of Abraham Lincoln.* London: Oxford

University Press, 1926. [Reissued, with] A Preface by Fletcher Pratt [and]

Photographs from the Meserve Collection, Cleveland: The World Publishing Company, [1952].

BIGELOW, JOHN, JR., *The Campaign of Chancellorsville*. New Haven: Yale University Press, [1910].

BROWN, DEE ALEXANDER, *Grierson's Raid*. Urbana: University of Illinois Press, 1954.

Campaigns of the Civil War, 13 volumes, New York: Charles Scribner's Sons, 1881-1885.

(Published and sold as sets under the title, *The Army in the Civil War, Subscription Edition*.)

I. *The Outbreak of the Rebellion* by John G. Nicolay

II. *From Fort Henry to Corinth* by Manning F. Force

III. *The Peninsula* by Alexander S. Webb

IV. *The Army Under Pope* by John Codman Ropes

V. *The Antietam and Fredericksburg* by Francis Winthrop Palfrey

VI. *Chancellorsville and Gettysburg* by Abner Doubleday

VII. *The Army of the Cumberland* by Henry M. Cist

VIII. *The Mississippi* by Francis Vinton Greene

IX. *The Campaign of Atlanta* by Jacob D. Cox

X. *The March to the Sea. Franklin and Nashville* by Jacob D. Cox

XI. *The Shenandoah Valley in 1864* by George E. Pond

XII. *The Campaigns of Grant in Virginia* by Andrew A. Humphreys

XIII. *Statistical Record of the Armies of the United States* by Frederick Phisterer

(A companion set, *The Navy in the Civil War* in 3 volumes was also issued.)

CATTON, BRUCE, *Mr. Lincoln's Army*. Garden City: Doubleday & Company, 1951.

CATTON, BRUCE, *Glory Road*. Garden City: Doubleday & Company, 1952.

CATTON, BRUCE, *A Stillness at Appomattox*. Garden City: Doubleday & Company, 1953.

(The three Catton volumes combine to present a history of the Army of the Potomac.)

FISKE, JOHN, *The Mississippi Valley in the Civil War*. Boston: Houghton Mifflin Company, 1900.

GRACIE, ARCHIBALD, *The Truth About Chickamauga*. Boston: Houghton Mifflin Company, 1911.

HANSON, JOSEPH MILLS, *Bull Run Remembers . . . The History, Traditions and Landmarks of the Manassas (Bull Run) Campaigns before Washington, 1861-1862*. Manassas: National Capitol Publishers, 1953.

HASKELL, FRANKLIN ARETAS, *The Battle of Gettysburg*. Boston: The Mudge Press, 1908. *Second Edition*, [Wisconsin History Commission: Reprints No. 1, Madison]: Wisconsin History Commission, 1910.

HORN, STANLEY F., *The Army of Tennessee: A Military History*. Indianapolis: The Bobbs-Merrill Company, [1941]. [New edition], Norman: University of Oklahoma Press, 1953.

MIERS, EARL SCHENCK, *The Web of Victory; Grant at Vicksburg*. New York: Alfred A. Knopf, 1955.

MITCHELL, JOSEPH B., *Decisive Battles of the Civil War*. New York: G. P. Putnam's Sons, [1955].

MONAGHAN, JAY, *Civil War on the Western Border, 1854-1865*. Boston; Little, Brown and Company, [1955].

PARIS, LOUIS PHILLIPPE ALBERT D'ORLEANS, COMTE DE, *History of the Civil War in America*. Translated, with the approval of the author, by Louis F. Tasistro. Edited by Henry Coppee [and John P. Nicholson]. 4 volumes, Philadelphia: Joseph H. Coates & Co., 1875-[88].

SCHAFF, MORRIS, *The Battle of the Wilderness*. Boston: Houghton Mifflin Company, 1910.

SHANNON, FRED ALBERT, *The Organization and Administration of the Union Army, 1861-1865*. 2 volumes, Cleveland: Arthur H. Clark Company, 1928.

VAN HORNE, THOMAS B., *History of the Army of the Cumberland*. Illustrated with Campaign and Battle Maps compiled by Edward Ruger. 2 volumes and atlas, Cincinnati: Robert Clarke & Co., 1875.

WILLIAMS, KENNETH P., *Lincoln Finds a General: A Military Study of the Civil War*. 4 volumes, New York: The Macmillan Company, 1949-1956.

(The first four volumes of a projected 7 or 8 volume work, based in the main on a study of the *Official Records.*)

WILLIAMS, THOMAS HARRY, *Lincoln and His Generals.* New York: Alfred A. Knopf, 1952.

VII. NAVAL OPERATIONS

BOYNTON, CHARLES B., *The History of the Navy During the Rebellion.* 2 volumes, New York: D. Appleton and Company, 1867-1868.

DURKIN, JOSEPH T., S.J., *Stephen R. Mallory: Confederate Navy Chief.* Chapel Hill: The University of North Carolina Press, 1954.

FOX, GUSTAVUS VASA, *Confidential Correspondence of Gustavus Vasa Fox, Assistant Secretary of the Navy, 1861-1865.* Edited by Robert Means Thompson and Richard Wainwright. 2 volumes, New York: Naval History Society, 1918-1919.

GOSNELL, H. ALLEN, *Guns on the Western Waters; The Story of River Gunboats in the Civil War.* Baton Rouge: Louisiana State University Press, [1949].

LEWIS, CHARLES LEE, *David Glasgow Farragut.* 2 volumes, *Volume I, Admiral in the Making. Volume II, Our First Admiral.* Annapolis: U. S. Naval Institute, 1941-1943.

LEWIS, CHARLES LEE, *Admiral Franklin Buchanan, Fearless Man of Action.* Baltimore: The Norman, Remington Company, 1929.

MORGAN, MURRAY, *Dixie Raider, The Saga of the C.S.S. Shenandoah.* New York: E. P. Dutton & Co., 1948.

The Navy in the Civil War, 3 volumes, New York: Charles Scribner's Sons, 1883-1885.

(Published and sold as sets, *Subscription Edition,* to match *The Army in the*

Civil War; and also sold individually.)
I. *The Blockade and the Cruisers* by James Russell Soley
II. *The Atlantic Coast by Daniel* Ammen
III. *The Gulf and Inland Waters* by A. T. Mahan

PORTER, DAVID DIXON, *The Naval History of the Civil War.* New York: The Sherman Publishing Company, 1886.

PRATT, FLETCHER, *Civil War on Western Waters.* New York: Henry Holt and Company, [1956].

ROBERTS, WALTER ADOLPHE, *Semmes of the Alabama,* Indianapolis: The Bobbs-Merrill Company, [c1938].

SCHARF, J. THOMAS, *History of the Confederate States Navy from its organization to the surrender of its last vessel.* New York: Rogers and Sherwood, 1887.

SEMMES, RAFAEL, *Service Afloat, or the Remarkable Career of the Confederate Cruisers, Sumter and Alabama . . .* Baltimore: The Baltimore Publishing Co., 1887. [Republished in condensed form as] *Rebel Raider.* Edited by H. Allen Gosnell, Chapel Hill: The University of North Carolina Press, 1948.

U. S. Navy Department. *The War of the Rebellion . . . Official Records of the Union and Confederate Navies.* 30 volumes and Index, Washington: Government Printing Office, 1894-1922.

WEST, RICHARD S., JR., *The Second Admiral: A Life of David Dixon Porter.* New York: Coward-McCann, 1937.

VIII. PERSONAL NARRATIVES, DIARIES, LETTERS AND SPEECHES

ALEXANDER, EDWARD PORTER, *Military Memoirs of a Confederate.* New York: Charles Scribner's Sons, 1907.

BEAUREGARD, PIERRE GUSTAVE TOUTANT, see ROMAN, ALFRED.

BILLINGS, JOHN D., *Hardtack and Coffee: or the Unwritten Story of Army Life . . .* Illustrated with . . . sketches by Charles W. Reed. Boston: George M. Smith & Co., 1887.

BLACKFORD, WILLIAM WILLIS, *War Years with Jeb Stuart.* Foreword by Douglas Southall Freeman. New York: Charles Scribner's Sons, 1945.

BORCKE, HEROS VON, *Memoirs of the Confederate War for Independence.* 2 volumes, London: William Blackwood & Sons, 1866. [Reprinted], New York: Peter Smith, 1938.

BOYD, BELLE, *Belle Boyd, in camp and prison.* 2 volumes, London: Otley, and company, 1865. [One volume edition]. New York: Blelock & Company, 1865.

BRYAN, GEORGE SANDS, *The Spy in America.* New York: J. B. Lippincott Company, [1943].

BULLOCH, JAMES DUNWODY, *Secret Service of the Confederate States in Europe:*

or, how the Confederate cruisers were equipped. 2 volumes, New York: G. P. Putnam's Sons, 1884.

BUTLER, BENJAMIN F., Autobiography and Personal Reminiscences of Major-General Benjamin F. Butler . . . Boston: A. M. Thayer & Co., 1892.

CADWALLADER, SYLVANUS, Three Years with Grant, As Recalled by War Correspondent Sylvanus Cadwallader. Edited, and with an Introduction and Notes by Benjamin P. Thomas. New York: Alfred A. Knopf, 1955.

CHASE, SALMON PORTLAND, Inside Lincoln's Cabinet; The Civil War Diaries of Salmon P. Chase. Edited by David Donald. New York: Longmans, Green and Co., 1954.

CHESNUT, MARY BOYKIN, A Diary from Dixie . . . Edited by Isabella D. Martin and Myrta Lockett Avary. New York: Appleton and Company, 1905. [Revised and enlarged edition] Edited by Ben Ames Williams, Boston: Houghton Mifflin Company, 1949.

COOKE, JOHN ESTEN, Wearing of the Gray; Being Personal Portraits, Scenes and Adventures of the War. New York: E. B. Treat & Co., 1867.

DANA, CHARLES A., Recollections of the Civil War . . . New York: D. Appleton & Company, 1898.

DAVIS, JEFFERSON, Jefferson Davis, Constitutionalist, His Letters, Papers and Speeches. Collected and Edited by Dunbar Rowland. 10 volumes, Jackson: Printed for the Mississippi Department of Archives and History, 1923.

DE FOREST, JOHN WILLIAM, A Volunteer's Adventures; A Union Captain's Record of the Civil War. Edited by James H. Croushore, Introduction by Stanley T. Williams. New Haven: Yale University Press, 1946.

DE LEON, THOMAS COOPER, Four Years in Rebel Capitals. Mobile: The Gossip Printing Co., 1890.

DOUGLAS, HENRY KYD, I Rode with Stonewall. Chapel Hill: The University of North Carolina Press, [1940].

EARLY, JUBAL ANDERSON, Autobiographical Sketch and Narrative of the War between the States, with notes by R. H. Early. Philadelphia: J. B. Lippincott Company, 1912.

FLETCHER, WILLIAM ANDREW, Rebel Private: Front and Rear. Beaumont, Texas: Greer Press, 1908. [New edition], With a Preface by Bell Irvin Wiley, Austin: University of Texas Press, 1954.

FREMANTLE, ARTHUR JAMES LYON, Three Months in the Southern States, April-June, 1863. London: William Blackwood & Sons, 1863. (Also published the same year in New York and Mobile.) [New edition published as] The Fremantle Diary, Editing and Commentary by Walter Lord, Boston: Little, Brown and Company, [1954].

GIBBON, JOHN, Personal Recollections of the Civil War. New York: G. P. Putnam's Sons, 1928.

GORDON, GEORGE H., Brook Farm to Cedar Mountain in the War of the Great Rebellion, 1861-1862. Cambridge: The Riverside Press, 1883.

GORDON, GEORGE H., A War Diary of Events in the War of the Great Rebellion, 1863-1865. Boston: James R. Osgood & Co., 1882.

GORDON, JOHN B., Reminiscences of the Civil War. New York: Charles Scribner's Sons, 1903. Memorial Edition, [with an Introduction by Stephen D. Lee and "A Memorial Sketch of the Last Hours, Death and Funeral of General John B. Gordon" by Mrs. Frances Gordon-Smith], 1904.

GOSS, WARREN LEE, Recollections of a Private. A Story of the Army of the Potomac. New York: Thomas Y. Crowell & Co., [1890].

GRANT, ULYSSES SIMPSON, Personal Memoirs of U. S. Grant. 2 volumes, New York: Charles L. Webster & Co., 1885. [Second edition, edited by Frederick D. Grant], New York: The Century Company, 1895. [One volume edition], Edited with Notes and an Introduction by E. B. Long, Cleveland: The World Publishing Company, [1952].

(Not only a great work in the military field, but a truly remarkable literary effort—belongs on any list of 100 great American books.)

GREEN, JOHN WILLIAMS, Johnny Green of the Orphan Brigade, The Journal of a Confederate Soldier. Edited by A. D. Kirwan. Lexington: The University of Kentucky Press, 1956.

HANCOCK, CORNELIA, South After Gettysburg; Letters of Cornelia Hancock.

Edited by Henrietta Stratton Jaquette. Philadelphia: University of Pennsylvania Press, 1937. [New edition] With a Foreword by Bruce Catton, New York: Thomas Y. Crowell Company, 1956.

HITCHCOCK, HENRY, *Marching with Sherman, Passages from the Letters and Campaign Diaries* . . . Edited, with an introduction by M. A. DeWolfe Howe. New Haven: Yale University Press, 1927.

HOOD, JOHN B., *Advance and Retreat: Personal Experiences in the United States and Confederate States Armies.* New Orleans: Published for the Hood Orphan Memorial Fund, 1880.

JOHNSTON, JOSEPH E., *Narrative of Military Operations, Directed, during the Late War between the States.* New York: D. Appleton & Company, 1874.

JONES, JOHN BEAUCHAMP, *A Rebel War Clerk's Diary, at the Confederate States Capital.* 2 volumes, Philadelphia: J. B. Lippincott & Company, 1866.

(Also issued in a one-volume edition, same plates and same date.)

New and Enlarged Edition, Edited, with an Introduction and Historical Notes by Howard Swiggett, 2 volumes, New York: Barnes & Noble, 1935.

LINCOLN, ABRAHAM, *Abraham Lincoln: His Speeches and Writings.* Edited with critical and analytical notes by Roy P. Basler. Preface by Carl Sandburg. Cleveland: The World Publishing Company, 1946.

LINCOLN, ABRAHAM, *The Collected Works of Abraham Lincoln.* 9 volumes, Roy P. Basler, Editor; Marion Dolores Pratt and Lloyd A. Dunlap, Assistant Editors. New Brunswick: Rutgers University Press, 1953-1955.

(The definitive edition of the writings and speeches of our 16th President, prepared under the direction of The Abraham Lincoln Association.)

LONGSTREET, JAMES, *From Manassas to Appomattox; Memoirs of the Civil War in America.* Philadelphia; J. B. Lippincott Company, 1896. [Second edition, revised], 1903.

LYMAN, THEODORE, *Meade's Headquarters, 1863-1865: Letters of Colonel Theodore Lyman* . . . Selected and edited by George R. Agassiz. Boston: The Atlantic Monthly Press, 1922.

MARSHALL, CHARLES, *An Aide-de-Camp of Lee, being the Papers of Colonel Charles Marshall* . . . Edited by Major General Sir Frederick Maurice. Boston: Little, Brown and Company, 1927.

MCCARTHY, CARLTON, *Detailed Minutiae of Soldier Life in the Army of Northern Virginia, 1861-1865.* Richmond: Carleton McCarthy & Company, 1882.

MCCLELLAN, GEORGE BRINTON, *McClellan's Own Story.* New York: Charles L. Webster & Company, 1887.

PORTER, HORACE, *Campaigning with Grant.* New York: The Century Co., 1897.

ROMAN, ALFRED, *The Military Operations of General Beauregard in the War between the States, 1861 to 1865.* 2 volumes, New York: Harper & Brothers, 1884.

(Actually an autobiography of General Beauregard though authorship is ascribed to Roman and the work is done in the third person.)

RUSSELL, WILLIAM HOWARD, *My Diary North and South* . . . in two volumes. London: Bradbury & Evans, 1863. [One volume American edition], Boston: T. O. H. P. Burnham, 1863. [New edition], Edited and Introduced by Fletcher Pratt, New York: Harper & Brothers, [1954].

SHERIDAN, PHILIP HENRY, *Personal Memoirs of P. H. Sheridan.* 2 volumes, New York: Charles L. Webster & Co., 1888. *New and Enlarged Edition,* with an account of his life from 1871 to his death in 1888, by Michael V. Sheridan, 2 volumes, New York: D. Appleton & Company, 1902.

SHERMAN, WILLIAM TECUMSEH, *Memoirs of General W. T. Sherman, written by himself.* 2 volumes, New York: D. Appleton & Company, 1875. *Second edition, revised and corrected.* 2 volumes, 1886.

(For a criticism of the first edition, see BOYNTON, HENRY VAN NESS, *Sherman's Historical Raid.* Cincinnati: Wilstach, Baldwin & Co., 1875.)

SORREL, G. MOXLEY, *Recollections of a Confederate Staff Officer.* With an introduction by John W. Daniel. New York: The Neale Publishing Company, 1905.

STRONG, GEORGE TEMPLETON, *The Diary of George Templeton Strong.* Edited by Allan Nevins and Milton Halsey Thomas. 4 volumes, New York: The Macmillan Company, 1952.

TAYLOR, RICHARD, *Destruction and Reconstruction: Personal Experiences of the Late War.* New York: D. Appleton & Company, 1879. [New edition] Edited by Richard B. Harwell, New York: Longmans, Green and Co., 1955.

TROBRIAND, PHILIP REGIS DE, *Four Years with the Army of the Potomac.* Translated by George K. Dauchy. Boston: Ticknor & Company, 1889.

WATKINS, SAM R., *1861 vs. 1882. "Co. Aytch," Maury Grays, First Tennessee Regiment; or, A Side Show of the Big Show.* Nashville: Cumberland Presbyterian Publishing House, 1882. [New edition], With an introduction by Bell Irvin Wiley, Jackson, Tennessee: McCowat-Mercer Press, 1952.

WELLES, GIDEON, *The Diary of Gideon Welles, Secretary of the Navy under Lincoln and Johnson.* Edited, with an introduction by John T. Morse, Jr. 3 volumes, Boston: Houghton Mifflin Company, 1911.

(For a critical evaluation of this work the reader is referred to "Is the Printed Diary of Gideon Welles Reliable?" by Howard K. Beale, in *American Historical Review*, XXX, April, 1925.)

WILSON, JAMES HARRISON, *Under the Old Flag.* 2 volumes, New York: D. Appleton & Company, 1912.

IX. BIOGRAPHIES OF OUTSTANDING CIVIL WAR FIGURES

ADAMS, CHARLES FRANCIS (1807-1888). ADAMS, CHARLES FRANCIS, JR., *Charles Francis Adams.* Boston: Houghton Mifflin Company, 1900.

BANKS, NATHANIEL PRENTISS. HARRINGTON, FRED HARVEY, *Fighting Politician, Major General N. P. Banks.* Philadelphia: University of Pennsylvania Press, 1948.

BEAUREGARD, PIERRE GUSTAVE TOUTANT. WILLIAMS, T. HARRY, *P. G. T. Beauregard: Napoleon in Gray.* Baton Rouge: Louisiana State University Press, 1955.

BENJAMIN, JUDAH PHILIP. MEADE, ROBERT DOUTHAT, *Judah P. Benjamin, Confederate Statesman.* New York: Oxford University Press, 1943.

BUTLER, BENJAMIN FRANKLIN. HOLZMAN, ROBERT S., *Stormy Ben Butler.* New York: The Macmillan Company, 1954.

DAVIS, JEFFERSON. DAVIS, VARINA HOWELL, *Jefferson Davis, Ex-President of the Confederate States of America. A Memoir by His Wife.* 2 volumes, New York: Belford Company, [1890].

––– STRODE, HUDSON, *Jefferson Davis: American Patriot 1808-1861.* New York: Harcourt, Brace and Company, 1955.

(The first volume of a projected two volume work.)

––– WINSTON, ROBERT W., *High Stakes and Hair Trigger; The Life of Jefferson Davis.* New York: Henry Holt and Company, [1930].

DOUGLAS, STEPHEN ARNOLD. JOHNSON, ALLEN, *Stephen A. Douglas:*

A Study in American Politics. New York: The Macmillan Company, 1908.

FORREST, NATHAN BEDFORD. HENRY, ROBERT SELPH, "*First with the Most*" *Forrest.* Indianapolis: The Bobbs-Merrill Company, [1944].

––– HENRY, ROBERT SELPH, editor, *As They Saw Forrest: Some Recollections and Comments of Contemporaries.* Jackson, Tennessee: McCowat-Mercer Press, 1956.

––– WYETH, JOHN A., *Life of General Nathan Bedford Forrest.* New York: Harper & Brothers, 1899.

FREEMAN, DOUGLAS SOUTHALL, *Lee's Lieutenant's: A Study in Command.* 3 volumes, New York: Charles Scribner's Sons, 1942-1944.

(Also published in a four volume subscription edition, with additional illustrations.)

GORGAS, JOSIAH. VANDIVER, FRANK E., *Plowshares into Swords; Josiah Gorgas and Confederate Ordnance.* Austin: University of Texas Press, 1952.

GRANT, ULYSSES SIMPSON. CATTON, BRUCE, *U. S. Grant and the American Military Tradition.* Boston: Little, Brown and Co., 1954. [Reprinted], New York: Grosset & Dunlap, [1956].

––– FULLER, JOHN FREDERICK CHARLES, *The Generalship of Ulysses S. Grant.* London: John Murray, 1929. [American edition], New York: Dodd, Mead & Company, 1929.

––– LEWIS, LLOYD, *Captain Sam Grant.* Boston: Little, Brown and Company, 1950.

HAMPTON, WADE. WELLMAN, MANLY WADE, *Giant in Gray; A Biography of Wade Hampton of South Carolina.* New York: Charles Scribner's Sons, 1949.

HENDRICK, BURTON J., *Statesmen of the Lost Cause; Jefferson Davis and His Cabinet.* Boston: Little, Brown and Company, 1939.

HENDRICK, BURTON J., *Lincoln's War Cabinet.* Boston: Little, Brown and Company, 1946.

HOOD, JOHN BELL. DYER, JOHN P., *The Gallant Hood.* Indianapolis: The Bobbs-Merrill Company, [1950].

HOOKER, JOSEPH. HEBERT, WALTER H., *Fighting Joe Hooker.* Indianapolis: The Bobbs-Merrill Company, [1944].

JACKSON, THOMAS JONATHAN. DAVIS, BURKE, *They Called Him Stonewall: A Life of Lt. General T. J. Jackson, C.S.A.* New York: Rinehart & Company, [1954].

—— HENDERSON, GEORGE FRANCIS ROBERT, *Stonewall Jackson and the American Civil War.* [With an introduction by Field-Marshall the Late Right Hon. Viscount Wolseley.] 2 volumes, London: Longmans, Green & Co., 1898. [One volume edition, without abridgement] New York: Longman's Green and Co., 1949.

JOHNSON, ANDREW. STRYKER, LLOYD PAUL, *Andrew Johnson; A Study in Courage.* New York: The Macmillan Company, 1929.

LEE, ROBERT EDWARD. DAVIS, BURKE, *Gray Fox: Robert E. Lee and the Civil War.* New York: Rinehart & Company, 1956.

—— FREEMAN, DOUGLAS SOUTHALL, *R. E. Lee: A Biography.* 4 volumes, New York: Charles Scribners' Sons, 1934-1935. *Pulitzer Prize Edition,* [with additional illustrations, sold by subscription only], 1936.

—— HORN, STANLEY F., editor, *The Robert E. Lee Reader.* Indianapolis: The Bobbs-Merrill Company, [1949]. [Reprinted], New York: Grosset & Dunlap, [1954].

—— MIERS, EARL SCHENCK, *Robert E. Lee: A Great Life in Brief.* New York: Alfred A. Knopf, 1956.

LINCOLN, ABRAHAM. ANGLE, PAUL M., editor, *The Lincoln Reader.* New

Brunswick: Rutgers University Press, 1947.

—— NICOLAY, JOHN G. and JOHN HAY, *Abraham Lincoln: A History.* 10 volumes, New York: The Century Co., 1890. [Reprinted from the original plates], 1914.

—— RANDALL, JAMES GARFIELD, *Lincoln the President.* 4 volumes, New York: Dodd, Mead & Company, 1945-1955. (Volume IV was completed after Dr. Randall's death by Richard N. Current.)

—— SANDBURG, CARL, Abraham Lincoln: *The Prairie Years* [and] *The War Years.* 6 volumes, New York: Harcourt, Brace and Company, [1926-1939]. *One-volume edition,* [Revised, and with new material, 1954]. (A condensation of *The War Years* was published under the title, *Storm Over the Land: A Profile of the Civil War,* [1942].)

—— THOMAS, BENJAMIN P., *Abraham Lincoln: A Biography.* New York: Alfred A. Knopf, 1952.

LONGSTREET, JAMES. SANGER, DONALD BRIDGMAN and THOMAS ROBSON HAY, *James Longstreet, I. Soldier by Donald Bridgman Sanger. II. Politician, Officeholder, and Writer by Thomas Robson Hay.* Baton Rouge: Louisiana State University Press, 1952.

McCLELLAN, GEORGE BRINTON. ECKENRODE, H. J. and BRYAN CONRAD, *George B. McClellan, The Man Who Saved the Union.* Chapel Hill: The University of North Carolina Press, 1941.

MEADE, GEORGE GORDON, MEADE, GEORGE, *The Life and Letters of George Gordon Meade, Major General United States Army.* 2 volumes, New York: Charles Scribner's Sons, 1913.

MOSBY, JOHN SINGLETON. JONES, VIRGIL CARRINGTON, *Ranger Mosby.* Chapel Hill: The University of North Carolina Press, 1944.

PATRICK, REMBERT W., *Jefferson Davis and His Cabinet.* Baton Rouge: Louisiana State University Press, 1944.

PEMBERTON, JOHN CLIFFORD. PEMBERTON, JOHN C., III, *Pemberton: Defender of Vicksburg.* Chapel Hill: The University of North · Carolina Press, 1942.

POLK, LEONIDAS. POLK, WILLIAM M., *Leonidas Polk: Bishop and General.*

2 volumes, New York; Longmans, Green & Co., 1893. [Reprinted], 1915.

QUANTRILL, WILLIAM CLARKE. CONNELLEY, WILLIAM ELSEY, *Quantrill and the Border Wars*. Cedar Rapids: The Torch Press, 1910. [New edition] With an Introduction by Homer Croy, New York: Pageant Book Co., 1956.

SCOTT, WINFIELD. ELLIOTT, CHARLES WINSLOW, *Winfield Scott, The Soldier and the Man*. New York: The Macmillan Company, 1937.

SHELBY, JOSEPH ORVILLE. O'FLAHERTY, DANIEL, *General Jo Shelby, Undefeated Rebel*. Chapel Hill: The University of North Carolina Press, [1954].

SHERIDAN, PHILIP HENRY. O'CONNOR, RICHARD, *Sheridan the Inevitable*. Indianapolis: The Bobbs-Merrill Company, [1953].

SHERMAN, WILLIAM TECUMSEH. LIDDELL HART, BASIL HENRY, *Sherman, Soldier, Realist, American*. New York: Dodd, Mead and Co., 1929.

––– LEWIS, LLOYD, *Sherman, Fighting Prophet*. New York: Harcourt, Brace and Company, [1932].

SICKLES, DANIEL EDGAR. SWANBERG, W. A., *Sickles the Incredible*. New York: Charles Scribner's Sons, 1956.

SMITH, EDMUND KIRBY. PARKS, JOSEPH HOWARD, *General Edmund Kirby Smith, C.S.A.* Baton Rouge: Louisiana State University Press, [1954].

STANTON, EDWIN McMASTERS. GORHAM, GEORGE C., *Life and Public Services of Edwin M. Stanton*. 2 volumes, Boston: Houghton Mifflin Company, 1899.

(Inadequate, but until the new biography by Benjamin P. Thomas is completed, will have to do.)

STEPHENS, ALEXANDER HAMILTON. VON ABELE, RUDOLPH R, *Alexander H. Stephens, A Biography*. New York: Alfred A. Knopf, 1946.

STEVENS, THADDEUS. KORNGOLD, RALPH, *Thaddeus Stevens: A Being Darkly Wise and Rudely Great*. New York: Harcourt, Brace and Company, [1955].

STUART, JAMES EWELL BROWN. McCLELLAN, HENRY BRAINERD, *The Life and Campaigns of . . . J. E. B. Stuart*. Boston: Houghton Miffllin Company, 1885.

––– THOMASON, JOHN W., JR., *Jeb Stuart*. New York: Charles Scribner's Sons, 1930.

THOMAS, GEORGE HENRY. CLEAVES, FREEMAN, *Rock of Chickamauga, The Life of General George H. Thomas*. Norman: University of Oklahoma Press, 1948.

WHEELER, JOSEPH. DYER, JOHN P., *"Fightin' Joe" Wheeler*. University, La.: Louisiana State University Press, 1941.

X. SPECIAL STUDIES, MONOGRAPHS, MISCELLANEOUS WORKS

ADAMS, GEORGE WORTHINGTON, *Doctors in Blue; The Medical History of the Union Army in the Civil War*. New York: Henry Schuman, [1952].

ANDREWS, J. CUTLER, *The North Reports the Civil War*. [Pittsburgh:] University of Pittsburgh Press, [1955].

BRUCE, ROBERT V., *Lincoln and the Tools of War*. Foreword by Benjamin P. Thomas. Indianapolis: The Bobbs-Merrill Company, [1956].

CRAVEN, AVERY, O., *The Coming of the Civil War*. New York: Charles Scribner's Sons, 1942.

EISENSCHIML, OTTO, *Why Was Lincoln Murdered?* Boston: Little, Brown and Company, 1937.

EISENSCHIML, OTTO, *The Celebrated Case of Fitz John Porter*. Indianapolis: The Bobbs-Merrill Company, [1950].

GRAY, WOOD, *The Hidden Civil War; The Story of the Copperheads*. New York: The Viking Press, 1942.

HESSELTINE, WILLIAM B., *Civil War Prisons: A Study in War Psychology*. Colombus: Ohio State University Press, 1930.

HESSELTINE, WILLIAM B., *Lincoln and the War Governors*. New York: Alfred A. Knopf, 1948.

HORAN, JAMES D., *Confederate Agent, a discovery in history*. New York: Crown Publishers, [1954].

HUNT, AURORA, *The Army of the Pacific*. Glendale: The Arthur H. Clark Company, 1951.

JONES, JOHN WILLIAM, *Christ in the Camp: or, Religion in Lee's Army*. Richmond, B. F. Johnson, 1887.

JONES, VIRGIL CARRINGTON, *Gray Ghosts*

and *Rebel Raiders*. Foreword by Bruce Catton. New York: Henry Holt and Company, 1956.

KANE, HARNETT T., *Spies for the Blue and Gray*. Garden City: Hanover House, 1954.

JORDAN, DONALDSON and EDWIN J. PRATT, *Europe and the American Civil War*. With an Introduction by Samuel Eliot Morison. Boston: Houghton Mifflin Company, 1931.

KORN, BERTRAM WALLACE, *American Jewry and the Civil War*. With an Introduction by Allan Nevins. Philadelphia: The Jewish Publication Society of America, 1951.

LEECH, MARGARET, *Reveille in Washington*. New York: Harper & Brothers, [1941].

MAXWELL, WILLIAM QUENTIN, *Lincoln's Fifth Wheel: The Political History of the United States Sanitary Commission*. Preface by Allan Nevins. New York: Longmans Green & Co., 1956.

MONAGHAN, JAY, *Diplomat in Carpet Slippers; Abraham Lincoln Deals with Foreign Affairs*. Indianapolis: The Bobbs-Merrill Company, [1945].

NEVINS, ALLAN, *The Statesmanship of the Civil War*. New York: The Macmillan Company, 1953.

PHILLIPS, ULRICH BONNELL, *American Negro Slavery: A Survey of the Supply, Employment and Control of Negro Labor as Determined by the Plantation Regime*. New York: D. Appleton and Company, 1918. [Reprinted], New York: Peter Smith, 1952.

QUARLES, BENJAMIN, *The Negro in the Civil War*. Boston: Little, Brown and Company, [1953].

STARR, LOUIS M., *Bohemian Brigade; Civil War Newsmen in Action*. New York: Alfred A. Knopf, 1954.

WILEY, BELL IRVIN, *Southern Negroes 1861-1865*. New Haven: Yale University Press, 1938. [Reprinted], New York: Rinehart & Company, [1953].

WILEY, BELL IRVIN, *The Life of Johnny Reb, The Common Soldier of the Confederacy*. Indianapolis: The Bobbs-Merrill Company, [1943].

WILEY, BELL IRVIN, *The Life of Billy Yank: The Common Soldier of the Union*. Indianapolis: The Bobbs-Merrill Company, [1952].

INDEX

This index is confined to the chronological summary of the war, pages 1-137. Biographies of the leading figures of the war will be found in alphabetical order starting on page 153.

Adams, Charles Francis, 14, 41, 72
Agriculture Department established, 37
Aiken House, *illus.*, 132-3
Alabama, C. S. S., 40, 44; sinks *U. S. S. Hatteras*, 56; sunk, 93
Alabama, secession of, 7
Anderson, Robert, 5, 6; surrenders Fort Sumter, 11
Andrews, James J., 32
Antietam, Battle of, 45; *illus.*, 46-7
Appomattox, surrender meeting, 130
Arkansas, C. S. S., 40
Arkansas, reconstruction, 84; secession of, 14
Army of the Potomac, 40
Army of Virginia, 40

Atlanta, falls to Union, 106; siege of, 100; *illus.*, 104-5, 112-3, 114-5

Baker, Edward D., 19
Ball's Bluff, Battle of, 19, 22
Banks, Nathaniel, 28, 36
Battle, *see individual names*
'Battle Hymn of the Republic,' 26
Beauregard, P. G. T., 11, 15, 32, 89, 92; replaced by Bragg, 40
Beaver Dam Creek, Battle of, 37
Bell, John, 5
Belmont, Battle of, 22
Benjamin, Judah P., 28
Bentonville, Battle of, 122
Big Bethel, Battle of, 15

Blair, Francis P., Jr., 14
Blockade, 11, 18
Blockade runner, *illus.*, 108-9
'Bloody Angle,' 89
Boonville, Battle of, 15
Booth, John Wilkes, 130, 131
Bragg, Braxton, 40, 44, 77; letter from Davis, 123
Bragg, Thomas, 28
Breckinridge, John C., 5
Brice's Cross Roads, Battle of, 93
Britain, declared neutral, 14
Brown, Isaac N., 40
Buchanan, James, 5, 6
Buckner, Simon B., 26
Buell, Don Carlos, 26, 32
Burnside, Ambrose E., 23, 48
Bull Run, First Battle of, 15, 18; *illus.*, 16-7; Second Battle of, 41, 44
Butler, Benjamin F., 14, 18, 32, 52; proclamation on women of New Orleans, 33

Cameron, Simon, 10, 23
Carrick's Ford, Battle of, 15
Cass, Lewis, 6
Cedar Creek, Battle of, 106
Cedar Mountain, Battle of, 41
Chancellorsville, Battle of, 58-9
Chantilly, Battle of, 44
Chaplin Hills, Battle of, 45
Charleston, falls to Union, 122; *illus.*, 128-9
Chase, Salmon P., 10, 93
Chattanooga, *illus.*, 76-7
Chestnut, James, Jr., 5
Chickamauga, Battle of, 72
Cobb, Howell, 6
Cold Harbor, First Battle of, 37; *illus.*, 94-5; Second Battle of, 92
Columbia, S. C., burned, 122; *illus.*, 124-7
Columbus, Ky., occupied by Confederacy, 19
Confederacy, formation of, 10; capital falls, 130; surrender of, 130
Constitution, Confederate, 10
Copperhead, origin of term, 40
Crater, Battle of the (before Petersburg), 93
Crittenden compromise, 6
Curtis, Samuel, 28
Cushing, W. B., 108

Dahlgren, Ulric, 84
Davis, Jefferson, becomes President, 22; changes cabinet, 28; elected provisional President, 10; inaugurated, 26; letter to Bragg, 123; offers negotiations, 121
Delaware, votes for Union, 7

'Dictator' mortar, *illus.*, 96-7
Donelson, Fort, Battle of, 23, 26
Douglas, Stephen A., 5; dies, 15
Draft riots in New York, 69
Du Pont, Samuel F., 58

Edwards' Ferry, Battle of, 19, 22
Election, 1860, 5; 1864, 108
Elkhorn Tavern, Battle of, 28
Ellsworth, Elmer E., 14
Emancipation Proclamation, 52; preliminary, 45
Everett, Edward, 5

Fair Oaks, Battle of, 36, 37
Farragut, David G., 32, 40, 101; letter to wife, 27
Fessenden, William P. 93
Fisher, Fort, falls to Union, 121
Fishing Creek, Battle of, 23
Five Forks, Battle of, 130
Florida, secession of, 7
Floyd, John B., 6, 26
Forrest, Nathan Bedford, 49; letter, 29
Fort, *names of forts are indexed under their second element*
Franklin, Battle of, 109
Franklin, W. B., 45
Frayser's Farm, Battle of, 37
Fredericksburg, Battle of, 49; *illus.*, 50-1
Freedman's Bureau, 122
Frémont, John Charles, 19, 22, 36, 89
Frietchie, Barbara, 44
Fugitive Slave Act, 7; repealed, 93

Gaines' Mill, Battle of, 37; *illus.*, 42-3, 94-5
Galveston, falls to Confederacy, 53
'General' (locomotive), 32
Georgia, secession of, 7
Gettysburg Address, 73, 76
Gettysburg, Battle of, 68-9; *illus.*, 66-73
Gladstone, William E., 48
Glendale, Battle of, 37
Glorieta, Battle of, 28
Grant, Ulysses S., 18-9; demands unconditional surrender, 26; heads Department of the Tennessee, 48; heads Division of the Mississippi, 73; named commander of all Union armies, 85; separated from command, 28; at Shiloh, 32
Greeley, Horace, 100
Grierson, Benjamin H., 58
Guntown, Battle of, 93

Habeas Corpus, partial suspension, 18; suspended, 56
Halleck, Henry Wager, 22, 32, 40, 85
Hamlin, Hannibal, 5
Hammond, James H., 5

INDEX

Harpers Ferry, falls to Confederacy, 11, 45; falls to Union, 15

Hawes, Richard, 45

Henry, Fort, Battle of, 23

Hill, A. P., 45

Hill, D. H., 44

Hooker, Joseph, 53, 72; Lincoln letter to, 61

Housatonic, U. S. S., sunk by submarine, 84

Howe, Julia Ward, 26

Hunter, Robert M. T., 28

Island Number 10, falls to Union, 32

Jackson, Miss., falls to Union, 59

Jackson, Thomas J. (Stonewall), 15, 28; dies, 59; last dispatch, 59; nickname, 18; valley campaign, 36, 37

Johnson, Andrew, 93, 122

Johnson, Herschel V., 5

Johnston, Albert S., 28; dies, 32

Johnston, Joseph E., 15, 32, 36; surrenders, 130

Kearny, Phil, 44

Kennesaw Mountain, Ga., *illus.*, 98-9

Kentucky, neutrality resolution, 14; secession movement, 22

Kilpatrick, Judson, 84

Lane, Joseph, 5

Lawrence, Kans., raided by Quantrill, 69

Lee, Robert E., joins Confederacy, 14; named Commander-in-Chief, 121; surrenders, 130; takes over Army of Northern Virginia, 36; in West Virginia, 18, 19

Lexington, Mo., Battle of, 19

Libby Prison, escape, 85; *illus.*, 34-5

Lincoln, Abraham, assassinated, 130; election, first, 5; second, 108; inauguration, first, 10; second, 122; letter to Hooker, 61; nomination, second, 93

Little Rock, Ark., falls to Union, 72

Logan's Crossroads, Battle of, 23

Lookout Mountain, Battle of, 76

Louisiana, secession of, 7

Lyon, Nathaniel, 14; dies, 18

Magruder, John, 28

Manassas, First Battle of, 15, 18; *illus.*, 16-7; Second Battle of, 41, 44

Manpower, 15

March to the Sea, 108-9

Marye's Heights, 49

Maryland, invaded by Lee, 44

Mason, James, 19, 22

Mason and Slidell arrest, 22

Maximilian of Hapsburg, 89

McAllister, Fort, falls to Union, 109

McClellan, George B., 15, 26, 28; named General-in-Chief, 22; nominated for President, 101; ordered to move, 23; visited by Lincoln, 40

McClernand, John A., 48

McCulloch, Benjamin, 18

McDowell, Irvin, 15, 36

McLaws, Lafayette, 45

McPherson, James B., 100

Meade, George Gordon, 62

Mechanicsville, Battle of, 37; *illus.*, 38-9

Memphis, Tenn., falls to Union, 40

Merrimac, 26

Middletown, Battle of, 106

Mill Springs, Battle of, 23

Missionary Ridge, Battle of, 76; *illus.*, 82-3

Mississippi, secession of, 7

Mississippi River, Union gains control, 4, 27

Missouri, secession movement, 19

Mobile, Ala., falls to Union, 130

Mobile Bay, Battle of, 101

Monitor, 26; sinks, 52

Monocacy River, Battle of, 100

Montgomery convention, 10

Morgan, John Hunt, 36, 40, 44; dies, 93; escapes, 76

Mortar, 'Dictator,' *illus.*, 96-7

Mosby, John S., 56

Murfreesboro, Battle of, 49, 52

Nashville, Battle of, 120; *illus.*, 118-9

Nevada, enters Union, 108

New Bern, falls to Union, 26

New Hope Church, Battle of, 89; *illus.*, 90-1

New Mexico, fighting in, 28

New Orleans, Butler's proclamation, 33; falls to Union, 32

New York City, draft riots, 69; neutrality proposal, 7

New York Herald field headquarters, *illus.*, 54-5

Norfolk Navy Yard, falls to Confederacy, 11, 14; falls to Union, 36

Oak Hills, Battle of, 18

Old Dominion, blockade runner, *illus.*, 108-9

Opequon Creek, Battle of, 106

Ox Hill, Battle of, 44

Palmetto Ranch, 'Battle' of, 131

Patterson, Robert, 15

Peachtree Creek, Battle of, 100

Pea Ridge, Battle of, 28

Peninsula Campaign, plans for, 26, 28; Union Army in, *illus.*, 34-5

Perryville, Battle of, 45
Petersburg, siege of, *illus.*, 96-7, 132-3, 136-7
Philippi Races, Battle of, 15
Pickett's Charge, 68
Pigeon's Ranch, Battle of, 28
Pillow, Gideon, 26
Pillow, Fort, falls to Union, 40; 'massacre' at, 88
Pine Bluff, Battle of, 73
Pittsburgh Landing, Battle of, 32
Pleasant Hill, Battle of, 85
Polk, Leonidas, dies, 93
Pope, John, 32, 40, 41
Porter, David D., 56
Porter, Fitz-John, 37, 41
Port Royal, S. C., falls to Union, 22
Potter House, *illus.*, 112-3
Price, Sterling, 18
Pulaski, Fort, falls to Union, 28, 32

Quantrill, William Clarke, 44
Queen of the West, 56

Randolph, George W., 28
Repair shop, army, *illus.*, 24-5
Richmond, capital of Confederacy, 14; falls to Union, 130
Rich Mountain, Battle of, 15
Ringgold, Ga., *illus.*, 80-1
Roanoke Island, falls to Union, 23
Rosecrans, William S., 15, 45
Rost, Pierre A., 14
Russell, Lord John, 14

Sabine Crossroads, Battle of, 85
St. Albans, Vt., raided by Confederates, 108
Sanitary Commission, U. S., headquarters, *illus.*, 62-3
Santa Fe, N. M., falls to Confederacy, 28
Savage Station, Battle of, 37
Savannah, Ga., falls to Union, 109; *illus.*, 116-7
Scott, Winfield, 22
Secession, 5*ff*; of Alabama, 7; of Arkansas, 14; of Florida, 7; of Georgia, 7; by Kentucky group, 22; of Louisiana, 7; of Mississippi, 7; by Missouri group, 19; of South Carolina, 6; of Tennessee, 14, 15; of Texas, 10; of Virginia, 11
Sedgwick, Fort, *illus.*, 136-7
Seven Days Campaign, 37
Seven Pines, Battle of, 36, 37
Seward, William H., 10, 14
Sharpsburg, Battle of, 45
'Shebang,' *illus.*, 62-3
Shenandoah, C.S.S., surrenders, 131

Shenandoah Valley, Jackson's campaign, 36
Sheridan, Phil, 85
Sherman, William T., letter to Wilson, 107
Shiloh, Battle of, 32
Sibley, Henry Hopkins, 28
Sioux uprisings, 52
Slaughter Mountain, Battle of, 41
Slidell, John, 19; *see also* Mason and Slidell arrest
Smith, C. F., 28
Somerset, Battle of, 23
South Carolina, secession of, 5, 6
South Mountain, Battle of, 45
Spotsylvania, Battle of, 89
Springfield, Battle of, 18
'Spring Hill Affair,' 109
Stanton, Edwin M., 23
'Stars and Bars,' 10
Stephens, Alexander H., 10, 122
Stevens, I. I., 44
Stone's River, Battle of, 49, 52
Stuart, J. E. B., 37
Sumter, Fort, Anderson occupies, 6; falls to Confederacy, 11; falls to Union, 130; *illus.*, 4-5, 8-9
Surrender of Lee, 130

Taney, Roger B., dies, 108
Taylor, Richard, surrenders, 131
Tennessee, secession of, 14, 15
Texas, secession of, 10
Thirteenth Amendment, 122
Thomas, George H., 23, 72
Tweed Ring, 53

Vanderbilt, Cornelius, 53
Vicksburg, Miss., 40; falls to Union, 69
Victoria, Queen of England, 14
Virginia, secession of, 11

Wagon Park, *illus.*, 86-7
Wallace, Lew, 32
Watts, Thomas N., 28
Welles, Gideon, 10

West Virginia, Constitution adopted, 26
White Oak Swamp, Battle of, 37
Wilderness, Battle of, 88
Wilkes, Charles, 22
Wilson's Creek, Battle of, 18
Winchester, Battle of, 106
Wood, Fernando, 7

Yancey, William L., 14
Yorktown, siege of, 28; *illus.*, 30-1

Zollicoffer, Felix K., 23
Zouaves, *illus.*, 20-1